Greenhill Books

FOR THE
GLORY OF ROME

FOR THE GLORY OF ROME

A History of Warriors and Warfare

Ross Cowan

Greenhill Books, London
MBI Publishing, St Paul

For the Glory of Rome
A History of Warriors and Warfare
First published in 2007 by
Greenhill Books/Lionel Leventhal Ltd
Park House, 1 Russell Gardens, London NW11 9NN
and
MBI Publishing Co., Galtier Plaza, Suite 200,
380 Jackson Street, St Paul, MN 55101-3885, USA

British Library Cataloguing-in Publication Data
Cowan, Ross
Warriors of the Roman Empire
1. Soldiers – Rome
2. Military art and science – History – To 500
3. Rome – Army – Military life
4. Rome - History, Military
I. Title
355. 1'0937

ISBN 978-1-85367-733-5

Library of Congress Cataloging-in Publication Data available

For more information on our books, please visit www.greenhillbooks.com,
email sales@greenhillbooks.com, or telephone us within the UK on
020 8458 6314. You can also write to us at the above London address.

Edited and typeset by Donald Sommerville

Printed and bound in Great Britain by
Creative Print and Design (Wales), Ebbw Vale

CONTENTS

ILLUSTRATIONS

ACKNOWLEDGEMENTS

I would like to thank Michael Leventhal and Henry Alban Davies of Greenhill Books for commissioning this title and guiding it towards publication. Editor Donald Sommerville expertly crafted my rough and ready manuscript into this handsome book. Dr. Duncan B. Campbell and Professor Lawrence Keppie freely lent their great expertise on the armies of the Hellenistic kingdoms and Rome, and sections of this book are the better for it. Needless to say, any errors are those of the author. When I was unable to consult his *A Commentary on Livy, Books VI–X. Volume 4: Book X* (Oxford, 2005), Professor Stephen P. Oakley kindly sent me copies of his files which greatly benefited my treatment of the battles of Camerinum and Sentinum (*see* Chapter II). From my vague outlines Graham Sumner painted the vivid reconstructions of Roman warriors which add so much to this volume. Johnny Shumate provided the splendid illustration of a *sarissa*-wielding phalangite, that determined opponent of the legionary at the battles of Heraclea, Ausculum and Malventum (*see* Chapter I). The enthusiasm and encouragement of Jim Bowers sped this book to a conclusion. Jim also provided the illustration of a *bellator* of *legio XXII Primigenia* in the grip of battle lust. Jasper Oorthuys and Steven D. P. Richardson supplied illustrative material, as always.

Acknowledgements

Special thanks are due to the Cowan family, Thomas McGrory and Krista Ubbels for their support and interest in this project.

This book is dedicated to the memory of David Gemmell. He wrote about warriors and heroes, many of them ancient Greeks and Romans. His novel *Ghost King* introduced me to the legend of the Ninth Legion and ignited my interest in the Roman army.

Ross Cowan

Mons Graupius

Burnswark
Hadrian's Wall
Carlisle

BRITANNIA

GERMAN
PEOPLES

Colchester
(Camulodunum)

BELGAE

ATLANTIC

OCEAN

Argentoratum

Danube

Avaricum

Alesia

GAUL

Battle with
the Helvetii

ARVERNI

Gergovia

PANNONIA

Placentia
Mediolanum
Vercellae

Cremona
Patavium

ILLYRICUM

Clastidium

NORTH ITALIAN
GALLIA

Arausio

Aquae Sextiae
Massilia

Pistoria

Intercatia

CELTIBERIANS

Sentinum

Lake
Trasimene

Camerinum

Perusia

Ausculum

Numantia

Picenum

Telamon

Ilerda

Falerii

Veii
Rome

Fidenae

Luceria

LUSITANIANS

HISPANIA

Aesernia

Nola

Cannae

Capua

Aquilonia

Caudine Forks

Sucro

Balearic Islands

Pompeii

SARDINIA

Munda

New Carthage

SICILY

Carthage

MAURETANIA

NUMIDIA

Thapsus

Zama

AFRICA

M e d i

N

LIBYA

Bu Njem

0   200 km

0   200 miles

THE ROMAN WORLD
Battles, Sieges and Other Sites of Importance

D A C I A

M O E S I A

Danube

Black Sea

THRACE

yrrhachium

MACEDON

Philippi

EPIRUS

Pydna

bracia

Actium

Pharsalus

Chaeronea

Orchomenus

Argos

Athens

Piraeus

Sparta

Creta

PONTUS

Elegeia

Adrianople

Constantinople

BITHYNIA

ASIA

CAPPADOCIA

Amida

Dara

Tigris

Carrhae

CILICIA

Euphrates

SYRIA

Ctesiphon

Maiozamalcha

Cyprus

Dura-Europos

editerranean Sea

Jerusalem

Alexandria

E G Y P T

Nile

INTRODUCTION

'He had forty-five scars at the front of his body, but none on the back.' (Pliny, *The Natural History*, 7.101)

T his book is about the fighting men of Rome (and also their valiant enemies). The Roman legionary might have defined himself as a soldier (*miles*) or as a warrior (*bellator*). He would not have discerned a conflict between the labels, but there is a modern tendency to draw a distinction: on the one hand, the soldier who fights as part of an organised unit; on the other, the warrior fighting his personal battles alone. Individualistic warriors, no matter how brave, usually succumb to the cohesive strength and steadfastness of the disciplined group of soldiers. Even when massed together, warriors cannot assume a formation better than a mob.

The Romans are often described by modern historians as professional soldiers and their opponents, especially the Gauls and Germans, as warriors, yet the Gallic Helvetii and Ariovistus' Germanic Suebians fought Caesar's legions in disciplined phalanxes.[1] For most of the Republican period the legions were composed of farmers and men with other common occupations; they served only for the duration of a campaign (though they were expected to serve in multiple campaigns between the ages of seventeen and forty-six). It was such part-time legionaries that met the professional Epirote phalangites at the battles of Heraclea and Ausculum.

The part-time legionaries fought in the maniple, a tactical unit usually of 120 men. Sometimes the legionaries fought shoulder to shoulder, the maniple becoming a block of united strength and power, driving forward like a wedge into the enemy battle line. Sometimes the legionaries in the maniple assumed a loose order, each man occupying six feet of space, free to fight as an individual but with support close at hand. Sometimes the legionary was expected to fight entirely alone, to turn and meet enemies coming from all directions. His equipment of heavy javelin, cut-and-thrust sword and a shield that covered him from shoulder to shin, was adaptable to the needs of group or individual fighting. A maniple could begin a charge as a cohesive close-order unit, but as it neared the enemy the legionaries in the front rank might sprint ahead and collide with the foe as individuals, using shields as battering rams, exploiting any gaps their volley of javelins had made in the opposing ranks, and hack their way forwards with swords. The Roman fighting man was thus a formidable combination of soldier and warrior. Roman military organisation created disciplined groups of soldiers who would fight together for a common goal, but, when opportunity allowed, it permitted the individual warrior to emerge and to sate his desire for personal glory.

Yet a fine balance had to be maintained. Roman commanders sometimes struggled to restrain their legionaries when the warrior mentality was in the ascendant; occasionally the warrior mentality overwhelmed commanders as well, and they charged forward impetuously when more restrained tactics were called for. Every Roman soldier yearned for a glorious reputation, but it was especially important for aristocratic officers. Military prowess was inextricably linked with political advancement. With senior magisterial office came the great military commands, the opportunity to lead legions and allied forces into battle, to display tactical acumen and to be seen engaging hand-to-hand with the best of the enemy. Victory assured personal and national glory of the highest order. Successive generations of nobles strove to build on the martial feats of their ancestors, to outdo rival noble clans and be the leading men in Rome. This competition ensured continuous warfare and the extension of Roman territory across Italy. Defeat in battle was disgraceful but it also presented a fine opportunity to exact righteous revenge. Every war the Romans fought was in some way 'just'.

The ordinary citizen did not usually complain when he was called from his fields to fight in yet another campaign. He also had a reputation to build or maintain. There would be the opportunity to take booty and slaves, and land might be distributed later. The Italian tribes and cities allied to Rome enjoyed similar benefits. This also necessitated that warfare had to be continuous, or nearly so. Success in war ensured the compliance of the Allies.[2]

However, the Romans did not view their aggression and imperialism so cynically. They would have been gravely affronted by the notion that greed and an insatiable desire for fame and glory motivated their actions. They were an honourable people. There was nothing wrong with competition and conquest; the gods approved. The trial of battle was the ultimate test and the fruits of victory were justly deserved. As a pious people the Romans always dedicated a share of the spoils to the gods.

The following pages introduce some of the most notable *milites* and *bellatores* of the Roman army: Servilius Geminus Pulex, victor of twenty-three single combats; Marcus Sergius Silus, who fought with a prosthetic iron fist; Gnaeus Petreius, the centurion who executed his commanding officer for cowardice; and Quintus Sertorius, proud of his empty eye socket because it was a mark of valour. Readers will also meet Caesar's proud centurions, mad emperors, charismatic kings and wily consuls.

There is considerable narrative treatment of the course of the Pyrrhic War, the Third Samnite War, Caesar's conquest of Gaul and the first stage of his civil war against the Pompeians, but the relevant chapters are not arranged in strict chronological order. These wars and campaigns serve to demonstrate the doggedness of Roman fighting men, their lust for glory and their desire to be seen as courageous by their peers. The material also reveals their passion for single combat, demonstrates their fundamental belief in the divine, and illustrates the concepts of loyalty and honour by which they lived and died.

Chapter I

THE PYRRHIC WAR

'They fought desperately with their swords against the Greeks' *sarissai*, careless of their lives, thinking only of wounding and killing the enemy.' (Plutarch, *Pyrrhus*, 21.6)

In 280 BC Pyrrhus of Epirus, spiritual heir of Alexander the Great, sailed to Italy. He came to defend the Greek colonies of the south from Roman aggression and to create an empire. He was one of the most famous men in the Greek world, a king and a general renowned for his courage, daring and tactical acumen. He was hero-worshipped by his soldiers. Few in the Greek world doubted that he would achieve his aim.

Rome had excited little interest in mainland Greece and the Hellenistic kingdoms. She was known for her republican constitution and as a power in Italy, but she was not an international player; most Greek leaders would have considered Syracuse in Sicily more important. Rome's legions had routed the armies of Gallic tribes and

Italic confederations, but when had they ever faced anything like a modern Hellenistic army? How could part-time legionaries defeat the Epirote warrior-king and his army of hardened professionals? How could they withstand the devastating combination of phalanx, elephant corps, light troops and cavalry? Yet it did not pay to underestimate the capabilities of Rome and her army. The Pyrrhic War thrust Rome on to the world stage and she rose to the challenge.

THE EAGLE OF EPIRUS

Pyrrhus of Epirus was king of the Molossians and, through a combination of force of arms, luck and his not inconsiderable charm, sometimes king of Macedonia. He claimed direct descent from Achilles, son of Zeus and hero of the Trojan War, and from that other belligerent demi-god, Heracles. He strove to live up to their example and win their fame, especially that of Achilles, 'not merely through his ancestry but through his prowess on the battlefield'.[1]

While still an infant Pyrrhus was ousted from his princely throne and then restored by the army of the Illyrian king who had adopted him. He was usurped again as a teenaged king and exiled but made a name for himself as a soldier in the wars of the *Diadochi* – 'the Successors'. They were the companions of Alexander the Great who fought perpetually over their old master's fragmenting empire: Ptolemy, Antigonus Monophthalmos (the 'One-Eyed'), Seleucus, Cassander and Lysimachus. A mature Pyrrhus returned to Epirus to kill the usurper and throughout the 290s and 280s BC spent his time seizing large chunks of neighbouring kingdoms or defending his own.[2] He was partial to fighting single combats with enemy generals and, on those rare occasions when he was not on campaign, he read military manuals or wrote about tactics and his own exploits. Pyrrhus' writings were bestsellers in antiquity and much plundered by later Greek, Carthaginian and Roman generals for inspiration: Hannibal described Pyrrhus as his teacher.[3] 'No one has ever shown better judgement in choosing his ground, or in marshalling his forces,' said the Carthaginian commander. Pyrrhus' elder contemporaries were more cautious in their praise. When asked who was the best general, Antigonus the One-Eyed, a commander to both Philip II and Alexander the Great, saw the promise in the young officer who had recently joined his army and replied, 'Pyrrhus – *if* he lives to be old.' Hannibal also respected Pyrrhus' ability to win men over.

Pyrrhus was a thorough autocrat (at least when he could escape the confines of Epirus) and dangerously impulsive (few of his endeavours were seen through to a conclusion before he embarked on another adventure), but he was also chivalrous and possessed of a magnetic and charismatic personality which drew men and women to him. He was always conspicuous on the battlefield in his gaudy armour, horned helmet and flamboyant purple and gold cloak. In that age of warriors there were always men willing to follow him on the next adventure, but Pyrrhus was even confident of his powers to inspire unwilling conscripts. 'You pick out the big men,' he told his recruiting officers. 'I'll make them brave!' Nor were the great men and women of the age immune to his powers of persuasion. 'He was adept at turning his superiors to his own advantage,' wrote Plutarch. Thus, only a year after being sent to Ptolemy of Egypt as a political hostage (298 BC), he had charmed Ptolemy's queen, married his step-daughter and returned to Epirus at the head of a Ptolemaic army.[4]

Pyrrhus was obsessed with war and its dangerous glamour. He revelled in planning and tactics, and lusted after the adrenaline rush of combat and the glory and prestige that came with victory.[5] He was not the most powerful or successful of the Hellenistic kings who succeeded Alexander the Great, but he was reckoned the most like Alexander in spirit and deeds.[6] Pyrrhus was in fact a cousin of the famous king. Alexander's mother, Olympias, was of the Molossian royal house.

Although Pyrrhus was the staunchest Epirote patriot, he was chafed by the confines of his kingdom. Pyrrhus was never called king of Epirus as the Roman sources erroneously refer to him. He was king of the Molossians, the principal tribe of Epirus, and acknowledged *hegemon* (leader) by the lesser tribes of the Thesprotians and

Chaonians; the three tribes were known collectively as the Epirote Allies. The kings of the Molossians were bound by a strict constitution, which even included clauses allowing the people to depose the monarch and expel his family – as happened to the young Pyrrhus in 317 and 302 BC. The king had to consult with the Epirote Alliance before he could call out the army and embark on a campaign, hence the desire of Alexander the Molossian (*see below*) and especially Pyrrhus to conquer territory outside Epirus, where they could rule in the true autocratic fashion of contemporary Hellenistic monarchs. It is telling that Pyrrhus made his lavish capital at Ambracia, close to but beyond the bounds of his native land; his chief minister, Cineas, was not an Epirote but a Thessalian; and the alliances that the king attempted to forge, for example with the Romans after Heraclea, were intended to be alliances with Pyrrhus alone, not Pyrrhus as the representative of the Epirotes.

In 289 BC Pyrrhus, aged about thirty, fought one of the most celebrated single combats of the age against Pantauchus, the feared general of Demetrius Poliorcetes ('the Besieger'). Demetrius (son of Antigonus the One-Eyed) had recently seized the throne of Macedon, occupied Aetolia in central Greece, and was marching on the Aetolians' ally, Epirus. Pyrrhus counter-marched against the invading force, but somehow both kings managed to by-pass each other – seemingly deliberately on the part of Pyrrhus. The Epirote continued his advance south into Aetolia, where Demetrius had left Pantauchus with a large force of occupation. Pantauchus met Pyrrhus' army at an unspecified location and, perhaps seeking to reduce the conflict to a decisive battle of champions, challenged Pyrrhus to single combat. The arrogant Pantauchus was confident in his strength and courage but Pyrrhus took heart from his descent from Achilles:

> At first they hurled their spears, then, coming to close
> quarters, they plied their swords with might and skill. Pyrrhus
> got one wound, but gave Pantauchus two, one in the thigh

and one along the neck, and put him to flight and overthrew him. However, he did not kill him, for Pyrrhus' companions dragged him away. Then the Epirotes, exalted by the victory of their king and admiring his valour, overwhelmed and cut to pieces the phalanx of the Macedonians, pursued them as they fled, slew many of them, and took 5,000 of them alive. (Plutarch, *Pyrrhus*, 7.4–5)

Strangely enough, the surviving Macedonians did not take unkindly to Pyrrhus' overwhelming victory.[7] Saddened by a long line of weak kings and usurpers, the oldest soldiers yearned for a return of the glory days of Alexander the Great:

This battle did not fill the Macedonians with fury and hate towards Pyrrhus for their losses. Rather, it persuaded those who witnessed his exploits or engaged him in the battle greatly to respect him and admire his bravery and to talk much about him. They compared his demeanour, his swiftness and all his motions to those of the great Alexander, and thought they saw him as a shadow, as it were, and imitation of that leader's impetuosity and might in conflicts. The other kings, they said, could only imitate Alexander in superficial details, with their purple cloaks, their bodyguards and the angle at which they held their heads, or the lofty tone of their speech: it was Pyrrhus alone who could remind them of him in arms and action. (Plutarch, *Pyrrhus*, 8.1)

As a result of this victory Demetrius was forced to evacuate Aetolia and abandon his plundering of Epirus, from where he raced to defend the borders of Macedonia. When the triumphant Pyrrhus returned home, the Epirotes honoured their king with a new title: the Eagle. Knowing when to return a compliment the king declared, 'Through you I am an eagle. It is by your arms that I am held aloft by swift pinions.' When the Eagle marched into Macedonia in 288 BC – a co-ordinated invasion with Lysimachus (*see below*) attacking from Thrace – the veterans of the Macedonian army were still so taken with him that they saluted Pyrrhus as king and Demetrius was compelled to flee. The rumour that the great Alexander had appeared to Pyrrhus in a vision and blessed his enterprises probably helped to sway them.[8] Pyrrhus and Lysimachus divided the kingdom between them, but soon Lysimachus' power began to tell.

Lysimachus had been a bodyguard of Alexander the Great. During one of his less stable moments (and there were many), Alexander had locked the unarmed Lysimachus in a cage with a hungry lion: Lysimachus killed the beast with his bare hands. On Alexander's death he seized the satrapy of Thrace. In time he consolidated a considerable empire stretching from the Danube to the Taurus Mountains, though his trans-Danubian campaigns came to an inglorious conclusion when he was captured and ransomed by a barbarian chieftain. Benefiting from wealthy Asian provinces such as Pergamum which he taxed rapaciously, the size of his treasury was legendary and it enabled him to finance a superb army and bribe the senior officers and officials of his opponents.

By 284 BC Lysimachus had thoroughly undermined Pyrrhus' position in Macedon, tampered with his officers and cut his supply lines.[9] Pyrrhus was forced back to Epirus, but the indefatigable king sought to expand his domains north into Illyria, adding to those lands he had already acquired through dynastic marriages to Illyrian princesses, and sought to reclaim Corcyra (Corfu). The island was the dowry of his second wife, Lanassa, daughter of Agathocles, the tyrant of Syracuse in Sicily, but Pyrrhus' polygamy alienated her and she had left him in 290 BC for Demetrius of all people, who garrisoned the island! (After his expulsion from Macedon Demetrius attempted to carve himself out another kingdom in Asia Minor but was eventually captured by Seleucus, the most successful of the *Diadochi*, and kept in luxurious confinement until he drank himself to death in 283 BC.)

Pyrrhus re-conquered Corcyra in 282 BC, but then found himself in an unaccustomed situation: except for powerful Lysimachus, he had no one to fight. The mighty Eagle discovered that ruling a peaceful and prosperous kingdom was not entirely to his liking and he yearned for adventure: 'Like Achilles, he could not endure inaction,' says Plutarch.[10] Early in 281 BC Lysimachus failed in his attempt to add the vast kingdom of Seleucus to his empire, and was killed in battle at Corupedium. Pyrrhus made ready to attack Macedonia but then arrived an embassy of Tarentines imploring the warrior-king to lead them in their Hellenic struggle against a barbarian city called Rome.

TARENTUM

Tarentum (Taras, Taranto) was established in 706 BC on the site of an ancient Mycenaean trading station by the best harbour in southern Italy. It was Sparta's only overseas colony and for centuries Tarentum struggled to match the martial prowess of her parent city. In about 473 BC Tarentum's ruling aristocrats were annihilated in a battle with the neighbouring Messapians, but the common people successfully defended the city and then re-established it as a radical democracy.

Already rich as a major producer of wool and purple dyed garments (greatly prized in antiquity as the colour of royal and magisterial robes), Tarentum supplemented her wealth by the manufacture of ceramics and metalwork, which were much sought after as luxury goods. On the hub of the major trade routes between east and west and with the money and manpower to maintain a considerable navy, the democratic city went on to become the leading mercantile power of southern Italy. Her coinage was the preferred standard in southern and Adriatic Italy and was found even beyond the Alps. She was jealous of her control of the sea and dominant over the other Italiote Greek cities in the region, including famous Croton, and Metapontum. In fact Tarentum controlled the Italiote League from about the end of the fifth century BC and levied troops from the cities. However, the expansion of the warlike Sabellian tribes from the central highlands into southern Italy put the territory of Tarentum under great pressure, and halted her attempts to expand into the rich pasture lands of Apulia. The territory of the Sabellian Samnites bordered Apulia and their main produce was wool. They would not tolerate competition.[11]

Tarentum resorted to the use of mercenaries to bolster her own army against her most persistent opponents, the Lucani, kin of the Samnites; the name means 'wolf men' because they believed Mamers (the name of the war god Mars in Oscan, the language spoken by the Sabellians) had sent his sacred wolf to guide them out of the central Italian highlands to a new homeland in the prosperous south. On paper Tarentum could field 20,000 hoplites and 2,000 cavalry (it is unclear if these were all Tarentine soldiers or levies from the cities of the Italiote League), but they were increasingly disinclined to leave the pleasures of the city and serve against demented Italic tribesmen who dedicated themselves to Mamers and thought it a great thing to die gloriously in battle.[12] So rich Tarentum employed only the best mercenary captains with the most professional armies. Among others, they hired Archidamus and Cleonymus of Sparta, and Alexander, king of the Molossians, uncle of both Alexander the Great and Pyrrhus. They all failed.

Archidamus, king of Sparta, was killed in battle against the Lucani at Manduria in 338 BC. Legend had it that the engagement was fought on the same day that Philip II of Macedon and his teenage son Alexander the Great routed the free Greeks led by Athens and Thebes at the battle of Chaeronea. There was no greater sign of Sparta's decline than that her king was serving abroad as a mercenary when formerly she would have led the defence of Greece.[13]

Alexander the Molossian had more success defeating the Lucani, the Samnites and Bruttii (a breakaway element of the Lucani, whose name apparently meant 'runaways'), but relations with the Tarentines collapsed when they realised his real intention was to establish an empire in southern Italy. They refused to send him any more troops or coin. While marching in foul weather by Pandosia, on the border between Lucania and Bruttium, Alexander's army was forced to separate into three contingents, perhaps unaware that it was being shadowed. The full Lucanian army, reinforced by the Bruttii, proceeded to wipe out each contingent. Alexander himself managed to fight his way clear with a small force, even killing the Lucanian general in one-on-one combat (for the distinction between this and single combat, *see* Chapter III), but when about to make good his escape across a river, the king was speared by a Lucanian exile serving in his ranks (331 or 330 BC). The vengeful Lucani and Bruttii hacked Alexander's corpse in two, sending one half to be displayed before the walls of Consentia, which Alexander had captured from the Bruttii, and venting their rage on the other half by bombarding it with javelins and stones.[14]

After initial successes against the Lucani, the Spartan prince Cleonymus also fell out with the Tarentines and seized and plundered the Italiote city of Metapontum. He proceeded to ravage the territory of the Sallentini in the heel of Italy, but a Roman army kicked him out. He tried to make good his losses by embarking on a plundering expedition up the Adriatic coast (302 BC). This came to grief when his forces attempted to raid the city of Patavium (Padua) in the territory of the Veneti. The citizens armed themselves and divided into two forces. One division defeated Cleonymus' marauders, while the other fell on his lightly defended fleet and destroyed most of the ships. Cleonymus escaped with only one-fifth of his fleet and is later found in the service of a certain king Pyrrhus. A tombstone from Patavium, dating from about 300 BC and decorated with a scene of two Venetic cavalrymen trampling a decapitated enemy, may commemorate a Patavian who fought in one of the engagements.[15] The Roman historian Livy (59 BC–AD 17) was a native of Patavium and the victory was still proudly celebrated in his day:

> There are now living in Patavium many who have seen the beaks of the ships [the bronze rams from the prows used to attack other ships] and the spoils of the Laconians [Spartans]

which were fastened up in the old temple of Juno. In commemoration of the naval battle a contest of ships is held regularly, on the anniversary of the victory, in the river that flows through the city. (Livy, 10.2.14–15)

TARENTUM VERSUS ROME

The Tarentines caused the war with Rome by attacking a squadron of ten Roman warships sailing towards the harbour of Tarentum in the autumn of 282 BC. The small fleet was perhaps en route to Roman colonies on the Adriatic coast or making a reconnaissance of Magna Graecia ('Great Greece' as the Greek colonised region of coastal south Italy and Sicily was known), although it is not inconceivable that its purpose was aggressive. The growing power of Rome was anathema to Tarentum. The Romans had started to interfere in southern Italy and were undermining Tarentine authority and influence.

As we have seen, the Romans helped the Sallentini in 302 BC to eject Cleonymus and in c. 286 BC accepted an invitation by the Italiote city of Thurii to protect her from the Lucani and Bruttii. The Sabellians were scared off but Rome was soon involved in yet another major war in northern Italy against the Gauls (284–282 BC); the Lucani were emboldened to renounce their old treaty with Rome and their general Sthenius Statilius laid siege to Thurii with a mixed force of Lucani and Bruttii. Thurii despaired and threw her lot in with Rome to become an Ally. Entering the Roman Alliance meant retaining considerable local autonomy (although those who had become 'Allies' after being defeated in war were essentially subjects), but ceding all control of military and foreign policy to Rome, and making an annual contribution of men and materiel for the Roman army or navy. Such was the price of protection. Thurii would not appeal to Tarentum. Since her foundation in 444 BC Thurii had vied with Tarentum for prestige and power in Magna Graecia, even briefly leading the Italiote League when Alexander the Molossian broke from Tarentum. To the Thurian mind, to ask for Tarentum's help would be to invite domination of a worse sort than that of Rome.

The consul Fabricius Luscinus marched to relieve Thurii and fought a great battle with Sthenius Statilius' army in the summer of 282 BC. The Romans believed that Mars himself fought with them that day. Statilius drew up his army on the open ground before the city and offered battle, but neither his efforts nor those of the Roman consul could persuade the legionaries to press their attacks. When it seemed that the consul would have to concede a technical defeat and leave the enemy in possession of the field, Father Mars decided to intervene:

> A young man of great stature emerged from the ranks and urged the Romans to take courage and, when he saw they were hesitant, snatched up a ladder and made his way through the enemy ranks to their camp, set up the ladder and climbed the rampart. Then he shouted in a voice of thunder that a step had been taken to victory. He brought our men to the place for the capture of the enemy camp, and also brought the Lucani and Bruttii for its defence. (Valerius Maximus, *Memorable Deeds and Sayings*, 1.8.6)

Having brought the two sides to battle on the ramparts of the camp, this remarkable young man again appeared when the fighting reached stalemate and 'gave to the Romans to be slaughtered or made prisoner' 25,000 of the enemy (doubtless an exaggeration), including Sthenius Statilius. Twenty-three enemy standards (*signa*) were also taken, a great prize because they were sacred to the gods. It was a complete victory and the consul held a parade the following day to reward his brave soldiers. He was keen to honour the young giant with a rampart crown, but the soldier was not on parade or among the bodies of the dead. The later Roman officer and historian Ammianus Marcellinus, knowing well the pride of Roman soldiers, stated that if the man who had led the assaults was an ordinary soldier 'from consciousness of his exploit he would have presented himself of his own accord' to receive the award. The soldiers began to suggest that Father Mars himself had come to them; a man so big could only be a god! The rumour became 'fact' when a helmet decorated with two feathers – the crest of Mars – was discovered. The consul then led his army in a joyous celebration of thanks-giving.[16]

A garrison was installed in Thurii to ensure that its pro-Roman aristocrats remained in control. Tarentum was enraged. She was the protector of the Italiote Greek cities and, as a radical democracy, did not take kindly to the bolstering of aristocracies, especially in Thurii! So when the populace, who were apparently watching a performance in the theatre overlooking the harbour, spotted the Roman ships, the demagogue Philocharis easily spurred them on. He reminded them that Rome was breaking a fifty-year-old treaty by sailing into Tarentine waters (made with Alexander the Molossian; the Romans probably considered it long expired), and conceivably declared that Fabricius, fresh from his triumph at Thurii, had sent the ships to support the noble families in Tarentum and help them overthrow the democracy. The Tarentines raced down to the wharves and manned their warships. They may have lost their liking for soldiering but they remained skilful sailors, and promptly sank four Roman ships and captured another. The Roman admiral was among the casualties and the captives were executed or sold as slaves. Thoroughly energised, the normally reticent Tarentine army then marched on Thurii. The heavily outnumbered Roman garrison was forced to depart ignominiously, the Thurian aristocrats were exiled and the city was sacked. Rome had been humiliated.

A senatorial embassy was dispatched from Rome to demand reparation. The envoys arrived at Tarentum during the raucous Bacchanalia festival (winter 282/1 BC) and were jeered by the drunken revellers – they were especially insulting about the purple stripes on the senators' formal togas.[17] The embassy was finally granted a hearing by the city council in the theatre. Here the Romans received similar treatment and were mocked for their poorly pronounced Greek. The council would concede nothing. As the Romans made to leave the theatre, a notorious drunkard called Philonides barred the way of the chief envoy Postumius Megellus, a former consul and man of great distinction. Philonides pulled up his tunic and bared his backside at the envoy, then voided his bowels explosively. Some of the faeces spattered Postumius' toga, and the theatre erupted with laughter and applause. The Roman, unsurprisingly, was not amused. In slow and deliberate Greek he declared: 'Laugh while you can. You will be crying when you wash this garment clean with your blood!'[18]

ENTER THE EAGLE

The Tarentine embassy to Epirus presumably failed to relate this unseemly incident to king Pyrrhus – ambassadors were supposed to be sacrosanct. 'They told him,' relates Plutarch, 'that they needed a commander of reputation and good sense.' Pyrrhus was flattered. Hoping to lure the Eagle over the sea, they would supply a fleet of infantry and cavalry transports. The wily Tarentines had already supplied Pyrrhus with transports for the assault on his old wedding present – Corcyra. The island fell to Pyrrhus and he was now under obligation to return the favour.[19] The Tarentines declared that Italy was far richer than Greece, and 370,000 Italiote Greek and Italian warriors would flock to his standard as soon as he set foot in southern Italy. The Italian Allies included the Lucani, Bruttii, Samnites and Messapians, all temporarily reconciled to Tarentum because of the threat posed by expansionist Rome.

The Romans had waged three great wars against the proud Samnites, seizing much of their territory, but hostilities had broken out again when Rome suffered a temporary but serious setback against the Gauls at Arretium (*see below*). The Samnites had once threatened Tarentum but now looked to her for support. During the Third Samnite War Tarentum maintained an apparently neutral position, but foreseeing that Samnite defeat would remove the

THE PYRRHIC WAR, 280–275 BC

Arretium

Ancona

Volsinii

Ausculum
Picenum

Tiber

Rome

Praeneste

Anagnia

LATIUM

Ferentinum · Fregellae

S A M N I U M

Arpi

Ausculum

Aufidus

Capua

Malventum

Venusia

A P U L I A

Naples

M E S S A P I A

L U C A N I A

Tarentum

Metapontum
Heraclea
Siris

Adriatic Sea

T y r r h e n i a n

S e a

Thurii

B R U T T I U M

Croton

I o n i a n

S e a

Heircte
Panormus

Messana

Locri

Mt Eryx

Rhegium

Lilybaeum

S i c i l y

Tauromenium

Enna

Catana

Leontini

Syracuse

Cossyra

N

0   50 km

0   50 miles

(albeit belligerent) buffer zone between her and Rome, she probably helped to finance the Samnite war effort. As for the Lucani, it was their appeal to Rome against Samnite aggression that had triggered the Third Samnite War (*see* Chapter II). It well suited Rome for the Lucani to drain the resources of Tarentum while Rome fought the Samnites in central Italy, but the subsequent establishment of a Roman military colony at Venusia on confiscated Samnite territory bordering Lucania and Apulia, as well as the intervention at Thurii sorely aggravated the Lucani. They had long made strenuous efforts to conquer it and their 'ally' had stolen their prize. The colony at Venusia would also have antagonised Tarentum. It was on the edge of her sphere of influence and she had long nursed ambitions of expansion into Apulia.

Plutarch says that Pyrrhus and the Epirote Alliance were greatly encouraged by the number of troops the Tarentines said could be called upon. Tarentum could deliver the fleet but the suggested allied manpower was imaginary and what troops there were did not appear until Pyrrhus had scored his first victory. Surely an old campaigner like Pyrrhus realised the Tarentines were exaggerating, though Plutarch's claim may have derived from a source which drew on Pyrrhus' memoirs. But if Tarentum could not deliver men, she and the Italiote Greek cities could deliver cash. We know from inscribed temple records that from September 281 until Pyrrhus left Italy in 275 BC, the city of Locri gave almost 300 tons of silver coin to 'the king . . . for the common cause'; that was enough to pay an army of over 20,000 men for six years and that was just the contribution of a single city! Rich Tarentum undoubtedly paid more (her payments to Pyrrhus began even before he crossed the Adriatic), and would also have subsidised the war costs of the Samnites and others, who were effectively acting as mercenaries.

The start date of Locri's payments is most interesting; she actually had a small Roman garrison until 280 BC (perhaps only 200 legionaries – like Thurii, Rhegium and Croton, Locri had appealed to Rome for protection against Sabellians). The first payment in

September 281 BC may have been instigated by the anti-Roman faction in the city and coincided with the arrival of Cineas at Tarentum, but the size of the exactions also caused discontent.[20] (There is also the possibility that, when the Italiote cities sided with Pyrrhus in 280 BC or from 279 BC when he demanded large contributions to his war chest, payments were backdated to when his first forces landed in Italy to 'liberate' it.)

Impulsive as ever, Pyrrhus began to dream of conquering an empire in the West to rival the one Alexander the Great had carved out in the East. First Italy, then Sicily, Carthage and Libya, and from this mighty power base he would reclaim the ultimate symbolic prize of Macedonia! According to Pausanias, Pyrrhus also envisaged the struggle as a new Trojan War: the descendant of mighty Achilles versus the Roman descendants of the Trojan refugee Aeneas. According to a foundation myth that was in a process of evolution throughout most of the Republican period, Mars was the Father of the Romans, but Rhea, the Latin princess Mars raped and to whom she bore Romulus and Remus, was a descendant of wandering Aeneas.[21]

Pyrrhus' mind was made up when he received a typically ambiguous response from the oracle of Zeus at Dodona about the success of the proposed expedition. The priestesses, deciphering the words of Zeus from the wind-rustled leaves of the god's sacred oak and the movements of doves on its branches, delivered this response: 'You, if you cross over to Italy, Romans shall conquer.' Receiving an equally double-sided response from the great oracle of Apollo at Delphi ('you . . . the Romans can defeat'), Pyrrhus believed that he would be victorious.[22] He decided to hold the embassy hostage just in case the Tarentines had second thoughts about their invitation.

He presented the proposed expedition to the Epirote Alliance in terms of a Hellenic crusade to liberate Magna Graecia and thus secured the army. He renounced his claims on Macedonia and in return received the promise of troops and twenty Indian war elephants from a relieved Ptolemy Ceraunus (a son of Ptolemy I of

Egypt and called the 'thunderbolt' on account of his daring), who, having just assassinated Seleucus, had barely had time to warm his new throne. Other Hellenistic monarchs enthusiastically contributed troops (or the promise of reinforcements to replace his losses), ships and money for the chance to keep the ambitious and unpredictable Epirote out of their affairs for a while. Antiochus, son of Seleucus, and probably Ptolemy II of Egypt (elder brother of Ceraunus) supplied yet more coin to Pyrrhus' war chest. Antigonus Gonatas, son of Demetrius, who maintained his father's considerable dominions in southern Greece, had his own designs on Macedonia and made doubly sure that Pyrrhus crossed the Adriatic by supplying extra transport ships.[23]

The Eagle sent an advance force of 3,000 men across the Adriatic to Tarentum under the command of his suave chief minister, the Thessalian Cineas, and general Milo (late 281 BC). This force prevented the aristocratic faction seizing control of the city from the democrats and making amends with Rome. A Roman army was devastating the territory of Tarentum, carrying off livestock, burning crops and cutting down vines. The Romans deliberately avoided the property of aristocrats known to favour an alliance with Rome, but the army departed when the professional Epirotes took control of the city. Tarentum was too strongly fortified to take by storm, either by land or sea. The Tarentine navy harried the retreat of the Roman army as it marched along the coastal road, bombarding it from the sea with catapults. Then the Tarentines, perhaps with the aid of the Epirote advance force, laid an ambush for the Romans as they retreated towards Venusia. On both occasions the consul Lucius Aemilius Barbula forced his Tarentine captives to form a protective screen while his army marched on. The Tarentines, not wishing to kill their own, were forced to abandon their attacks.[24]

Once inside Tarentum, Milo seized the acropolis to serve as Pyrrhus' headquarters, and the Epirote officers made themselves hugely unpopular by requisitioning the finest houses as their quarters and making sexual advances on the women and young folk of their hosts. Pyrrhus soon followed with 20,000 heavy infantry, 3,000 cavalry and 2,500 archers and slingers, and the 20 war elephants, but his fleet was scattered by a storm – he refused to wait for calmer spring weather – and in typically adventurous fashion he managed to get himself shipwrecked on the Iapygian peninsula (Calabria), then made his way overland to Tarentum. He used this unplanned excursion to make up the storm losses by recruiting the local Messapians. The citizens of Tarentum, naïvely expecting that Pyrrhus' soldiers would do all the fighting on land for them, were dismayed to find themselves also pressed into service. Pyrrhus was careful not to form them into separate units in case they were tempted to mutiny, but distributed them through the Epirote ranks. A strict drillmaster, the king closed down all the entertainments in the city, including the theatre from which Tarentum had launched its attack on Rome, and made the citizens train daily. Those who refused to serve were executed. The noble and influential Tarentines who had favoured reconciliation with Rome were arrested. Some were put to death, others shipped to Epirus.[25]

THE BATTLE OF HERACLEA[26]

When it was reported that a Roman army, commanded by the new consul Valerius Laevinus, was marching southwards through Lucania and devastating the country as it went, Pyrrhus boldly left the city and advanced to meet the Romans in the plain between Pandosia and Heraclea, the latter city a major outpost of Tarentum dominating a crossing of the River Siris. None of the promised allies arrived to bolster the Epirote army and its Tarentine conscripts. The Samnites had been fighting the Romans since 284 BC and were involved in on-going operations. Also, the continued presence of Aemilius Barbula's army at Venusia made it difficult for them to send any force directly to Pyrrhus. The Lucani and Bruttii were also constrained by the army at Venusia, but more so by another force that Laevinus had planted at an unspecified strategic point in Lucania 'to prevent its people sending aid to his opponent'.[27] Other tribes and Italiote cities would wait and see what the Epirotes were made of, though one wonders if the vindictive Tarentines forced the Thurians to supply troops. Despite the lack of reinforcements Pyrrhus thought it shameful to hold back and allow the Romans to advance any further. Laevinus also thought it shameful to waste any time in getting to grips with Pyrrhus. Moreover, he was conscious of the need to fight the war as far as possible from Rome and the territory of her Allies (mostly in central Italy). If he was defeated closer to Rome the city would be in danger and the Allies might be encouraged to revolt.

Modern historians sometimes assert that Pyrrhus' army was out-numbered by the Romans. The Roman army was composed of two legions, each of *c.* 4,000–5,000 men, and *c.* 16,000–20,000 Allies, assuming that the ratio of Allies was 2:1, but the ratio of Allies to Romans varied. If the number of Allies were equal to the legionaries – a common enough occurrence – the Roman army would have numbered only *c.* 18–20,000.

As we have seen, Pyrrhus lost some men while crossing the Adriatic, though it seems the ships were mostly scattered by the storm rather than sunk. These losses were made good by the Messapii, and most of the scattered fleet eventually made it to Tarentum. Coupled with the 3,000 Epirotes already in Tarentum, the large-scale conscription of Tarentines and the possible presence of Italian mercenary bands, Pyrrhus' army at Heraclea numbered at least 25,000 soldiers, and was conceivably much larger. Even so, it is obvious that Pyrrhus would have preferred more men.[28]

From his camp Pyrrhus sent a messenger with a letter to Laevinus. The epistle bade the Roman to disband his army and come to Pyrrhus, who would arbitrate the dispute between Rome and Tarentum and compel the guilty party to make amends. The king offered Rome his friendship but simultaneously emphasised his skill as a general and the prowess of his army. Pyrrhus gave the consul ten days to make a decision; he hoped that Laevinus would dither and therefore exhaust his provisions. Pyrrhus was also hopeful that reinforcements might yet appear. However, Laevinus wasted no time and sent the messenger back with a letter declaring that he had never heard such arrogant nonsense. He had no need of a court of arbitration with Pyrrhus as its judge; he would face trial in the court of Mars, the progenitor of the Roman people, meaning the field of battle.[29] Laevinus then continued his advance and established camp on the opposite bank of the Siris. Pyrrhus watched this development with interest. He was taken aback by the discipline of the Roman soldiers and amazed at the construction of the fortified camp with its ditch and rampart and orderly rows of tents. Pyrrhus was hardly a stranger to such camps – he was famous for employing them – but he had not expected to see the earthworks thrown up so quickly and professionally by men whom he considered to be barbarians. He is said to have commented to his 'friend' (*philos* – divisional commander) Megacles that 'The discipline of these barbarians is not barbarous.'[30]

* * *

That the Roman army was so good at camp building, even in the face of the enemy, was the result of going to war every year. Even when there was no enemy to fight the Senate would send out the legions and Allies on raiding expeditions to keep the men 'sharp'. It was probably also thought expedient to keep the Allies occupied lest they be tempted to turn their considerable manpower on Rome. For example, 303 BC was a rather lean year for warfare but the keen ears of the two consuls heard whispers of bandits in Umbria. Something that required a policing operation was used as excuse to mount a full-scale expedition involving both consular armies:

> So that their year might not go by without any war whatever,
> the consuls made a little expedition into Umbria, because of
> a report that armed men were issuing from a certain cave and
> making raids upon the farms. The soldiers carried their
> standards into the cave, and there in the murk received many

wounds, particularly from rocks that were hurled at them. Finally they found the other mouth of the cavern – for there was a way of going through it – and heaped up faggots at both entrances and set them on fire. In this way about 2,000 armed men perished in the cave from the smoke and the heat, for they finally rushed into the flames in their very efforts to escape. (Livy, 10.1.4–6)

One wonders if some of the 2,000 'bandits' were actually refugees who had fled the Roman incursion.

In 299 BC the legions and cohorts again marched into Umbria and besieged Nequinum. It was the town's misfortune to be situated on a strategic crossing of the River Nar. Its capture would ensure Roman domination of Umbria and prevent its tribes making troublesome alliances with Etruscans and Gauls. The siege, however, was carried out almost in a leisurely fashion and when the town was finally taken – by treachery rather than by storm – it was thoroughly looted. Latin colonists were then sent to re-establish it as Narnia.[31]

Giving the soldiers practice in siege warfare and the opportunity to plunder seems also to have figured heavily in the Romans' considerations. At this time legionaries were not professional soldiers. They were citizens called away from their farms and businesses for the duration of a campaign: if the state wanted to wage war every year it had to be made profitable for the soldiers. Fabricius Luscinus believed that his campaign against the Lucani and Bruttii in 282 BC was all the more successful because he had managed to capture and plunder many enemy towns 'from which he enriched his army'.[32] Livy attributes a notable appeal to the gods by a consul when he led his army into a Samnite ambush (311 BC):

The consul rode up to the place where the fighting was most serious, leapt down from his horse and called upon Jupiter and Mars and the other gods to witness that he had not come here seeking glory for himself, but only plunder for his soldiers. (Livy, 9.31.10)

Between the ages of seventeen and forty-six Roman citizens of sufficient property qualification – equipping oneself with arms and armour was an expensive business – were liable to be called up for sixteen or twenty annual campaigns, though only in emergencies would a man serve in many consecutive annual campaigns. Men aged over forty-six remained under obligation to serve, forming the garrisons of Rome and important colonies. The Roman army had yet to develop into a 'professional' organisation, namely permanent legions composed of full-time salaried soldiers, but with such a heavy service requirement it always had a high proportion of experienced veterans. Although the Allies usually supplied half, and sometimes more, of the manpower of the Roman army, the actual proportion of troops sent by each individual state was considerably less than Rome levied from her own citizens. On the other hand, the Allies might serve a greater number of campaigns and were sometimes subject to harsher discipline.[33]

Rome's citizen and Allied manpower was huge. Herein lay the secret of her success. Her armies were composed of tough veterans and even if an army was destroyed it could quickly be replaced. This was the case in 284 BC. The Senones destroyed the consular army of the militarily inexperienced Caecilius Metellus at Arretium in Etruria, but the following year the Romans raised new legions and won a crushing victory over the Gauls at Lake Vadimon. As we have seen, in 282 BC another consular army was sent to relieve Thurii despite continuing fighting against Samnites, Etruscans and Gauls. In 280 BC the census recorded 287,222 Roman citizens (the actual number of males liable for legionary service may have been only half of this), added to which were thousands upon thousands of Latin citizens and other Allies. Pyrrhus probably did not know what he was letting himself in for.[34]

* * *

Meanwhile one of Pyrrhus' scouts was captured and brought to Laevinus. The consul paraded the complete army for the bemused scout and declared Rome had many more armies like it. He then sent him away with an invitation for Pyrrhus to visit the camp: 'Tell the king that Laevinus, the Roman consul, asks that he send no more spies but to come himself and see with his own eyes the power of Rome.'[35] Despite this show of confidence, Laevinus was worried. Many of the Roman legionaries and Allies were awed by the reputation of Pyrrhus and fearful of his war elephants. They had never seen such beasts before and, having no better name, called them 'Lucanian Cows'.[36] Laevinus knew that, if he delayed, the morale of his men would plummet and Sabellian reinforcements might reach Pyrrhus. He decided to force an immediate crossing of the river and bring Pyrrhus to battle on the plain. He set about motivating the soldiers (*cohortatio*).

Roman soldiers liked to be reminded of four things when their general made a speech. First, that the gods were on their side. The Romans believed that they were a chosen people, sired by Mars and favoured by Jupiter, but when the enemy were close at hand they needed to be reassured, thus the general and priests accompanying the army would watch for favourable omens and sacrifice to the gods. Second, the soldiers liked to be told that they were courageous while their opponents were pathetic weaklings. Zonaras tells us that Laevinus' speech 'contained many exhortations to courage'.[37] Third, that they would be victorious. Fourth, and not least, the general would emphasise that, in the event of victory, plunder and slaves and perhaps even land would be for the taking.

Laevinus attempted to cross the river by the ford in front of the camp, but Pyrrhus had anticipated this move and posted a strong force on the opposite bank. For a time the Epirote force succeeded in holding the Romans back and Pyrrhus used the delay to array his battle line on the plain. Reconstructions of the battle sometimes assume that the elephants were on the wings of Pyrrhus' army, guarding the exposed flanks of his phalanx. However, Zonaras says they were kept in reserve, and indeed they played no part until the end of the battle, perhaps being deliberately kept out of sight, so their appearance would have the maximum shock effect.[38] Unable to force the crossing, Laevinus ordered his cavalry to ride out of sight, as if they were being sent on a plundering expedition. They were then to find other fords, circle around the Epirote position at the original ford and attack from behind. They were successful. The Epirotes broke in panic and the Roman infantry surged across the river.

Pyrrhus had by now deployed his battle line and sought to destroy the head of the Roman infantry column before the rest of it had time to cross and deploy into line. He spurred forward with his 3,000 cavalry but his move was countered by the Roman and Allied cavalry that had surprised the Epirotes at the ford. The king ordered his men to close up and led the charge. This was met with stubborn resistance by the Roman and Allied horse. Sensing that the fight was finely balanced, the king was everywhere at once, directing the fighting and supporting the hard-pressed with his bodyguard:

> While personally engaging in combat and repelling all his attackers, he did not become confused in his decisions nor lose his presence of mind. He directed the action as though he were watching it from a distance, but he was everywhere himself, and always managed to be at hand to support his troops wherever the pressure was greatest. (Plutarch, *Pyrrhus*, 16.7–8)

Pyrrhus was wearing typically extravagant battle gear and attracted the attention of a *turma* (squadron) of Ferentani cavalry.[39] The Allied troopers shadowed Pyrrhus' every move, waiting for an opportunity to attack. When the Ferentani seized their chance and charged, Pyrrhus' bodyguards closed up around him, but Obsidius (or Oblacus), prefect of the *turma*, broke through their ranks and bore down on the king, grasping his lance with both hands. Leonnatus the Macedonian, one of the royal bodyguards, counter-charged Obsidius and killed his horse but, even as the horse collapsed under him, Obsidius' lance took the king's mount full in the chest. Pyrrhus' bodyguards dragged him off the stricken horse and away from the fighting. Obsidius was surrounded and eventually cut down. Seeing him fall, the Ferentani went berserk and managed to retrieve his body. Thinking their king dead, Pyrrhus' cavalry broke off from the fighting, though the king had already mounted another horse and was riding back towards his infantry.

Pyrrhus was evidently taken aback by Obsidius' assault. We have seen that the king was an accomplished monomachist (Greek for duellist) but this battle was too important for him to risk his life unnecessarily. He swapped his magnificent armour and purple cloak (maybe a gift from the Tarentines) for Megacles' plain breastplate, felt cap, such as was worn under a helmet to absorb the force of blows, and brown cloak. The loyal officer was then charged with riding up and down the battle line to hearten the Epirotes and Tarentines and to draw the attention of the Roman cavalry, allowing the real Pyrrhus to direct the advance of the phalanx without being hindered by glory-seeking warriors.[40]

The Roman army completed its crossing of the Siris and deployed into battle line. Pyrrhus was impressed by the sight of it, rank upon rank of tough legionaries and Allied soldiers equipped with tall *scutum* shields, short swords and long *pila* – a heavy javelin with a long iron head which, if thrown with enough force at close range, could punch through shield and armour and flesh. The veteran legionaries in the third and final line of maniples (the *triarii*) were armed with long thrusting spears. If the battle turned into a rout they would form a phalanx and cover the retreat of the army. Proud centurions, chosen for their valour and steadiness and laden with military decorations, were in the front ranks shouting encouragement to the men in their maniples. At the rear of the maniples the *optiones*, the centurions' deputies, were ready to shove any laggards back into line. Above them shone the standards of the legions: the minotaur, the horse, the boar, the wolf of Mars and the eagle of Jupiter. Their helmets sported the tall feathers that proclaimed them as the sons of Mars.

Due to the nature of the Romans' more open manipular formation (the Romans allowed each man plenty of room to use javelin and sword freely, and intervals were maintained between each maniple of 120 or 60 men), their battle line was perhaps longer than the Epirotes and we may presume that Pyrrhus had deployed his cavalry and light troops (archers and slingers) to cover the flanks of the phalanx. Still, he was certain his phalanx would crash through the legions and Allied cohorts. Moreover, the Romans now had the river at their backs; if they were forced into retreat they would have nowhere to go.

The 'Macedonian' phalanx was so-called because Philip II of Macedon had developed the formation out of the old hoplite phalanx of eight to twelve ranks (in which the Roman legion itself had once fought and some of Rome's enemies, such as the Etruscans, still used a form of it). It was the instrument with which Alexander the Great had conquered the Persian Empire. The basic unit of the Macedonian phalanx was the *speira* of 256 men arranged in files of sixteen and with a front of sixteen. Block after block of *speirai* combined to form a seemingly impenetrable wall of iron pike heads. The best soldiers formed the front and rear ranks, veteran officers and under-officers who could be relied upon to advance fearlessly and prevent any raw recruits peeling away from the rear of the formation. Those in the front rank bound the phalanx together and were called the 'edge of the sword'. Each phalangite was armed with a *sarissa* (pike) some sixteen feet long. The *sarissai* of the first four ranks projected beyond the phalanx, while those of the remaining ranks were held vertically and helped to break up volleys of missiles. The phalangites were arrayed almost shoulder to shoulder and needed both hands to use their *sarissai*, so their shields were strapped to their left arms and also supported by a neck strap. The Macedonian phalanx was a superb combination of moral and physical power. Few troops could stand the sight of a seemingly solid wall of phalangites bearing down on them, fearing they would be impaled or trampled. Few again could withstand the actual collision of the phalanx; when its sixteen ranks gained momentum it would simply shove battle lines of lesser depth and cohesion off the field.[41] Aemilius Paullus, who fought the Macedonians at Pydna in 168 BC, said he had never been confronted by anything as frightening as the phalanx:

> He saw that they were swinging down their small shields from their shoulders to cover their front and levelling their *sarissai* to meet the attack of his shield-bearing troops [legionaries equipped with the *scutum*]. He saw the strength of their interlocked shields and the fierceness of their attack and was both amazed and filled with fear. He had never seen a more terrifying sight. Later he would often speak of that day, of what he saw and his emotions. (Plutarch, *Aemilius Paullus*, 19.3)

Yet, like all formations, the phalanx was vulnerable at the flanks, especially the unshielded right, and if *speirai* or files were forced to part because of rough ground an enemy could get in among the ranks and cause slaughter; the unwieldy *sarissai* were useless at such close quarters. The phalangites were also equipped with swords but they were not accustomed to the one-on-one combat favoured by the Romans and other Italians.

Pyrrhus expected that his phalanx would bulldoze the relatively open Roman formation, but this hope was not fulfilled. The Roman legion met the Macedonian phalanx for the first time at Heraclea, and it says much for the courage of the veterans of both armies, the two ranks of warriors at the front of each formation who could actually see their enemy, that they stood their ground despite alien and terrifying tactics. The Roman soldiers met the phalanx with volley after volley of heavy *pila* and other missiles. (The sources do not mention it, but the Romans were surely also suffering from the missile barrage of Pyrrhus' archers and slingers; the ancient composite bow was as deadly as the famed medieval longbow, and sling bullets (*glandes*) are so-called for good reason.) However, so long as the Epirotes kept their tight formation on the level plain the Romans could not get past the massive pikes. It was usual for a legionary to throw his *pilum*, draw his sword and charge at the run, using his shield like a battering ram and crashing into the enemy.

Once in the enemy formation he would set to work with his sword, stabbing and cutting, spreading terror and dismay; no other people used the sword with such grim determination as the Romans. This was not possible at Heraclea: each legionary had to negotiate a serrated alley of *sarissa* heads before he could confront a phalangite, and the full impact of the *pila* barrage was probably broken by the hedge of swaying pike shafts. Yet neither could the Epirotes break through the more open and mobile Roman formations or even push them back for long. Thus the two lines of infantry charged, collided, fought, shoved back and forth, broke off and then did it all over again. This happened seven times. Then Megacles was killed.[42]

Megacles had done his work well, inspiring the troops with his 'royal' presence and leaving Pyrrhus free to direct the attacks of the phalanx. He was a continual target for attack by Roman and Allied warriors and, despite his being well protected by Pyrrhus' bodyguards, a trooper called Decius eventually succeeded in landing a mortal blow on him. The royal helmet and purple and gold cloak were torn from his corpse and displayed triumphantly. The consul Laevinus seized the opportunity, thrust his sword into a nearby corpse and rode along the Roman line shouting that the blood on the blade belonged to Pyrrhus![43] The Roman army was exultant. The soldiers charged again, no doubt bellowing war cries and drumming *pila* and swords against shields in typical Roman and Italic fashion. Laevinus then ordered a contingent of cavalry he had held in reserve to go around the flank of the Epirote army and fall on it from behind.

The Epirotes and Tarentines saw Megacles fall and believed Pyrrhus was dead. Their resistance faltered. Only those troops immediately around Pyrrhus in the phalanx knew the king was alive. Pyrrhus immediately threw off his felt cap and spurred out of the battle line, riding down its length and declaring he was still with them. Spotting Laevinus' detached force of cavalry, Pyrrhus signalled the war elephants forward from their place in the reserve. The Roman horses became uncontrollable as soon as they caught the alien scent of the elephants, many throwing their riders. The cavalry turned in panicked flight – directly into the path of the advancing Roman infantry. Chaos ensued as the cavalry tried to get through the leading ranks of the infantry, while the rear ranks were still pressing forward. The terrible elephants followed, trampling men and horses underfoot or impaling them with their tusks, while the soldiers in the towers strapped to the backs of the elephants rained down missiles or lunged at the Romans with long *sarissai*. The Roman army turned in panic.

It was time now for the kill and Pyrrhus sent in his Thessalian cavalry to complete the rout. They speared and cut down the Roman soldiers as they ran towards the river. In ancient warfare most casualties were inflicted during the rout. The more reliable accounts of the battle tell us that 7,000 Roman soldiers were killed and 1,800 captured, many of the latter being nobles serving in the cavalry. As well as those killed by the Thessalian cavalry, many must have been knocked down and trampled by their comrades during the panicked flight or drowned attempting to cross the Siris. Plutarch says that the pursuit did not end until nightfall, but Zonaras and other sources state that Pyrrhus had to abandon the pursuit at the river when one of the war elephants was injured and its distress infected the other animals. Orosius relates that Minucius, a centurion of the *hastati* (the first line of maniples in the legionary battle formation), cut the trunk from the elephant and so ensured the escape of the Roman army. However, another source places this episode at Ausculum, fought in 279 BC.[44]

AFTER THE BATTLE

The following day Pyrrhus surveyed the human debris on the battlefield and received a tally of his own casualties. He had lost almost 4,000 men, many of them his best Epirote officers and veteran soldiers – presumably casualties of the initial fighting at the river crossing, and from the more exposed front ranks of the phalanx. Pyrrhus could not easily replace these men whereas the Romans could call up more and more citizen and Allied troops. The figure, and the admission that the dead men were his best, probably derive from Pyrrhus' own account of the Italian campaigns in his *Hypomnemata* ('memoirs'). For the king's 3,500 casualties at the subsequent battle of Ausculum, Plutarch states that the figure was taken by Hieronymus of Cardia from Pyrrhus' memoirs. Hieronymus was a contemporary of Pyrrhus and wrote an extensive history about the *Diadochi* which is now only known from fragments. In contrast to most generals of the ancient world, Pyrrhus appears to have prided himself on accurately recording his losses. It was usual to inflate the losses of the defeated and minimise those of the victor. An extreme example is the Roman general Sulla, who claimed to have slaughtered 100,000 Pontic soldiers at Chaeronea in 86 BC, while losing only fourteen killed or missing – and two were later found alive, reducing the number of casualties to twelve! Sulla would have been horrified by the dedicatory inscription that Pyrrhus set up at the temple of Zeus in Tarentum which referred to his heavy losses at Heraclea: 'Those men who before were unconquered . . . I have conquered and have been conquered by them.'[45]

That Pyrrhus lost almost 4,000 men demonstrates how hard the Romans and the Allies fought at Heraclea. Later Roman historians revelled in the tale of Pyrrhus' inspection of the dead on the field of Heraclea.[46] Typical is the account of Florus. Pyrrhus is found marvelling at the corpses of the legionaries:

> The wounds of all of them were on their chests; some shared deaths with their foes, all had their swords still in their hands, a threatening mien still marked their features, and their anger yet lived even in death. So struck was Pyrrhus with admiration that he exclaimed, 'How easy were it for me to win the empire of the world if I had an army of Romans, or for the Romans to win it if they had me as their king!' (Florus, *Epitome*, 1.13.17–18)

Thinking it disgraceful that such brave men should be left to rot in the fields, the king ordered their corpses cremated. He also asked the Roman captives to join him but was politely refused. The weapons of the Romans were collected and sent to Dodona to be dedicated to Zeus with the inscription, 'King Pyrrhus and the Epirotes and the Tarentines to Zeus Naius [took these spoils] from the Romans and their allies.' To the famous shrine of Athena at Lindus on Rhodes the king dedicated his flamboyant armour – the panoply that almost lost him the battle.[47]

Within days, news of the victory spread and representatives from the Samnites, Lucanians, Bruttians and Italiote Greek cities soon followed, congratulating Pyrrhus and finally offering their support. The Eagle was at first angry, grumbling that it was very well for them to appear now, but he could have done with their support at the battle. However, he soon became diplomatic; it is easy to imagine cool Cineas stepping in at this point to smooth things over. Not wishing to alienate his new allies (the Lucanians and Bruttii probably viewed him with some suspicion because he was the nephew of the hated Alexander the Molossian), Pyrrhus turned on his considerable charm and offered them a share of the spoils. He was hiding his real feelings, but he needed Sabellian warriors and Italiote cash to fulfil his imperial dreams.[48]

THE EAGLE FLIES NORTH

His army reinforced by Samnites, Lucani and Bruttii, and perhaps also by contingents from the main Italiote Greek cities – Croton, Metapontum, Locri – the Eagle marched north through Lucania and into Campania, long dominated by the Romans. The Epirote troops (and presumably also the Thessalian cavalry), aggrieved at having lost part of their hard-won booty to the new allies, spent much of the march plundering friendly territory and this persuaded any waverers in Campania to bar their gates. Pyrrhus hoped to win over the major Sabellian and Greek cities of Campania, Capua and Neapolis (Naples). However, Laevinus, having presumably retreated first to Venusia (or the stronghold he had established earlier in Lucania) where he treated his wounded and waited for the scattered remnants of his army to return, was sent reinforcements by the Senate and instructed to pursue Pyrrhus. A scathing Fabricius told the Senate that the Epirotes had not defeated the Roman army; it was Pyrrhus who had conquered Laevinus. The sentiment was echoed in the Senate's response to Cineas' embassy (*see below*): Pyrrhus might defeat one thousand Laevinuses but he would never conquer Rome. Frontinus states that, as punishment, the Senate ordered disgraced Laevinus to winter his army at Saepinum, a Samnite town destroyed by Rome in 293 BC, but the order is perhaps viewed better as a measure to inhibit hostile moves by the Samnites.[49]

On learning of the defeat, the Senate enforced an emergency levy, even recruiting *proletarii*, that is poor citizens normally exempt from legionary (but not all military) service on account of their not having enough money for the necessary arms and armour. Laevinus' reinforced army beat Pyrrhus in the race to Capua and the Eagle turned away from its strongly defended walls (he was evidently without a siege train). Similarly rebuffed at Neapolis, Pyrrhus wasted no time and again swung his march north. His intent was not to capture Rome. If he faltered before Capua and Naples, how could he storm Rome? His ultimate destination was Etruria, where Rome was still fighting against the cities of Volsinii and Vulci, and the king hoped to form a northern coalition and so exert pressure on Rome on two fronts and force her to submit without fighting another major battle. However, the other consul, Tiberius Coruncanius, either managed to defeat the Etruscans in the nick of time or, perhaps more likely, he patched up a truce and moved his army south against Pyrrhus. Some sources claim Pyrrhus reached the hill-town of Praeneste in Latium, only twenty miles east of Rome, and from its lofty walls he could see the city itself. It seems more likely that the nearest he came was Anagnia, some forty miles to the south-east of the city (indicating that he was marching along the Via Latinia), where he was informed of the new situation in Etruria.[50]

Despite the protestations of his allies – presumably loudest from the Samnites who had long dreamed of ravaging Latium – Pyrrhus retreated back the way he came, harassed all the time by Laevinus. The consul finally offered battle when the king's army entered Campania. Pyrrhus looked on Laevinus' army with some surprise; it was now bigger than it had been at Heraclea. He declared that the legions were like the Lernaean hydra: if you cut them up into small pieces, they only grew whole again. Pyrrhus did not wish to fight a pitched battle with Coruncanius hot on his heels – if he dallied he might well find himself surrounded – but nevertheless ordered his troops and corps of elephants to form line of battle, and had them raise an immense clamour, clashing weapons against shields and shouting war cries, the elephants and trumpeters making a cacophony of noise. The Romans responded with an apparently even greater *clamor* (war cry). Zonaras says that this so terrified Pyrrhus' men that they refused to come to close quarters with the Romans; Pyrrhus withdrew 'as if the omens were bad'. Laevinus did not try to force a fight. With Coruncanius not yet on the scene the disgraced consul was probably unwilling to risk a second defeat closer to Rome, and with Pyrrhus abandoning the field, the moral victory belonged to the Roman. He could claim to have driven the king away and thus saved Rome. The Eagle returned to Tarentum having accomplished nothing.[51]

NEGOTIATIONS

It was by now autumn and envoys from Rome were sent to Tarentum to negotiate the release of the soldiers taken prisoner at Heraclea. Pyrrhus was keen to reach a speedy conclusion. The resources and resolve of Rome were far greater than he had expected.[52] He directed Cineas to return to Rome with the envoys and to seek a general peace, taking with him a number of the prisoners as a goodwill gesture. As a young man Cineas had been the most able pupil of the great Athenian orator Demosthenes; Pyrrhus declared that Cineas' eloquence had won him more cities than he had taken by the spear. Now Cineas turned the full force of his talents against the Senate. Although some of the senators understood Greek, he presumably spoke through an interpreter. He offered peace and military alliance with Pyrrhus on condition that the Romans recognise the independence of Tarentum and the Italiote Greeks, agree not to make aggressive moves or meddle in their affairs again, and that they evacuate occupied Samnite and Lucanian territory in southern Italy, limiting the Romans' sphere of influence to central Italy. The military alliance aspect of the terms is interesting. The alliance was with Pyrrhus alone, not the Epirotes. The king would come to the aid of Rome if she was threatened by an aggressor, even suggesting that he would help in the completion of her northern Italian conquests, but the reality was that Pyrrhus wanted the legions to fight in his wars. To demonstrate the king's peaceful nature and generosity, Cineas (artfully glossing over Pyrrhus' hasty retreat from Latium) declared that the king had not attacked Rome despite having ample opportunity to do so, and would now release all the captives without ransom.[53]

A few senators were tempted, perhaps those with whom Cineas had sought private audiences and given gifts to prior to addressing the Senate, but old Appius Claudius Caecus ('the blind') was aghast. Learning that a foreign enemy was dictating terms, he bade his slaves carry him through the Forum in a litter, then he was helped into the Senate House by his many sons and sons-in-law who were members of the august assembly. Having made a suitably dramatic entrance, the forceful and influential ex-consul berated the senators for even contemplating such terms. 'I used to think my blindness a misfortune,' he said. 'Now I wish I was deaf as well.' Rome would not be dictated to by a foreign enemy, he continued, Pyrrhus must be driven from Italian soil! Caecus reminded the younger senators that the Romans of his generation had beaten all comers. When threatened by the aspirations of Alexander the Great they did not worry: 'If Alexander the Great had come to Italy and fought us when we were young men and our fathers were in their prime, he would not now be celebrated as invincible. He would either have been killed or fled, and so made Rome even more glorious!' Caecus spat that Pyrrhus in no way compared to Alexander. Although Pyrrhus promised to be Rome's ally in Italy, what use was his army when it could not hold even a small part of Macedonia from Lysimachus? If Rome accepted his alliance her enemies would think her weak. The Samnites and Tarentines would be laughing at Rome. Caecus' conclusion was that Pyrrhus and Rome's other enemies had to be punished. The speech became famous and was still drawn on for inspiration by Romans in the first century BC.

The Senate voted unanimously to reject the proposal and to expel Cineas from the city immediately. He was told that the Romans would 'wage implacable war upon Pyrrhus for as long as he remained in Italy'. Once the king was back in his own country they would consider his overtures for friendship. The diplomatic gifts Cineas gave to the ladies of the great Roman families were now interpreted as bribes (which they were) and he returned to Tarentum with the Roman prisoners. When Pyrrhus asked Cineas what manner of men the Roman senators were he said, 'They are like kings.'[54]

In the winter another Roman delegation led by Fabricius Luscinus, conqueror of the Lucanians, sought the release of the prisoners before they were deported to Epirus or sold into slavery.[55] Pyrrhus was still eager for a settlement. He sent an honour guard to meet the embassy as it crossed into Tarentine territory, and when it approached the city came out to welcome the envoys in person. Pyrrhus was greatly impressed with the charismatic and incorruptible Fabricius. His attempts to bribe the Roman with gold and the promise of a high command failed miserably. 'If I were to serve you,' joked Fabricius, 'those men who now advise and honour you would surely find me preferable and have me for king!' For a second time Pyrrhus paroled a number of prisoners, allowing them to return to Rome for the Saturnalia, the festival of Saturn celebrated on 17 December. Unless peace was made, the Senate agreed to return the men by a certain date and would execute any who refused to go back.[56]

THE BATTLE OF AUSCULUM

The captives were duly returned. Frustrated by the Romans' refusal to negotiate a peace, Pyrrhus spent the winter of 280–279 BC preparing for a new campaign. In the spring he advanced northwards into Apulia, taking numerous towns along the way, either by storm or submission.[57] He perhaps followed the coastal route up to Barium (Bari), with the Tarentine fleet supporting him. Pyrrhus' intention seems to have been to by-pass the Roman stronghold of Venusia, then, turning inland and following the line of the River Aufidus, to advance through rebellious Samnium and on to Latium and Rome. However, the new consuls for 279 BC, Publius Sulpicius Saverrio and Publius Decius Mus, perhaps having united their armies at Venusia, headed-off Pyrrhus at Ausculum in northern Apulia before he could enter Samnium.

Plutarch's account of the battle is the most straightforward and is the only source to reveal that the fighting was spread over two days. The consuls took up position on rough wooded ground where Pyrrhus' phalanx could not deploy, and his elephants and cavalry found the terrain difficult to negotiate. A deep river with steep wooded banks also benefited the Romans, though Plutarch does not specify if it protected a flank of the Roman army or completely separated the two forces. Pyrrhus' army sustained heavy casualties and broke off fighting at sunset. During the night Pyrrhus sent contingents of troops to occupy certain points on the rough ground. These had presumably played an important part in the day's fighting, though what they were – ridges, a ford on the river? – Plutarch does not say. Nor is it clear whether the Romans had manned these key areas or if the complete army had retired into its fortified camp.

Whatever the case, on the following morning, with Pyrrhus' troops now occupying parts of the rough terrain, the Romans were compelled to come down on to the more level ground where Pyrrhus was offering battle. Pyrrhus had chosen his ground well because there was apparently no room for the Romans to make flanking manoeuvres.

The king's phalanx was now arrayed in close order, with the cavalry presumably on the wings. Plutarch states that the slingers and archers took up position in the spaces between the war elephants. It is not clear where the elephants were positioned but Plutarch emphasises that the Romans were desperate to defeat the phalanx before the beasts were brought into action. Colliding with the phalanx head-on, the legionaries and Allies fought furiously, but, after using up their *pila*, their swords made little impact against the much longer reach of the *sarissai*. The Roman army finally began to fall back where Pyrrhus himself was leading the attack (and was wounded by a *pilum* for his efforts), but it was the appearance of the elephants that put the Roman army to flight. The Romans lost 6,000 men, the consul Decius probably among them, but many others reached the safety of the nearby camp. (This perhaps also suggests that the river did not run between the Roman and Epirote camps.)

Plutarch derived the casualty figure from Hieronymus, who also reported that, according to Pyrrhus' memoirs, the king's casualties were 3,505, again mostly his best Epirote officers and phalangites. Almost all of his original *philoi* were now dead. When a soldier congratulated him on the victory, Pyrrhus made the famous se: 'If we are victorious in one more battle with the Romans, we shall be utterly ruined.'[58] It is from this statement that we derive our expression 'Pyrrhic victory' to describe a victory which costs the winner more than the loser, but the expression was not actually coined until 1875. The ancients termed such victories 'Cadmean' after the legend of Cadmus, who sowed the dragon's teeth with the intention of 'growing' inhabitants for his new city of Thebes, but the new Thebans emerged from the earth as fully armed warriors and attacked each other. When the pointless battle was over, only five were left. The expression was also applied to Cadmus' descendants Polynices and Eteocles, who killed each other when fighting for

control of Thebes. Diodorus thought that Pyrrhus' victories were
Cadmean:

> All of Pyrrhus' victories were Cadmean. For the Romans,
> though defeated, were in no way humbled, since their
> dominion was so great. Pyrrhus, on the other hand, had
> suffered the damage and disaster that commonly go with
> defeat. (Diodorus Siculus, 22.6.2)

It should also be noted here that the main sources – Dio, Diodorus
and Zonaras – apply the 'Pyrrhic victory' statement to Heraclea, but
it makes more sense for the king to have said it after the second
costly victory at Ausculum.[59]

AUSCULUM, DAY 2: DIVERGING ACCOUNTS

Dionysius of Halicarnassus, Zonaras and Frontinus all give accounts
of the second day of fighting at Ausculum. They supply the details
missing from Plutarch: the size and composition of the opposing
armies; where the infantry, cavalry and elephants were positioned in
the battle lines; and the specific tactics used by Pyrrhus and the
consuls. However, the sources contradict each other.

Dionysius gives a detailed breakdown of the battle lines. On
Pyrrhus' right flank were Macedonian infantry. Beside them were
Italian mercenaries hired by Tarentum, Ambracians, and Tarentines
equipped with distinctive white shields. These contingents fought as
a phalanx. Beside the Tarentines were a mixed force of Lucani and
Bruttii. The centre of the line was composed of Epirotes and Greek
mercenaries from Aetolia, Acarnania and Athamania. The left was
formed by the Samnites, suggesting that they were in greater
numbers than any of the other allies or mercenaries. Also, the
Samnites were the only Italian troops to be equipped with the tall
scutum. The total number of infantry is given as 70,000.

Dionysius continues that the cavalry were positioned on the
wings: the Samnite, Thessalian, Bruttian and Italian mercenary
squadrons on the right; the Ambracian, Tarentine citizen, and Greek

mercenary horse (the Macedonian cavalry is described as mercenary) on the left. The light troops and nineteen war elephants (indicating that one was killed at Heraclea) were divided into two groups, one behind each wing, 'in a position slightly elevated above the plain'. Pyrrhus himself was surrounded by the royal *agema* of 2,000 picked horsemen, positioned behind the battle line and ready to intervene wherever his troops were hard-pressed by the Romans. The combined number of cavalry exceeded 8,000.

Frontinus, evidently using a different source from Dionysius, says that, according to the Homeric verse where the worst troops are put in the centre, the Samnites and Epirotes formed the right flank (traditionally the strongest in an ancient army), the Bruttii, Lucani and Messapians on the left, and the Tarentines in the centre. The elephants *and* cavalry were held in reserve. There were no Greek mercenary contingents. The size of the army is given as 40,000.

For the Roman army, Dionysius and Frontinus both suggest four consular legions (two per consul) of c. 5,000 men per legion. However, Dionysius adds 50,000 Latin and other Allies, whereas Frontinus gives only 20,000, equalling the number of legionaries. Both sources agree that the Allies were distributed between the legions, perhaps filling the intervals between the maniples so as to present a continuous front, and with the cavalry on the wings. Frontinus suggests that legionaries were held in reserve, though this might be a vague reference to the typical triple-line formation of the manipular legion.

Another source adds further confusion. The soldier and historian Polybius wrote in the mid-second century BC (he was a political detainee of the Romans 168–150 BC). He was much closer to the events than Plutarch and the other writers, and also had the advantage of being an eye-witness to phalanxes and legions similar to the type deployed in the Pyrrhic War. In a discussion of the superiority of the legion over the Macedonian phalanx, Polybius notes that in Italy Pyrrhus alternated the maniples of his Italian allies (Samnites and Lucanians) with the units of his phalanx in an attempt to create a less rigid battle line. This gives the impression of a far more composite formation than described by Dionysius and Frontinus.

It is certainly possible that Pyrrhus levied a force from his province of Ambracia and employed mercenaries from Aetolia and other areas within his sphere of influence in north and central Greece, as well as demanding troops from the Hellenistic kings who had eagerly subsidised his expedition in 281 BC, but as reinforcements for his depleted Epirote phalanx and light troops (the Acarnanians were renowned skirmishers). Plutarch notes that Pyrrhus could not expect the Epirote League to send him any more troops or money. We have seen how Pyrrhus was supplied with immense amounts of coin by his Italiote Greek allies but one wonders if this would have stretched to maintain Dionysius' array of 78,000 (more if one includes the garrison troops, for example the strong force Pyrrhus maintained in Tarentum to ensure its loyalty, garrisons in the recently captured Apulian towns and so on). All in all, Frontinus' estimate of 40,000 in each army seems more acceptable.[60]

Frontinus does not give an account of the actual fighting but Dionysius goes into considerable detail. The cavalry battle is viewed as a sideshow to the infantry clash. Having sung a hymn to their gods of war and raised their battle cries, the soldiers advance. The right wing of each army is the stronger but the left wings still give a good account of themselves, keeping order and falling back slowly. The Macedonians on Pyrrhus' right wing push back the First Legion and its Latin Allies, but in the centre, the Fourth Legion drives back the Epirote phalanx. Pyrrhus orders up the war elephants to aid the Epirotes (Dionysius does not specify which contingent of elephants and light troops). Seeing the elephants advancing, the Romans resort to their 'secret weapon':

> Beyond the battle line the Romans had stationed the light-armed troops and the 300 wagons they had prepared for the

battle against the elephants. The wagons had upright beams
on which were mounted movable transverse poles that could
be swung round as fast as thought in any direction. On the
ends of the poles were tridents, sword-like spikes or scythes,
all made of iron. Other wagons had cranes that swung down
heavy grappling irons. Many of the poles had attached to
them forward-facing grapnels, wrapped in tow and smeared
with pitch, which men were to light as soon as they came
near the elephants and then rain blows against the trunks and
faces of the beasts. Also standing on each four-wheeled
wagon were many archers, slingers and stone throwers; and
more were on the ground beside the wagons. (Dionysius of
Halicarnassus, *Roman Antiquities,* 20.1.6–7)

The improvised anti-elephant wagons are momentarily successful
against the elephants, but the oxen are hamstrung by the light
infantry accompanying the elephants and the wagon crews quickly
overwhelmed. The surviving Romans flee towards their own battle
line and try to force their way in, causing great confusion. Dionysius
then turns his attention to another part of the field; the survival of
his account in excerpts means that we hear no more of the elephant
assault. The Third Legion routs the mixed force of Lucani and
Bruttii; when they flee the White Shield Tarentines follow. Pyrrhus
sees his battle line rupturing and sends part of his *agema* and
cavalry from the right wing to stem the rout.

Zonaras' account tallies up to a point with Dionysius. The
Romans gradually push the enemy back and Pyrrhus sends in the
elephants. However, Pyrrhus deliberately avoids where the wagons
are stationed and attacks the other end of the line. Before the
elephants even reach them the cavalry horses panic and flee, but the
infantry stand firm and resist the elephants.[61]

The wagons do not feature in the brief account of Florus, which
is somewhat surprising considering his delight for the fantastic and
gruesome. Instead he gives the far more likely scenario of the

Romans concentrating their *pila* on the elephants and throwing flaming torches at the wood or wicker towers strapped to their backs. Gaius Numucius, a *hastatus* of the Fourth Legion demonstrates the mortal nature of the elephants by hacking the trunk off one of them. (*Hastatus* could simply mean one of the men in the front line of maniples, the *hastati*, but it was also a centurion's title.) Orosius adds that by concentrating flaming missiles which 'became embedded in their hind quarters and sensitive parts, the elephants became maddened and a source of destruction to their own side'.[62]

Returning to Dionysius, we learn that a force of Daunians from Arpi in northern Apulia, arriving too late to join the battle on the Roman side, decide to attack Pyrrhus' lightly defended camp. This they take with relative ease, pillage it thoroughly and set fire to anything they cannot carry, including tents, food and medical supplies, and slaughter the baggage animals. A fugitive from the camp rides to inform Pyrrhus, who sends cavalry and elephants to retake the camp. Before these arrive the Daunians retreat to the summit of a hill, too steep for the elephants and cavalry to assault. Pyrrhus' men then decide to turn on the Third and Fourth Legions who are still in pursuit of the Epirotes, Sabellians and Tarentines. The Romans break off their pursuit and take up position on a thickly wooded hillside. Again, the elephants and cavalry cannot operate freely, but their accompanying light troops cause the legionaries great trouble. Pyrrhus dispatches some of the Samnites and Greek mercenaries to help finish off the Romans, but one of the consuls sends in cavalry and, the battle on the plain seemingly forgotten (but remember that Dionysius' account is pieced together from excerpts), another general engagement develops when the cavalry arrives to support the legions. The armies fight without decision until nightfall, then Pyrrhus recalls his troops and returns to his ruined camp. Zonaras states that Pyrrhus' main battle line lost its will to fight when its men saw their camp in flames. Both sources agree that Pyrrhus' total casualties were much higher because his wounded were forced to camp under the open sky, without food or medical treatment – the Daunians had presumably killed the physicians in the camp.[63]

The Daunian attack on Pyrrhus' camp is about the only element of the accounts of Dionysius and Zonaras that can be accepted at face value. Plutarch, who read Dionysius' complete account of the battle and could compare it to the versions of Hieronymus and others, appears only to have considered this and Pyrrhus' wounding by a *pilum* as genuine; he is clearly sceptical of Dionysius' casualty figures (reported as 15,000 on each side) and the assertion that the battle took place on a single day. Despite its omissions, Plutarch's account of the battle, or battles, of Ausculum is by far the most reliable. The anti-elephant wagons and the chasing of half of Pyrrhus' army off the field may well be the patriotic inventions of later Roman writers. Indeed, some even portrayed Ausculum as an overwhelming Roman victory, with Pyrrhus losing half his army. Dionysius did not go that far but preferred to have the battle end in stalemate. That also is false. Pyrrhus forced the Romans off the battlefield and so won a clear victory, but his forces were so badly mauled in the process that he was not prepared to assault the Roman camp and withdrew back to Tarentum.[64]

DEVOTIO AT AUSCULUM?

There is one last problematical feature of the battle of Ausculum: did the consul Publius Decius Mus perform, or threaten to perform, *devotio*? *Devotio* was a ritual sacrifice whereby a general offered his life and the lives of his enemies to the gods of the Underworld by charging to the enemy and throwing himself on to their weapons. His death would secure theirs and so grant victory to the Romans. Decius' father had devoted himself in this way at the battle of Sentinum (*see* Chapter II), the act demoralising and terrifying the enemy – Gauls and Samnites. Zonaras, summarising the lost account of Dio, reports that prior to the fight at Ausculum, a rumour swept through Pyrrhus' camp that Decius was going to devote himself. The Greek troops probably did not understand the concept immediately, but the

Italians, particularly the Samnites who had faced a *devotus* sixteen years before at Sentinum, started to panic and the fear spread to other troops. Pyrrhus managed to reason with the troops. 'How can one man by dying prevail over so many? Incantations and magic are not superior to weapons and men.' He ordered that if any man in the ritual toga of a *devotus* was spotted, he was not to be harmed but taken alive. The king then sent a message to Decius warning him not to attempt the act. Decius responded that he had no need to perform *devotio*, because Pyrrhus would be conquered in other ways.

This all sounds quite feasible. The *devotio* of Decius' father is factual, and his grandfather probably devoted himself at the battle of the Veseris in 340 BC (*see* Chapter II). It would be surprising if the soldiers on both sides did not speculate if the consul would attempt to devote himself. Even if he did not intend to perform *devotio*, his heritage combined with death in battle would automatically suggest that he had died as a *devotus*. No account of the battle proper refers to *devotio*, and it remains unclear if Decius survived the battle. A Decius Mus was perhaps consul in 265 BC, but scholars are divided as to whether it was the same man or even if there was a consul of this name.

Cicero believed Decius died in battle but was (perhaps deliberately) vague on the matter of *devotio*. The modern scholars Skutsch and Cornell suggest a *devotio* was attempted but failed and was consequently 'hushed up' by Roman historians. Skutsch suggests that Decius had the misfortune to survive – a particular disgrace. Cornell doubts that a Decius Mus was consul in 265 BC. The only source is the late and unreliable *De Viris Illustribus*, which has a Decius Mus (no *praenomen* is given) sent to put down the revolt of Volsinii in 265/4 BC, but a triumphal inscription demonstrates that the consul sent to Volsinii was in fact Marcus Fulvius Flaccus. Cornell is therefore happy to accept Cicero's statements that Decius was killed at Ausculum, proposing that, if a *devotio* was attempted, it was a failure because it did not bring about a Roman victory.[65]

CEASEFIRE

When Pyrrhus returned to Tarentum he found news and an embassy waiting for him. The news reported the death in battle of Ptolemy Ceraunus against an army of migrating Gauls; the Macedonians were in dire need of a king and Pyrrhus' own realm of Epirus was threatened. The embassy was made up of Greeks from Sicily, led by the representatives of Syracuse. Knowing that Pyrrhus was the son-in-law of Agathocles, the late tyrant of Syracuse and scourge of the Carthaginians who sought to dominate all Sicily, they implored Pyrrhus to lead them, offering to put their cities, armies and fleets in his hands. Carthage had taken full advantage of the factional strife that erupted in Syracuse and the other Greek cities on Agathocles' death in 289 BC. With a fleet of 100–130 ships blockading Syracuse from the sea, and a substantial army laying siege to the landward walls, the Carthaginians seemed about to realise their centuries-old aspiration of adding the eastern portion of Sicily to their empire.

Pyrrhus was looking for any excuse to rid himself of the Roman war, and now two great opportunities had arrived at once. He pondered the matter for some time, tempted by the empty throne of Macedon and the prospect of heroically driving the Gauls out, but he settled on aiding the Sicilian Greeks, seeing Sicily as the stepping-stone to his ambition of conquering Carthage and its North African territories. Hardy Epirus could look after itself, but how to come to terms with Rome? A traitor in Pyrrhus' ranks provided the opportunity.

After Ausculum the Roman army remained in northern Apulia. In 278 BC Fabricius was again consul with Aemilius Papus and they took the field against Pyrrhus. When the armies were camped opposite each other, Nicias, the personal physician of the king, got a message to Fabricius. He offered to poison Pyrrhus and 'so end the war without further effort on the part of the Romans' – for a suitably large reward, of course. Fabricius was disgusted and sent a warning to Pyrrhus. The physician was executed and the grateful king made a gift of all his Roman prisoners of war to Fabricius and sent envoys to negotiate a conclusion to the war. The consuls would not accept the prisoners as a gift, but exchanged them for an equal number of Tarentine and Samnite captives. Nor would they speak of peace (they could not because a pact against Pyrrhus had just been made with Carthage), but some sort of ceasefire seems to have been patched up for, by the summer, Pyrrhus was making his way to Sicily. The Romans were happy to let him go for it meant they could redress the situation in Samnium, Lucania and Bruttium without his interference, though they may have agreed to leave Tarentum be.[66]

The freed captives were not welcomed back with open arms; they were called 'Pyrrhus' ugly little presents'. The Romans expected their soldiers to conquer or die, not allow themselves to suffer the ignominy of capture. The men were demoted and shunned. *Equites* (cavalrymen, often nobles) were reduced to the status of legionaries. Legionaries were forced to serve with the slingers – the boys too poor to afford legionary equipment or non-citizen auxiliaries. They were not allowed to share the comforts of the camp but were forced to sleep in the open beyond the security of the ramparts. Only when they had brought back the spoils from two conquered enemies would they be restored to their original status. *Spolia* (spoils – arms and armour of a defeated enemy) were normally taken in single combat, so the disgraced soldiers were being forced to prove their valour in isolation without the support of their comrades. This hard line was maintained later in the century. The so-called Cannae Legions, unjustly disgraced because they managed to escape the carnage at Cannae in 216 BC, were exiled by the Senate to Sicily. The legionaries implored Claudius Marcellus to let them fight the Carthaginians and regain their honour, 'as once those who were taken prisoner by Pyrrhus at Heraclea afterwards fought him and justified themselves', but Marcellus' attempt to sway the Senate was unsuccessful.[67]

THE SICILIAN ADVENTURE

The Tarentines (and allies) were rather annoyed at Pyrrhus' decision to go to Sicily and demanded that he finish the job in Italy or leave Tarentum as he found it, as a free democracy. The king's contempt for, and irritation with, the Tarentines now spewed forth. 'He ordered them to keep silent and await his convenience,' says Plutarch, then sailed off to Sicily – in sixty or seventy Tarentine vessels. Pyrrhus took only about half of his surviving Epirote force, 8,000 men according to Appian, and his war elephants. Milo retained the rest of the army in Tarentum and the other Italiote cities to ensure their loyalty while the king was away.[68]

All of Pyrrhus' dreams seemed to come true on Sicily. After he landed at Tauromenium, its *tyrannos* (many such despots had sprung up in the Greek cities following Agathocles' death) put himself and his army under Pyrrhus' command. Then Catana gladly gave troops and money. Pyrrhus marched down the road from Catana to Syracuse while the fleet followed along the coast. The approach of the king's still small army caused the Carathagian army to abandon its siege and depart, and the Carthaginian fleet broke off its blockade before it was trapped between the Tarentine fleet and the 141 Syracusan war vessels bottled up in the Great Harbour. Pyrrhus effected a reconciliation between the warring leaders of Syracuse and took command of its 10,000 troops and substantial navy. He was even saluted as king of Sicily.

In 277–276 BC Pyrrhus moved against the Carthaginian possessions in central and western Sicily. With the addition of troops from Acragas and Leontini his field army now numbered 30,000 infantry and 2,500 cavalry (the total number of troops available was probably greater). First to fall was Enna in the centre of the island. At Mount Eryx the king invoked the aid of Heracles and personally led his *philoi* in the assault. Pyrrhus was the first man up the scaling ladders and over the wall, yet he sustained no wounds and killed many of the Carthaginians. Next to fall were Heircte and Panormus

(Palermo), effectively reducing the once vast Carthaginian possessions to the strongly fortified harbour of Lilybaeum on the western extremity of the island. Before embarking on its siege, Pyrrhus turned his attention to the Mamertini, the 'sons of Mamers' (the war god Mars). They were Campanian mercenaries who had served Agathocles and were discharged on his death. However, instead of returning to Italy, they seized Messana (modern Messina) and set about terrorising the north-east of the island. Pyrrhus defeated them in several engagements and put an end to their exactions. He then returned to Lilybaeum but after two months the city was still not taken – it was almost impregnable on its landward side. The king rejected the alternative of a lengthy blockade by sea and decided instead to take the war to Carthage itself.

Despite his spectacular successes, Pyrrhus' popularity with the Silician Greeks plummeted when he seized rich estates for his *philoi* and forced the cities to accept Epirote officers as magistrates and councillors. Already simmering at this Epirote takeover, the Greeks' discontent boiled over when Pyrrhus demanded more troops, ships and rowers, and cash for his planned assault on Carthage. Many of the cities withdrew their support and began to side with the Mamertines and even looked to hated Carthage for aid against Pyrrhus. The infuriated king, seeing his conquests dissolve before his eyes, executed those suspected of collusion with Carthage and the Mamertines. The refusal of the Greek cities to co-operate meant he could not oppose the landing of a fresh army from Carthage, although Justin claims that Pyrrhus defeated it in one last battle before departing from Syracuse in late 276 or early 275 BC. But he did not leave completely empty handed. He departed with 110 warships and numerous troop transports, and probably retained a considerable number of mercenary soldiers.[69]

He sailed north towards Rhegium but was intercepted by a Carthaginian battle fleet. The majority of his warships were sunk or captured (Pyrrhus' flagship turned up later in a Carthaginian fleet), but it seems that they fought long and hard enough to allow the troop transports to flee. The transports and forty surviving warships may have finally docked at Locri where Pyrrhus had left his son Alexander (by Lanassa) before crossing to Sicily. The sequence of events from Pyrrhus' landing at Locri to his eventual return to Tarentum is not entirely clear but is dominated by a battle against the *legio Campana* and the Mamertines, and the sacrilegious robbing of the temple of Persephone.

The Mamertines had sent 10,000 warriors across the straits to reinforce the Campanian Legion, a 4,000-strong unit of Campanians, which ostensibly held Italiote Rhegium for Rome. This 'legion' (its precise status is unclear) had forcibly prevented Rhegium from siding with Pyrrhus after his victory at Heraclea. Subsequently left to their own devices, the Campanians took inspiration from the Mamertine seizure of Messana and set themselves up as the rulers of Rhegium and its territory, yet, being fearful of the ultimate consequences of their actions, they acted intermittently in the interests of Rome against Pyrrhus. While the king was in Sicily the legion had attempted to capture Locri and other of the Italiote cities from their Epirote or allied garrisons.

Once back in Italy Pyrrhus marched on Rhegium, determined to rid himself of the troublesome enemy stronghold on the edge of his territory. However, the Campanian Legion and Mamertines ambushed Pyrrhus' army as it was strung out in rough country. Two of the war elephants were killed and the rearguard sustained heavy casualties, then Pyrrhus intervened:

> Riding up in person from the van, Pyrrhus sought to ward off the enemy, and took great risks in contending with men who were trained to fight and were inspired with high courage. When he was wounded in the head by a sword and withdrew a little from the fighting, the enemy were all the more elated. One of the Mamertines ran forward, far in advance of the rest, a man who was huge in body and resplendent in armour. In a bold voice he challenged Pyrrhus to come out, if he were

still alive. This angered Pyrrhus and, wheeling round despite his guards, he pushed his way through them, full of wrath, smeared with blood, and with a countenance terrible to look upon. Before the barbarian could strike, Pyrrhus dealt him such a blow on the head with his sword that, what with the might of his arm and the excellent temper of the blade, it cleaved right down through the body, so that at one instant its sundered parts fell to either side. This checked the barbarians from further attacks. They were amazed and confounded at Pyrrhus and thought him some superior being. (Plutarch, *Pyrrhus*, 24. 2–4)

Back in Locri Pyrrhus demanded more cash, presumably to pay his mercenaries and the dejected Epirotes. The contribution from the treasury of the temple of Zeus Olympios was no longer enough because the other allies were refusing to pay their contributions. He was persuaded by some of his *philoi* to break into the treasury of the temple of Persephone, the vengeful queen of the Underworld, and seize its untouched treasures. Pyrrhus wrote in his memoirs that this act of impiety lost him the war with the Romans and later commentators suggested that the wrath of the goddess resulted in Pyrrhus' final demise in Argos. The treasure was loaded onto ships to be sent to Tarentum, but almost as soon as the ships had put to sea a terrible storm blew up and drove the ships back to port. The war vessels escorting the treasure ships were all sunk. Pyrrhus immediately realised that this was the revenge of the goddess and restored the treasure to the temple.[70]

MALVENTUM: THE LAST BATTLE

Pyrrhus' extended sojourn on Sicily exposed the Samnites, Lucani and Bruttii to the full fury of Rome. In 278 BC Fabricius and Papus won enough victories over the Sabellians to justify triumphal processions in Rome. Yet more victories were won in 277 BC (although the Samnites did inflict a serious reverse on the Romans in the heavily forested Cranita Hills), and some Italiote Greek cities were taken or won over to alliance with Rome. Croton was perhaps taken from its Epirote garrison by a ruse, and it was maybe also at this time that Heraclea itself became a favoured ally of Rome, granted almost total autonomy and probable exemption from military or naval contributions. By 276 BC Rome's position in Italy was almost what it had been before the arrival of Pyrrhus, despite a serious outbreak of plague in the city which made legionary recruitment difficult. The despairing Samnites and increasingly terrified Tarentines sent envoys to Pyrrhus' headquarters at Syracuse. It was these appeals that helped persuade him to abandon the Sicilian adventure.[71]

Pyrrhus arrived back in Tarentum, maybe in spring 275 BC, with 20,000 infantry and 3,000 cavalry. He wasted little time, says Plutarch, adding the best of the Tarentines to the army, then marched against the Romans. As Plutarch mentions only Tarentine troops we might wonder if the Epirote troops under Milo had already rejoined the king for the campaign against Rhegium.[72]

The king advanced boldly into subdued Lucania where he detached a contingent to distract the forces of the consul Cornelius Lentulus, and then proceed on to Malventum in Samnium where the other consul, Manius Curius Dentatus, was encamped. Pyrrhus was not strong enough to take on both the consular armies, each 20,000–30,000 strong (the recent plague may support the lower figure), so he planned to knock out Dentatus before Lentulus could reinforce him. Few Samnites were able, and fewer were willing, to join the king; the recent Roman campaigns had shattered their power, says Plutarch. They were angry with Pyrrhus for abandoning them after they fought so hard at Ausculum and for taking so long to respond to their appeals, but the king appears to have reckoned that one more victory in their heartland would bring the Samnites and other allies back onside and keep his dream of an Italian empire alive.[73]

Curius Dentatus was determined to shatter Pyrrhus' dream. The tough old soldier had brought the Third Samnite War to a conclusion in 290 BC, and in the same year he conquered the Sabines. Following the disaster at Arretium, Curius did not exact revenge on the Senones by simply defeating them in battle; he drove the famous tribe, which had sacked Rome itself in 390 BC, completely out of Italy (284/283 BC). When conducting the levy for his legions early in 275 BC, the consul was met with an apathetic response, especially from younger citizens. Even the bellicose Romans were tiring of war. They had been fighting without pause since 284 BC and the heavy casualties at Arretium, Heraclea, Ausculum and, to a lesser extent, Cranita, were sustained by a citizen body that had not even recovered from the costly victories of the Third Samnite War and had recently been brought low by a recurrence of plague. But Curius got his men. The consul proceeded to select men by lot from each voting tribe. When a man of the tribe Pollia was so selected but failed to respond to the summons, Curius first confiscated his property and then sold the unfortunate man into slavery. As a result of this salutary example Curius had little difficulty filling up his legions.[74]

Malventum was (and remains) a site of considerable strategic importance commanding mountain passes and river valleys. It was the hub of communications in southern Samnium, with roads and drover's trails leading to central and northern Samnium, to Capua and Campania, to Venusia and Apulia, and in almost every other direction. It thus presented a considerable prize to Pyrrhus, but Curius considered that the surrounding country was rough enough to prevent the king employing his phalanx effectively.[75]

Curius was certainly aware that Pyrrhus was in the vicinity, but bad omens prevented the consul from marching the Roman army out of its camp. The *haruspices*, priests who divined the future from reading the entrails of sacrificial animals, declared that the sacrifices were inauspicious. Curius therefore stayed put and Pyrrhus took full advantage, selecting from his army the bravest men and most ferocious war elephants and led them on a night march with the intention of occupying the high ground behind Curius' camp, then making a surprise attack on the Roman camp while the legions were otherwise distracted by the phalanx. The audacity of the plan would have suggested its success to ever-optimistic Pyrrhus, but the continuing wrath of Persephone, the natural obstacles of Mother Earth, and human frailty conspired against it:

> Pyrrhus took a long circuitous route through heavily forested country, his torches burned out, and his soldiers lost their way and straggled. This caused such delay that at daybreak he was in full view of the enemy as he advanced on them from the heights. (Plutarch, *Pyrrhus*, 25.3)

> It was bound to happen, as might have been expected, that soldiers burdened with helmets, breastplates and shields and advancing against hill positions by long trails that were not even used by men but were mere goat paths through woods and crags, would keep no order and, even before the enemy came in sight, would be weakened in body by thirst and fatigue. (Dionysius of Halicarnassus, *Roman Antiquities*, 20.11.1)

It happened that the omens read by the *haruspices* finally came good that morning for Curius. Already hearted by the good omens, the Romans and Allies were exultant to see dreaded king Pyrrhus delivered before them in disarray with exhausted troops. Curius led a strong contingent of his army up the slope against the Epirotes, easily dispatching the leading ranks and putting the rest to flight. Two of the war elephants were killed and, presumably during the pursuit of the broken troops, another eight were driven into something like a box canyon, where they were surrendered to the Romans by their mahouts (identified as Indians by Dionysius). The Epirote (and Tarentine?) soldiers driven into similar terrain were less fortunate; they were slaughtered. The king, however, escaped down the slopes and rejoined his main army.

Curius returned to the level ground in front of his camp, where he arrayed the full army, with the exception of some veteran legionaries left to guard the ramparts, and met the advance of

Pyrrhus' main army. The fighting here was furious. The Romans and Epirotes were each successful at various points along the engaged battle lines. One Epirote assault headed by the remaining war elephants was particularly successful and the Roman troops at this point buckled and fell back on the camp. Now the veteran legionaries intervened. Dionysius says they were *principes*, that is the men who made up the second battle line in the manipular formation, but adds that they were equipped with *hastae*, heavy thrusting spears, which suggests that they were actually the *triarii*. The *hasta* was the weapon of the *triarii*, the third or reserve line of the legion, who were most likely to be left guarding the camp. The veteran warriors surged down the ramparts to stem the rout, throwing their spears like *pila* at the elephants. One young elephant turned about when it was struck on the head; its squeals of pain attracted the attention of its dam, which also turned and went in search of her calf, and the other war elephants followed, maddened by the spears, javelins and torches with which the Romans were bombarding them. The elephants charged back through the Epirote battle line and Pyrrhus' army disintegrated. Like that of the Romans at Heraclea, the flight of the Epirotes and Tarentines appears to have been so complete that they did not bother to regain their fortified camp. When the consul and his officers inspected the abandoned camp, its layout excited much interest and subsequently stimulated changes in the design of Roman camps.[76]

Pyrrhus is said to have escaped from Malventum with only a few horsemen. He made his way back to Tarentum and sent an embassy to Antigonus Gonatas, now king of Macedonia, demanding more money and troops. If he did not receive them, the king threatened, he would return to Epirus and look to Antigonus' dominions for the territorial expansion he had sought from the Romans. At first sight this suggests Pyrrhus intended to keep up his war with Rome but he had probably decided to abandon Italy and was making deliberately unreasonable demands (Antigonus may well have supplied reinforcements after Heraclea and Ausculum) in order to give him a 'just' cause for war and another chance to sit on the throne of Macedon. Indeed, despite his setbacks in Italy, Pyrrhus' great spirit was said to have been undiminished. The failure against the Romans had already been written off; the indomitable king now believed that his destiny lay in Macedonia and Greece! When the envoys returned with Antigonus' inevitable refusal, the Eagle made ready to depart, perhaps as early as autumn 275 BC.[77]

Pyrrhus sailed from Tarentum for Epirus (presumably still using Tarentine vessels) with only 8,000 infantry and 500 cavalry, a mere third of the force brought over five years before. However, the numbers suggest that he had perhaps managed to extricate more soldiers from the disaster at Malventum than the sources allow (though the bulk of the men may have been from the detached force detailed to occupy Lentulus' attentions in Lucania). The king had enough men to leave a substantial garrison in Tarentum under the command of his son Helenus and loyal Milo. This was to give the impression that he intended to return but Helenus was soon recalled (274 BC). However, Pyrrhus probably did hope to hold Tarentum for as long as possible. Its trade revenues could be taxed to his advantage, and its navy employed in his campaigns; despite the war, the city was presumably still operating as a commercial port and it was not until 272 BC that it was blockaded from the sea by a Carthaginian fleet. Indeed, much of the subsequent Tarentine discontent with Milo seems to have been caused by his exactions. As a parting gift Pyrrhus gave to the Tarentines a chair which had straps made from the cured skin of the treacherous doctor Nicias, a warning to those who aspired to the restoration of the democracy.[78]

The rule of Milo became so unpopular that the Tarentines took up arms against him. By 272 BC Milo was happy to hand the city over to the Roman consul Papirius Cursor (the victor of Aquilonia; *see* Chapter II) and sail back to Epirus with a considerable amount of tax he had exacted from the Tarentines. The city did not suffer unduly. It was made a naval ally of Rome and a legion was permanently stationed in the acropolis to ensure its loyalty.

In 273–272 BC the final flames of Samnite, Lucanian and Bruttian opposition were stamped out and colonies were soon planted on their territory. All were forced into the Roman Alliance; their military manpower and natural resources, for example the vast timber and pitch reserves of the Bruttii, were to be exploited by Rome. By 272 BC the pragmatic Italiote Greek cities had also entered into the Roman Alliance but mostly on advantageous terms as naval Allies. The adherence of Messapia and parts of Apulia to Pyrrhus was used by the Romans as an excuse for war in 267–266 BC and their peoples were made allies, willing or not. Within a decade of Pyrrhus' departure all peninsular Italy was under Roman domination, either by direct conquest or alliance. The defeat of Pyrrhus, the king most likened to the great Alexander, brought Rome to the wider attention of the Mediterranean world. Ptolemy II of Egypt was the first of the Hellenistic kings to open diplomatic relations with the new Western power.[79]

Curius Dentatus' triumphal procession for the victory at Malventum was delayed by campaigns against the Sabellians. In 274 BC he finally marched through Rome at the head of his victorious army, its captives and spoils displayed for all to see (Curius' share of the spoils paid for Rome's second aqueduct, the Anio Vetus).[80] Nothing excited the Roman crowd more than the appearance of the war elephants, the bane of the Romans at Heraclea and Ausculum, but now their slaves:

> These huge beasts with towers on their backs, which they had feared so much, now followed the horses which had conquered them, and with heads bowed were not wholly unconscious that they were prisoners. (Florus, *Epitome*, 1.13.28)

THE END OF THE EAGLE

What happened to the Eagle of Epirus? In 274 BC he again became king of Macedonia, once more causing the defection of a substantial part of the Macedonian army and defeating Antigonus in battle. Yet, despite this success, the wrath of Persephone was still upon the king. His popularity plummeted when his Gallic mercenaries plundered the tombs of the Macedonian kings at Aegae. The king then attempted to undermine Antigonus' domination of much of central and southern Greece, espousing the claim of his general Cleonymus to the throne of Sparta. This was the same Cleonymus hired by Tarentum and ejected from Italy by the Romans and Patavians thirty years before. Intending to establish Cleonymus essentially as a puppet ruler, Pyrrhus was beaten back from Sparta, where his rash son Ptolemy was killed having charged into the centre of the city.

When Antigonus marched into the Peloponnese with an army and established himself at Argos, Pyrrhus managed to fight his way into the town and, as usual, led from the front. He speared a young Argive soldier. Like many other non-combatants, the soldier's mother was watching the street fighting from a house-top. She saw her son fall and despairingly lifted and threw a roof tile at Pyrrhus. Some said the woman had been possessed by Demeter, the daughter of Persephone. The tile struck him on the neck just below the rim of his helmet, its impact sufficient to knock him unconscious. He fell from the saddle and was set upon by a small group of Antigonus' men. The king was regaining consciousness when he was decapitated. According to Plutarch the killing blow was momentarily delayed because the expression on Pyrrhus' face was so fierce that it frightened the executioner. Such was the end of the Eagle (autumn 272 BC). He probably supposed that ultimately he would die in battle, but he could hardly have imagined that an old woman would deliver him defenceless into the hands of his enemies.

Pyrrhus' head was given to Alcyoneus, son of Antigonus. He carried the head triumphantly and presented it to his father, but Antigonus was not exultant. He raged at Alcyoneus for condoning such a barbarous act, then drove him away with blows of his staff. Antigonus wept for Pyrrhus; he had been a worthy opponent but one who somehow always squandered his victories:

> Antigonus used to liken him to a player with dice who makes
> many fine throws but does not understand how to use them.
> (Plutarch, *Pyrrhus*, 26.2)

Pyrrhus' head was reunited with his body and cremated with honour. It is uncertain if Helenus took Pyrrhus' ashes back to Epirus or Ambracia, for a tradition was maintained in Argos that the king's charred bones were housed in the sanctuary of Demeter. In death Persephone and her child would not let go of the king.[81]

* * *

The Romans respected Pyrrhus and they continued to be fascinated by him for centuries after his death. He was a despot from across the sea, an invader, but he also embodied the qualities they most admired: he was a warrior, a man of honour and great *virtus* (manly courage and excellence).[82] When Pyrrhus praised the valour of the Romans after Heraclea, declaring that with such men he could conquer the world, his enemies were secretly pleased; Pyrrhus had confirmed their *virtus* and announced it to the world. The king conferred on the Romans a reputation for courage, steadfastness and heroism that still endures.

When Pyrrhus looked across the Siris and saw the legions for the first time, he felt a twinge of concern. But he would also have thrilled in the realisation that across the river stood worthy opponents, warriors who would not flee at the first onset. Even so, he was surprised at the high cost of his victory. A similar result at Ausculum depressed the king; pitched battles were supposed to decide wars, but the realisation was dawning that Rome would not play by the rules that governed warfare in the Hellenistic world. She would not, could not, concede defeat, and she would raise another army and he would be worn down. After Malventum Pyrrhus could have gathered together a new mercenary army and resumed the war, but he knew the game was up and tried his luck elsewhere.

Hannibal of Carthage declared that Pyrrhus was his teacher (via the medium of Pyrrhus' memoirs and tactical works), but the pupil ignored the master's findings when he embarked on his own invasion of Italy. The Romans were defeated in many battles, their aggressive tactics often working in Hannibal's favour, but they never sued for peace. The legions renewed themselves like the Hydra. After years of fruitless campaigning, Hannibal found himself bottled up and was forced to abandon Italy. He returned to Africa and found a Roman army waiting. He was defeated decisively at Zama in 202 BC.

Finally, Pyrrhus' dream of a Western empire forced the Romans to consider the world beyond Italy, and the riches and threats that it contained. In 264 BC they accepted an invitation from the Mamertines to protect them from Carthaginian aggression. As Pyrrhus had sailed to Italy to liberate his Greek brothers, Rome sent her legions to Sicily to aid her Italic brethren. Twenty-three years later Sicily (with the exception of Syracusan territory) became Rome's first overseas province. In another century the Mediterranean had become a Roman lake. Rome had achieved everything Pyrrhus had dreamed of, and more.

Chapter II

DIVINE INTERVENTION

'He drove before him fear and panic, blood and carnage.' (Livy, 10.28.16)

The rumour that Pyrrhus was killed because of the intervention of a goddess would not have surprised the Romans. The intercession of the gods was a reality to them and most apparent on the battlefield. The most important of Rome's gods and goddesses – Jupiter, Mars, Bellona – were believed to have aided the legions in battle. Sometimes the Romans would call on darker gods to aid them, but the divinities of the Underworld demanded a heavy toll of blood. The Romans did not shy away from paying it.

THE BATTLE OF SENTINUM, SPRING 295 BC

The Third Samnite War broke out in 298 BC following the attempt of the Samnites to bring the Lucani over to their League, initially by diplomacy, then by force. The Lucani appealed to Rome and declared their willingness to enter into the Roman Alliance. The Romans accepted because they realised another war with the Samnites was inevitable: the two powerful warrior nations with expansionist policies simply could not co-exist. If Rome accepted the appeal, war would result instantly, but the position of Luciana meant that Samnium could be assaulted from the south, indeed the existence of the Alliance would mean Rome had a ring of Allies around the Samnites. If the Samnites were left unopposed and succeeded in forcing the Lucanians into their League, the Bruttii and other southern Italian peoples would surely follow, and the Samnites' already considerable military resources would far outstrip those of Rome. The Third Samnite War was a struggle for the right to dominate peninsular Italy and the battle of Sentinum was one of the defining engagements, and not just for the great numbers involved or the decisive tactics employed. It was defined above all by divine intervention.[1]

* * *

The consuls learned of the defeat of Cornelius Scipio Barbatus' advance force when Gallic cavalry rode up to taunt the Roman column, singing songs of victory and with the freshly severed heads of legionaries impaled on their spears or hanging from their horses' tack. Quintus Fabius Rullianus, also called Maximus ('Greatest') for his skill in war, now consul for the fifth time, had sent Barbatus ahead with a legion to secure the Allied city of Camerinum in Umbria. If the army of Samnites and Senonian Gauls captured the pro-Roman city it would encourage malcontents in Umbria to join the powerful confederacy assembled against Rome by the Samnite general Gellius Egnatius. Rullianus was thankful that the numerous hoplites of the Etruscan cities had been prevented from joining the confederates by the diversionary operations of the propraetors Fulvius Centumalus and Postumius Megellus (later abused by the Tarentines as envoy in 282 BC) around Clusium and Perusia.

Scipio Barbatus appeared to be the man for the job. He boasted that his good looks were equal to his *virtus*, but his military capabilities were proven: as consul in 298 BC he had scored the first major Roman successes in the Third Samnite War. Barbatus established his camp in the vicinity of Camerinum, blocking the likely route by which the enemy would advance on the city, but the sudden appearance of the huge confederate army caused him abruptly to abandon the position for a hill sited between the camp and the city. He thought the heights would be easier to defend than a camp on level ground, but Gellius Egnatius had anticipated the Roman commander. In his haste to reach the hill Barbatus failed to send scouts ahead to reconnoitre the position; as the legionaries ascended the hill they came to a ridge where they were suddenly face to face with Samnite and Gallic warriors already sent up the other side by Egnatius. The rest of the confederate army swarmed up behind the Romans. The legion, probably *c.* 4,000 strong, was surrounded by about 40,000 enemy warriors. The Romans were on the point of annihilation and only the timely appearance of the united consular armies of Rullianus and Publius Decius Mus saved Barbatus. Egnatius withdrew before he too was trapped on the hill. Barbatus' good looks were seemingly intact but his reputation for excellence was somewhat dented.

The Samnite general chose not offer battle, perhaps still hopeful that Etruscan and other reinforcements might reach him; some of the tribes of central Italy were discontented with Rome and had possibly given his army aid as it marched northwards to rendezvous with the Gauls. Once the confederate army had descended from the hill Egnatius withdrew towards Sentinum, several days' march to the north.[2]

Rullianus and Decius led their forces in pursuit of the Samnites and Senones. The arduous training that Rullianus had insisted his legions undergo in the winter months now showed its worth as the Romans snapped at the heels of the Samnite and Gallic host, and Decius' legions must have been equally tough, entering the territory of Sentinum in two or three days and establishing camp four Roman miles from the enemy.[3] The consuls were conscious that reinforcements could yet reach Egnatius – maybe more Gauls, and the Etruscans might defeat the propraetors and march over the Apennine passes – so they endeavoured to bring on battle before the enemy force was swelled to overwhelming proportions. For two days the consuls sent troops to harass the enemy. The Samnites and Senones responded in kind, neither side winning any real advantage but, as the consuls – Rullianus in particular – intended, Gellius Egnatius' men were suitably provoked and on the third day descended *en masse* from their camp to offer battle. The following description of the battle derives almost exclusively from Livy.[4]

Gellius Egnatius and his Samnites formed the left wing of the confederate army, the Senones formed the right. Gallic cavalry were positioned on the right flank and Samnite cavalry, although not mentioned by Livy, were presumably on the left. Rullianus took up position on the Roman right with his First and Third Legions against the Samnites, Decius took the left against the Senones with the Fifth and Sixth Legions and the legionary cavalry (perhaps from all four legions) covered his flank. It has been estimated that each legion at Sentinum contained 4,500 men – presumably a 'Polybian' legion of 4,200 infantry and 300 cavalry. The size of legions could vary, but the 4,000 infantrymen and 600 cavalrymen Rullianus selected from volunteers in Rome at the start of the year may reflect the preferred complement of legions levied during the Third Samnite War. The total number of legionaries was therefore in the region of 16,000–18,000. Livy states that the number of Allied troops (both infantry and cavalry) in the army was greater than the number of Roman legionaries but does not specify by how much. Even if the Allies only outnumbered the Romans by a few thousands the army could have contained 35,000–40,000 warriors. Except for the cavalry, including 1,000 picked Campanian troopers who covered Rullianus' flank, the position of the Allied infantry cohorts in the Roman battle line is not made clear, though it seems probable that in accordance with Rullianus' strategy they were all held in reserve behind the legions (*subsidium*).[5]

The concern of the consuls about reinforcements reaching the enemy and becoming outnumbered suggests that the Samnites and Senones had at least an equal number of men, perhaps somewhat more, but not the overwhelming superiority that some ancient historians supposed. Livy records with disapproval that a number of historians enlarged the Roman army by the addition of the legions of the proconsul Volumnius Flamma and put the combined numbers of the enemy (including Etruscans and Umbri) at 646,000.[6] If Rullianus and Decius really were substantially outnumbered at Sentinum it seems unlikely that they would have been so keen to offer battle on a plain with an army arranged with a relatively narrow front that a superior enemy with a longer front might easily envelop at the flanks. If the combined number of casualties, prisoners and fugitives from Sentinum is accepted as reasonably accurate, it suggests that the confederates had at least 38,000 warriors. The armies were probably the largest that either side had ever fielded and Sentinum was to be the greatest battle yet fought on Italian soil.

In keeping with the scale of the battle about to be fought, it attracted divine attention. As the armies faced off, Father Mars sent a sign:

> As they stood arrayed for battle, a deer, pursued by a wolf that had chased it down from the mountains, fled across the plain and between the two battle lines. The animals then turned in opposite directions, the deer towards the Gauls and the wolf towards the Romans. For the wolf a space was opened between the ranks, but the Gauls killed the deer. Then one of the Roman front-rankers [*antesignanus*] called out, 'Where you see the animal sacred to Diana lying slain, that way flight and slaughter have shaped their course. On this side the wolf of Mars, unhurt and sound, has reminded us of the race of Mars and of our founder Romulus.' (Livy, 10.27.8–9)

The Romans were elated by this portent of the demise of the Senones and, Decius' men in particular, hastened to advance.

Rullianus' legionaries came up slowly and in good order and met the furious counter-charge of the Samnites defensively, shields locked and perhaps even using their *pila* like thrusting spears to hold the Sabellian warriors at bay.

The northern command against the Samnites and Senones had originally been assigned to Rullianus and he only called for Decius' support when he realised that the enemy army was too big for his two legions and Allies to handle so, despite the equal status of the consuls, Rullianus should be considered the supreme commander at Sentinum.[7] Rullianus believed that, if the Roman army fought defensively, the Samnites and Senones would eventually exhaust themselves against the unyielding wall of the legions; as soon as the confederates showed signs of faltering, he would send in the fresh Allied cavalry and cohorts from the reserve to assault their flanks. Assaulted on three sides the exhausted enemy would inevitably break. Exhorting the troops before the battle, Rullianus cried out, 'The enemy are more than men at the start of a fight, but by the end they are less than women!'

Decius had presumably agreed to these tactics but abandoned them as soon as the battle began; he had privately determined on two courses that would bring victory to Rome. He first sent his legions in a wild charge against the Gauls, no doubt carried out in classic Roman style at the run, the legionaries pausing momentarily to throw their *pila* and draw their swords, then resuming their run to cover the last few paces and colliding shield boss to shield boss with the Gallic warriors. But the Senones gave as good as they got, replying in kind with their javelins and stoutly resisting the legionary onslaught with great slashing blows of their long swords. Eventually the infantry action petered out, the exhausted combatants gradually breaking off contact and edging back to their original positions.

Disappointed in his hopes for a quick victory, Decius called on the Roman cavalry to follow him in a charge against the enemy horse. He appealed especially to the young nobles commanding the *turmae* (squadrons): 'Yours will be a double share of glory if victory comes first to the left wing and to the cavalry!'

With Decius at their head the Roman cavalry twice charged the Senonian troopers. The second charge scattered the Gauls and they were driven far from their station on the flank of the infantry. The Romans turned their horses and began to force their way into the ranks of the infantry, but within moments the Roman cavalry were met with an unpleasant surprise. The Senones had held their war chariots in reserve behind the main battle line and now they charged the Roman horsemen who were milling around at the rear and flanks of the Gallic infantry. The Roman cavalry horses were panicked by the sudden clatter of the chariots. The Romans now fled in complete disorder back to their own lines. It seems that they tried to find shelter in the intervals between the leading maniples and perhaps even the spaces separating the lines of *hastati* and *principes* and *triarii* (the first, second and third battle lines of the legion). The chaos this caused to the legionary formation was compounded when the Gallic chariot drivers forced their teams in behind the Roman troopers.

Enemies were normally wary of trying to exploit the seemingly tempting intervals between the maniples; anyone advancing into the gap would be met by the light javelins of the young skirmishers (*velites*) who were stationed there, as well as a crossfire of *pila* from the legionaries in the maniples to either side and the frontal charge of the maniple in the next line which was positioned to cover the gap.[8] The fugitive Roman cavalry made it impossible for this system of defence to work. The legionaries were trampled by the panicked mounts of their own cavalry and crushed by the hooves and wheels of the Gallic chariot teams, and the warriors stationed beside the chariot drivers lunged at the Romans with their long spears. The Senonian infantry followed immediately upon the chariots and completed the rout.

The Roman front rankers broke and ran, throwing the rest of the legionary formations into confusion as they fled. Decius, who had presumably been caught up in the initial flight of the Roman cavalry, vainly attempted to halt the retreat then decided that the time had come for him to embark on his second course of action: *devotio*. His father had devoted himself at the Battle of the Veseris in 340 BC and secured victory for the Romans against the rebellious Latins, now the son would attempt it at Sentinum. Throughout the battle Decius had kept beside him the *pontifex* (one of the chief priests) Marcus Livius Denter. The consul declared that he could no longer avoid the fate of his family and in order to save the Roman army must devote, that is sacrifice, himself. 'Now I will offer up the legions of the enemy, to be slaughtered along with me, as victims to Tellus [Mother Earth] and the divine Manes [gods of the Underworld].' Decius then commanded Denter to recite the prayer of devotion, essentially a magic rite which would seal the destruction of he Gauls and Samnites through the death of the consul. Livy asserts that Decius proceeded to don the ritual costume of the *devotus*, the *cinctus Gabinius*, a toga hitched up in such a way to make it less cumbersome and allow a man to ride a horse and wield a lance, but it is doubtful that Decius, in the midst of the collapse of his legions, would have had time to do so. It seems more likely that he was already wearing the costume, concealed beneath his cuirass and general's cloak, and so ready to reveal in the event of the failure of his first plan.

Denter completed the terrible prayer of *devotio*, the same as that with which Decius Mus senior had devoted himself at the Veseris:

> 'Janus, Jupiter, Father Mars, Quirinus, Bellona, Lares, divine Novensiles, divine Indigites, you gods in whose power are both we and the enemy, and you, divine Manes, I invoke and worship you, I beg and crave your favour, that you prosper the might and victory of the Roman people and visit on their enemies fear, shuddering and death. As I have pronounced these words on behalf of the Republic of the Roman people, and of the army and the legions and auxiliaries . . . I devote

the legions and auxiliaries of the enemy, along with myself,
to the divine Manes and Tellus.' (Livy, 8.9.6–8)

At Sentinum the younger Decius added further imprecations to
the vow of death:

'I will drive before me fear and panic, blood and carnage. The
wrath of the heavenly gods and the infernal gods will curse
the standards, weapons and armour of the enemy, and in the
same place as I die witness the destruction of the Gauls and
Samnites!' (Livy, 10.28.16–17)

On uttering these words Decius, like his father before him,
spurred his horse through the broken Roman troops and, grasping a
heavy spear in his right hand, charged into the midst of the
oncoming Senonian infantry. Livy claims that as soon as the consul
had impaled himself on their weapons the battle changed course in
the Romans' favour. The death of a general normally signalled
collapse, but Decius' death rallied the broken Roman troops and they
turned to meet their erstwhile pursuers, who were apparently
paralysed by Decius' actions.

One wonders how many of the legionaries, who were in full flight,
actually witnessed Decius' charge to the death. Livy says their flight
was gradually halted by the frantic efforts of Livius Denter who, with
the authoritarian voice of a former consul (302 BC), was riding
through the ranks bellowing that Decius was devoting himself to the
gods and so bringing about the destruction of the enemy: 'Everything
with the enemy is madness and despair!' We should also consider the
possibility that the centurions and the veterans of the *triarii* at the
rear of the legions did not succumb to the panic and were holding
firm, forming their phalanx and providing a rallying point for the
fugitives. Rullianus, who played the role of consummate general
throughout the battle, sent Scipio Barbatus and Gaius Marcius Rutilus
(another former consul) to lead forward the Allies in the reserve as
soon as he became aware that Decius' legions were in disarray. The

arrival of the Allies may also have coincided with Denter's rallying cries and so helped to stem the rout. As soon as Barbatus learned of Decius' death he too called on the troops not to let the consul's deed be for nothing; they must dare everything for the sake of the Republic.

Livy's description of the Senones' reaction to Decius' charge and death seems entirely fantastic: 'Those in the press around the body of the consul seemed without reason . . . and others were in a daze, unable either to fight or run away.' But is this entirely fictitious? The Roman historian (and the earlier annalists he used as his sources) would be keen to emphasise how the quite literal devotion of the Roman consul secured divine aid, but one wonders if the Senones were actually aware that they had killed a *devotus*. For more than a century the Senones had been encroaching into the territory of the proud Picentes, who took their name from the sacred woodpecker (*picus*) of Mars that had led them to their homeland in eastern Italy. It was probably the involvement of the hated Senones in Egnatius' confederacy that persuaded the Picentes not to join him but to side with Rome. There is strong evidence to suggest that the Picentes knew of the ritual of *devotio* and had used it in battle; they probably had occasion to use it against the Gauls. The *devotio* procedure of the Picentes was presumably essentially similar to that of the Romans: a commander or king invoking the gods, vowing to sacrifice himself and the forces of the enemy; the donning of ritual costume or armour; and the lone charge to the death. Therefore it is not impossible that the Senones at Sentinum recognised these features in Decius' death and the realisation that they had been offered in sacrifice to the gods caused their pursuit to falter. It would not matter that the gods involved were not Celtic (although the Senones were by now quite Italicised); we have already seen how easily terrified the Epirotes became when it was rumoured that the third Decius Mus (son of the Sentinum consul) intended to devote himself at Ausculum in 279 BC.[9]

However, by the time Denter (whom Decius had commissioned as propraetor and placed in command of the consular army), Scipio

Barbatus and Marcius Rutilus had brought up the Allies and quieted and reorganised the surviving legionaries, the Senones had regrouped themselves and formed a strong *testudo* (tortoise) of overlapping shields which even the divinely inspired Romans could not charge successfully. The Romans began to collect all the *pila*, spears and javelins lying on the battlefield and bombarded the Gallic formation. This had little effect. Most of the weapons stuck in the shields of the Senonian warriors, with only a few causing casualties.

Meanwhile on the right, the tactics of Rullianus were entirely successful. Gradually the javelin volleys, battle cries and charges of the Samnites grew less intense; the warriors became weary and sullen as the *hastati* of the legions refused to budge. Eventually, when Rullianus judged that the strength and resolve of Egnatius' men were sufficiently weakened, the consul ordered the prefects of the Allied *turmae* to move into position to attack the left flank of the Samnites (the Allied horse had presumably weakened the Samnite cavalry sufficiently); when he gave the signal they were to press home their charge. The consul then commanded the legionaries to push forward gradually – a final test of the strength of the enemy. The valiant Samnites had spent their last reserves of energy and were easily dislodged from their position. Convinced that the Samnites were ready to break, Rullianus called up all his reserves of Allied infantry cohorts, arranged them alongside the legions and at last gave the long-awaited order to charge. The cavalry prefects were given their signal to attack and the simultaneous frontal and flank assaults shattered the Samnite army. The Samnites, defeated by their own efforts, fled in a mass toward the confederate camp. The Senones were now completely exposed.

The Gallic *testudo* was holding firm against the missile barrage but Rullianus, finally aware of Decius' death, determined on the fulfilment of his colleague's vow and sent 500 of his picked Campanian horsemen to circle around the *testudo* and attack it from the rear. The *principes* (the second line of maniples) of the Third Legion were instructed to follow the cavalry and charge into any gap the surprise cavalry attack succeeded in making. 'Make havoc of them in their panic,' he said. Evidently the attack was entirely successful, for the consul was soon turning his attention to the confederate camp. There was a crush at the narrow gateway where Samnite warriors were trying to force their way in. Gellius Egnatius himself was unable or unwilling to reach apparent safety within the camp and improvised a battle line before the ramparts to meet Rullianus' assault.

On approaching the enemy camp Rullianus vowed a temple and the spoils of battle to Jupiter the Victor in return for total victory; it seems that the god was listening. Egnatius' line was swept aside, the Samnite general himself cut down, and the camp stormed with huge loss of life. Some 5,000 Samnites did manage to flee from Sentinum but one-fifth of their number were lost as they retreated home, principally in the territory of the bellicose Paeligni, who were allied to Rome.[10] The Senones, surrounded by the Romans, were presumably even less fortunate. Livy puts the total number of Samnite and Senonian dead at 25,000; another 8,000 were taken captive and destined for the slave markets. If we add the 5,000 Samnites who escaped, the confederate army numbered at least 38,000. The casualties to Rullianus' consular army were relatively light, 1,700 killed, but Decius' army lost 7,000 and the majority must have been from his two legions and cavalry. Opening his account of the battle of Sentinum, Livy wrote that the opponents were finely balanced and Fortuna, that most fickle of deities, had yet to decide on which side to grant her favour. Now she had decided but even for the victors the price was high.

In accordance with his vow, Rullianus had the spoils gathered from the enemy, piled up and burned in sacrifice to Jupiter the Victor. (This was only a proportion for, following the triumph of Rullianus, his soldiers were each awarded from the spoils eighty-two Roman pounds of bronze and a cloak and tunic.[11]) Soldiers were sent to look among the dead for the body of the consul Decius but it could not be found. It was finally discovered the following day under a heap of Senones, carried to the Roman camp and met with loud lamentations from the soldiers. Rullianus put all other duties aside and immediately oversaw the funeral of his colleague, 'with every show of honour and well-deserved eulogies', says Livy. Zonaras adds that Decius was cremated, a funerary custom which was just coming into vogue at this time among the Roman elite, but he wrongly assumes that Decius' body was burned with the spoils. Whether whole or cremated, his remains would have been taken back to Rome and deposited in the family tomb of the Decii. However, there is the fascinating possibility that Decius was accorded the great honour of being buried under the altar of the temple of Victoria in Rome when it was dedicated by Postumius Megellus in 294 BC.[12]

DEVOTIO AND VOWS

A rational appraisal of the battle of Sentinum reveals that Fabius Rullianus Maximus emerged victorious through his initially defensive tactics, careful use of reserves, and because the exhausted Samnites were unable to resist a sudden cavalry attack to their flank as well as the assault of the legions to the front. They retreated from the battlefield in disarray and thus left the Gauls completely exposed. For some reason the Senones formed up into a *testudo* formation rather than attempt to retreat; the legions and Allies bombarded its front and flanks with *pila* and other missiles and, when the Campanian cavalry attacked the rear of the formation, the Senones' resistance collapsed. However, we should not ignore the divine/religious element. That a wolf chased a deer into the space between the rival armies at the start of the battle sounds like the exaggeration of a patriotic Roman historian. We should perhaps not doubt that a wolf was seen – they still roam the highlands of Italy, and Roman soldiers were always on the watch for favourable omens – but it was probably glimpsed in woodland or on a far-off hill. Even so, the effect on a superstitious and pious people should not be underestimated. We have already seen how the Romans believed that

Mars himself fought alongside them at Thurii in 282 BC. The divine twins Castor and Pollux were believed to have aided the Romans, even fought beside them, at the battles of Lake Regillus (484 BC) and Pydna (168 BC), and, according to some sources, Vercellae (101 BC). The great voice of Silvanus, god of the woods and fields, emanating from the Forest of Arsia and declaring that the Romans would have the victory, was said to have terrified an Etruscan army, which was duly defeated (509 BC).[13]

Decius' act of *devotio* is not to be doubted and it was not unprecedented. It was clearly motivated by the successful *devotio* his father performed at the battle of the Veseris in 340 BC. Even if the Gauls at Sentinum did not comprehend why the younger Decius charged headlong onto their spears, the Roman soldiers certainly did – at least through the medium of Livius Denter – and accordingly were almost joyful at his death: they redoubled their efforts and started to fulfil the 'blood and carnage' element of Decius' vow, forcing the Senones to abandon their pursuit and form up into the defensive *testudo*.[14]

Rullianus' vow to Jupiter the Victor was neither the first nor the last of its kind made during the Third Samnite War, though it was made when victory was almost certain. When hard-pressed in battle against the Samnites and Etruscans in 296 BC, Appius Claudius Caecus dramatically lifted his hands to the heavens, called on the war goddess Bellona and vowed to her a temple if she would grant the Romans victory. There was no obvious sign of divine intervention in this battle but Appius' continued appeals to the goddess inspired his troops and they thrust the enemy back. In 294 BC the army of Marcus Atilius Regulus was defeated and forced back into its camp in an encounter with a smaller Samnite force at Luceria. According to Livy the Samnites' rage made their strength equal to that of the larger Roman army. It was the consul's desperate vow of a temple to Jupiter, in his guise as Stator ('the Stayer'), that prevented the Roman army from breaking into flight and being destroyed in a second encounter. (A close reading of Livy's account indicates that the steadiness of the centurions was instrumental in the survival of Regulus' army.) When the vow was made the power of the god became evident immediately. The flight of the Roman soldiers halted and the Samnites were pushed back and caught between the frontal assault of the legions and Allies, among whom were Lucanians, and a classic cavalry assault to their rear. Apparently almost 8,000 were taken prisoner (the number of Samnite dead is not recorded), stripped and forced under the yoke but then released, a mercy for which Regulus was later censured and one of the reasons why his request for a triumph was denied. Perhaps there were rumours that the episode was invented to explain his lack of prisoners, but the main reason was that Regulus' losses at Luceria were huge (7,800 dead), so great in fact that we might call the losses Pyrrhic. Zonaras states that the humiliating punishment of the yoke so infuriated the Samnites (the same punishment which under Gavius Pontius they had famously inflicted on the Romans at the Caudine Forks in 321 BC), that they raised a new army by a *lex sacrata*, a sacred law, and vowed to defeat the Romans or be destroyed in the process.[15]

THE LINEN LEGION

Despite its importance Sentinum was not the decisive battle of the Third Samnite War. Even after the battle of Aquilonia (293 BC), where their last great army was destroyed, the Samnites held out for another three years. The army levied by the Samnites in 293 BC is of particular interest. The leaders of the Samnite League enforced the conscription of men of military age by a *lex sacrata*. The lives of those who ignored the summons, or subsequently deserted, were forfeit to Jupiter. Between 36,000 and 40,000 men were enrolled by this sacred levy and mustered in a camp outside Aquilonia, where 16,000 of the warriors were selected to form an elite unit called the Linen Legion (*legio linteata*) and bound by a terrible oath to stand their ground or die. Livy's description of the formation of the Linen Legion is justly famous but also highly suspect:

At the middle of the camp the Samnites had enclosed an area of about 200 feet with wicker hurdles and roofed it over with linen. In this place they offered sacrifice. On the conclusion of the sacrifice the general commanded to be summoned all those of the highest birth and deeds in arms. One by one they were introduced. Besides other ceremonial preparations, such as might avail to strike the mind with religious awe, there was a place completely enclosed, with altars in the centre and slaughtered sacrificial animals lying about, and around them was a guard of centurions with drawn swords. The noble was brought up to the altar, more like a victim than a participant in a rite, and sworn not to reveal what he saw or heard. They then compelled him to take an oath in accordance with a certain dreadful form of words, whereby he invoked a curse upon his head, and his family and household, if he did not go into battle where his generals led the way, or if he either fled from the battle line or saw any other fleeing and did not instantly cut him down. There were at first a few who refused to take the oath; they were beheaded before the altars and lay among the slaughtered animals – a warning to the rest not to refuse. When the Samnite nobles had been bound by this imprecation, the general named ten of them and bade each choose another, and so on, until they had brought their number up to 16,000. These were called the 'Linen Legion' from the roof of the enclosure in which the nobles had been sworn, and were given splendid arms and crested helmets to distinguish them from the rest. (Livy, 10.38.5–13)

Other sources confirm that the Samnites did form an elite *legio linteata* (perhaps after their fine white linen tunics rather than the linen-covered enclosure) or a *legio sacrata* (a legion bound by a scared oath, probably to Jupiter) to fight at Aquilonia but, as E.T. Salmon has emphasised, the ceremony attended by the Samnite nobles within the linen enclosure was secret and, although some

Samnite deserters apparently related the particulars to Papirius Cursor, Livy must have invented most of the details.

Papirius Cursor, the consul commanding the Roman army at Aquilonia, considered the Linen Legion to be *devotus*, but it is clear that its purpose was not to perform *devotio* on a massive scale but to stand its ground where before other Samnite armies had ultimately fled. Livy does a great disservice to the Linen Legion, stating that fear of divine punishment rather than courage made its members stand fast. The Linen Legion resisted the onslaught of the Roman legions courageously and even held firm when a second Roman army appeared. This was in fact a ruse by Cursor – the new 'army' was a few detached Allied cohorts and a huge number of pack mules raising dust to simulate the approach of a large force of infantry and cavalry. While the Samnites were distracted by the appearance of the new Roman army, Cursor ordered lanes be opened up in the Roman infantry lines and the cavalry allowed through to launch a sudden frontal charge on the enemy. This was a rare tactic; as we have seen cavalry normally attacked infantry in flank (ideally the unshielded right), the rear, or when it was in disarray, but the charge was successful and followed immediately by the infantry led by Volumnius Flamma and the ubiquitous Scipio Barbatus. Even in this confusion the cohorts of the Linen Legion held out but eventually the sworn warriors fled with the unsworn and were pursued to their camp or the town of Aquilonia itself. Here Barbatus completely atoned for his defeat at Camerinum, by leading the successful assault on the main gate at the head of a *testudo* formation.[16]

Unlike Claudius Caecus, Fabius Rullianus and Atilius Regulus, Papirius Cursor did not vow a temple to one of the gods at Aquilonia. He was so certain of victory and had successfully wound his troops up to a state of near-hysteria and blood lust (the 'joyous fury' of the consul and his troops in combat is a dominant theme of Livy's battle narrative), that in the course of the battle he merely offered Jupiter the Victor 'a thimbleful of mead before he himself drank the strong wine'. The god evidently approved of the confidence and humour, but then he was also sated by the blood of the Samnites whose lives were forfeit to him.

The other consul, Carvilius Maximus, was conducting a simultaneous operation at nearby Cominium, which had forced the Samnites to detach 8,000 men from the army at Aquilonia to relieve Cominium. Such were the spoils from this battle that Carvilius was able to melt down the bronze helmets, cuirasses and greaves of the Samnites for a huge bronze statue of Jupiter that dominated the Capitol in Rome. It was so big that it could be seen from the sanctuary of Jupiter Latiaris ('of the Latins') on the Alban Mount, twelve miles away.[17]

THUNDER AND LIGHTNING

Although the Romans revered Mars as their Father, it was Jupiter (Iuppiter or Iove) whom they held as the most powerful and important of the gods. The eagle (*aquila*) was sacred to Jupiter and consequently adopted as the standard of the legion. The eagle was always the chief standard of the legion but until 104 BC each legion had four other major standards (*signa*) – the wolf, the minotaur, the horse and the boar. During the second century BC it had become customary to leave these other standards in the *aedes* (shrine) of the camp. The wolf was obviously connected to Mars but the attribution of the others is less certain, though the bull-headed minotaur might also have a connection with Mars; the bull was another of the many animals closely associated with the god. The final abandonment of the other standards (though not of course the essential individual *signa* of the centuries or maniples) was the decision of Marius and presumably connected with the reforms in legionary training and organisation made in response to the catastrophic defeat inflicted by the Germans at Arausio in 105 BC.[18]

As befitted the symbol of the king of the gods, the eagle standard was made of precious metal. During the late Republic, and presumably earlier, it was made of silver. The eagle under which

Catiline's desperados fought at Pistoria in 62 BC was silver (this *aquila* dated back to Marius' reform and had 'flown' at the final defeat of the Germans at Vercellae in 101 BC), as were the eagles of the legions of Brutus and Cassius at Philippi (42 BC). Under the Empire the standard was made of gold, or at least gilded silver; the sight of the massed golden eagles of Aurelian's legions amazed the arrogant envoys of the Iuthungi army and stunned them to silence (*c.* AD 271).

But sometimes a golden representation was not enough. In an effort to carry a living symbol of the divinity at all times, the *aquila* of *legio II Parthica* seems to have been a live bird. The tombstone of the *aquilifer* (eagle-bearer) Felsonius Versus, an Etruscan in an age when few Italians served in the army, who died in a campaign against the Sassanian Persians (AD 242–244), shows the apparently live eagle of the Second Parthica in a rectangular cage with crossbars mounted on a regular standard pole.[19]

Like sightings of wolves, the flight and alighting of eagles was of great importance to Roman armies. According to the Elder Pliny, 'Hardly ever has a Roman legion encamped for the winter without a pair of eagles making their appearance on the spot.' Commanders would also search the skies for eagles before engaging in battle.

At the battle of Idistaviso (AD 16), where the Romans faced the army of Arminius, the sighting of no fewer than eight eagles flying towards the wood immediately behind the German battle line was taken as a sure sign of Jupiter's favour and a portent of victory. According to Tacitus, Germanicus, imperial prince and general, cried out 'Forward! Follow the birds of Rome, the guardian spirits of the legions!' Germanicus' eight legions did just that and routed Arminius' force. Arminius was the mastermind of the Roman defeat of the Teutoburg Forest in AD 9, when three legions and many auxiliary units were ambushed and destroyed. In AD 16 it was the turn of the Romans: through Jupiter's favour they 'slaughtered the Germans from the fifth hour of day until nightfall and for ten miles the ground was littered with corpses and weapons.'

Yet the appearance of eagles did not always bode well for a Roman army. When two eagles alighted on the *aquila* standards of the legions of Brutus and Cassius (called the 'Liberators' for their assassination of Julius Caesar), it was taken as a sign of divine approval and that the imminent battle against the army of Antony and Octavian at Philippi would be successful. But the eagles were seen by some to peck at the silver standards, clearly a bad omen, and the fighting at Philippi resulted first in a draw and the suicide of Cassius, then the outright defeat and suicide of Brutus (42 BC).[20]

Jupiter was the thunder god, hence the *aquila* of the legion clutched a thunderbolt in its talons. The eagles of the Pompeian legions at Munda (45 BC) held gold thunderbolts, the first stage towards the Imperial gold eagle. Various lightning devices were common on Roman shields, which can still be seen today decorating the great triumphal monuments in Rome, especially Trajan's Column. When thunder was heard or lightning observed, the Romans believed Jupiter was making his presence felt. A rumble of thunder could be interpreted as a sign of divine disfavour. For example, the election of Claudius Marcellus as suffect consul in 215 BC (replacing the consul Postumius Albinus who had been killed in battle) was declared suspect by the augurs when thunder was heard, forcing Marcellus to resign immediately. In AD 172 the Emperor Marcus Aurelius and his field army were besieged somewhere north of the River Danube by a Germanic host. The fortified Roman camp, constructed in the midst of enemy territory, was assaulted during a thunderstorm. The Germans, either Quadi or Marcomanni, brought up a siege tower and it seemed that the camp would be stormed. But what did the storm signify, Jupiter's displeasure with the Romans or the Germans? Marcus Aurelius took it as a sign of Jupiter's anger against the Germans and prayed to the god to send a thunderbolt to destroy the siege tower. Jupiter obliged. A scene on the Aurelian Column in Rome depicts the miracle: the tower is blasted by lightning and barbarian warriors lie dead beneath it.[21]

In the summer of AD 172 another Roman army was ambushed and surrounded by the Quadi. The Romans formed up into square formation and locked shields. The Germans eventually abandoned their attempts to break the formation, preferring to let the Romans use up what little water they had and succumb to their wounds and the heat. However, a sudden thunderstorm provided the Romans with plenty of water: as the legionaries held up their helmets to catch the rain, the infuriated Quadi charged but were destroyed by a deadly hail and bolts of lightning. Despite the lightning, the Romans did not attribute this miracle to Jupiter. The Aurelian Column shows a strange divinity made of cascading water rising up protectively over the Roman soldiers, while the flood he sends drowns barbarian warriors and horses. Harnouphis, an Egyptian priest in the retinue of Marcus Aurelius, claimed to have called upon the Egyptian deity Thoth-Shou (associated by the Greeks and Romans with the god Hermes/Mercury) to send the rain. Some time later the legend grew that Christian soldiers of the Twelfth Legion had called upon God to send the rain and smite the Germans and the legion was given the title *Fulminata* ('lightning bearer' or 'armed with lightning') in thanks. However, it is unlikely that this legion, based in the Near East, took part in the campaign and its title actually dated back to the late first century BC.[22]

The so-called Lightning and Rain Miracles almost certainly have some basis in fact, that is natural phenomena interpreted and, to a certain extent, exploited as instances of divine intervention. No doubt the 'miracles' grew in the telling, especially in the versions of Imperial propagandists, but even in our modern and apparently rational age episodes of severe weather can cause immense damage, inspire awe and terror, and are still described as 'acts of God'.

A clear example of the deliberate exploitation of a natural phenomenon occurred in 210 BC when Scipio (later Africanus) was assaulting New Carthage in Spain. Informed by local fishermen that the ebb tide would drain the lagoon on the seaward side of the city, Scipio selected 500 legionaries to make a surprise attack on that side of the city while its defenders were fully occupied with the main Roman assault on the strongly fortified landward side. When the tide turned, as Scipio knew it would, he feigned surprise and declared to his superstitious men that the sea god Neptune was clearing a way for them to cross. Inspired by the god and further aided by the Carthaginians' failure to guard the seemingly invulnerable seaward walls, the Romans duly captured the city.[23]

Another Roman general to exploit the superstitions of his troops was Quintus Sertorius, the Marian who waged war against Sulla's lieutenants in Spain, 80–72 BC. He had very few Roman legionaries and the bulk of his army was made up of Spaniards. The warriors were in awe of a rare white deer that Sertorius kept as a pet. The tame creature followed Sertorius everywhere and was not disturbed by crowds or noise. Sertorius played on suspicions that the deer was sent by the gods:

> He gradually tried to give the doe a religious importance by declaring that she was a gift of the goddess Diana, and declared that she revealed many hidden things to him, knowing that the barbarians [the Spaniards] were naturally prone to superstition. He also resorted to such devices as these. Whenever he had secret intelligence that the enemy had made an incursion into the territory which he commanded, or were trying to bring a city to revolt from him, he would pretend that the doe had conversed with him in his dreams, bidding him hold his forces in readiness. Again, when he got tidings of some victory won by his commanders, he would hide the messenger and bring forth the doe wearing garlands for the receipt of glad tidings, exhorting his men to be of good cheer and to sacrifice to the gods, assured that they were to learn of some good fortune. By these devices he made the people tractable, and so found them more serviceable for all his plans; they believed that they were led not by the mortal wisdom of a foreigner, but by a god. (Plutarch, *Sertorius*, 11.3–12.1)

Sertorius relied heavily on this deception, but when the doe went missing he took it as a bad omen; he became depressed and his skill as a general deserted him. When his hunters finally tracked it down Sertorius' vigour returned and he staged an event where the white doe, still presumed lost by his Spanish warriors, miraculously reappeared and bounded up to nuzzle its master. Sertorius' reputation for good fortune and status as one favoured by the gods was thus re-established for a time.[24]

Celestial phenomena could also have a profound effect on the minds of the ancients. In AD 14 the mutiny of the Pannonian legions collapsed when superstitious legionaries saw an eclipse of the moon as divine displeasure. The soldiers desperately sounded trumpets and clashed cymbals in an attempt to restore the moon, known to them as the goddess Luna, but when clouds gathered and entirely cut off the view of the eclipsed moon, they broke down screaming that the gods had abandoned them.

In AD 310 the Emperor Constantine appears to have witnessed a solar halo, a phenomenon caused by the refraction of the sun's rays through hexagonal ice crystals high in the atmosphere and producing the appearance of a halo around the sun. This Constantine initially took as a vision of the god Apollo or Sol Invictus, the 'Unconquered Sun' and he swiftly adopted Sol as his patron deity. However, in his victory over Maxentius at the Milvian Bridge in AD 312 Constantine recognised the helping hand of the Christian god. The emperor's interest in Christianity was by this date long established and the battle was prefaced by a dream instructing him to daub 'the heavenly sign of God', either an elaborate cross or a Chi-Rho symbol, on the shields of his soldiers. Following this dream and victory he reinterpreted the event of AD 310 as a vision of Christ and the Cross. He immediately set the Empire on a new course: the rejection of the old pagan gods and the adoption of Christianity as the official religion of the Roman state.[25]

* * *

The courage and determination of Roman fighting men won the battles of Sentinum and the Milvian Bridge. Human, not divine, intervention was ultimately decisive. Yet the belief in divine intervention, or approval, spurred on the courage and determination that won those battles. The potency of that Roman belief is still evident. The reverberations of the triumph of Christianity at the Milvian Bridge continue to shape the world.

Chapter III

SINGLE COMBAT

'Vexation drives him, the chance holds him to it, the fact helps him.' (Ennius, *Annals*, fragment 167)

'Once again Antony sent Octavian a challenge to single combat, but Octavian replied that Antony had many ways of dying.' (Plutarch, *Life of Antony*, 75.1)

The Romans traced a tradition of single combat back to the very foundation of their city and believed that certain duels had played a crucial role in the development of their power. Single combats could decide battles or at least inspire the Romans to victory. Enemies were dismayed by the prowess of Roman duellists; their actions embodied the unconquerable spirit of Rome and demonstrated the favour of the gods. However, the descriptions of most single combats were written years, even centuries, after they were fought. The surviving sources are often skimpy, fragmentary and in disagreement over certain points. Care must be taken to strip away anachronisms and literary conventions, and to separate the

facts from fiction. However, most of the descriptions derive from
what was probably an essentially accurate oral tradition.

LEGENDARY DUELS
THE FIRST ROMAN DUELLISTS

The first Roman duellist was Romulus himself. According to the
foundation myth believed by the Romans, Romulus and Remus were
the twin sons of the Latin princess Rhea who had been raped by the
god Mars; the infants were famously suckled by a she-wolf and went
on to establish a war band and settle the hills above the best
crossing of the River Tiber. The traditional date is 753 BC, but
archaeology has demonstrated occupation at various points on the
hills and valleys of Rome centuries before this. Having argued with
and slain Remus, Romulus established himself as king of the
formative Rome and welcomed all manner of cut-throats and
runaways to his banner, but few women came with them, and the
other towns in Latium rebuffed Romulus' pleas to supply the new
Romans with wives. The Romans then determined to seize wives for
themselves and treacherously invited the Sabines and their women-
folk to a festival; the infamous kidnap and rape of the Sabine
women followed.

Romulus consequently found himself at war with the Sabines and
their allies. First to march on Rome was Acron, king of nearby
Caenina. Impatient of waiting for the forces of the hesitating Sabine
king, Titus Tatius, Acron dispersed his troops to ravage the small
territory of Rome, but the king and his diminished force were
intercepted by Romulus with his full army. Acron hoped to extricate
his outnumbered force by reducing the inevitable fight to a battle of
champions and challenged Romulus to single combat. The Roman,
protected by a simple wolf-skin helmet, easily dispatched the other
king with his lance, then beheaded him; thus also began the Romans'
passion for taking heads as trophies. Acron's troops panicked and
fled. They were pursued back to Caenina and the town was sacked.
Although this single combat is apocryphal, the panic of the

Caeninenses reflects the reaction of the losing side in historical single combats. We have seen how the Mamertine army desisted from an attack when Pyrrhus killed its champion (275 BC), and in c. 361 BC a Gallic army retreated in shock when its champion was brutally slain by a Roman tribune (*see below*). Accordingly in the second legendary Roman duel, again fought as a result of the rape of the Sabine women, the Roman battle line collapsed when Hostius Hostilius was killed by the Sabine champion, Mettius Curtius.

After the sack of Caenina, the Romans marched triumphantly back to their little town and Romulus displayed the arms he had stripped from Acron's corpse on a sacred oak tree on the Capitoline hill. He proceeded to mark out the site for a temple to be dedicated to Jupiter. Here the *spolia opima* (spoils of honour) taken by Roman commanders from enemy kings in single combat would be offered to Jupiter, called Feretrius – the bearer of trophies.[1]

It is probable that the custom of *spolia opima* was established very early in Rome's history, the parading and dedication of the spoils being the first stage in the development of the ultimately elaborate triumphal processions. Although Romans of the first century BC understood *spolia opima* to refer only to the spoils taken from an enemy king, the custom might also suggest that when Rome was just another small town in Latium, her wars and disputes with neighbouring towns and tribes were sometimes settled by single combats between high-ranking champions – kings or clan chiefs or leaders of war bands. Such combats were agreeable to warrior and agricultural societies, limiting conflict but also satisfying the heroic ethos of aristocrats. The practice of battle by champions was fairly common in the Mediterranean, the most famous example being the battle between 300 chosen hoplites of Sparta and 300 Argives at Thyrea in c. 546 BC. However, the result of the combat was accepted by neither side – two Argives lived but the sole surviving Spartan was the last to leave the field, and claimed possession of it by erecting a trophy of spoils – and resulted in a full-scale battle. This was a risk inherent to all battles of champions.[2]

Another apocryphal Roman duelling tale tells how the Roman king Tullus Hostilius (traditionally reigned 672–640 BC and the grandson of the Hostilius killed by Mettius Curtius) and Mettius Fufetius, newly dictator of the Latin city of Alba Longa, agreed to unify their states but each declared that his state should be dominant in the new union. The only way to settle the dispute was by a battle of champions and the rulers swore to abide by its outcome. Three brothers were chosen from each army: the Horatii brothers from the Roman and the Curiatii from the Alban. As Livy tells it, the Albans had the better of the combat at first and killed two of the Horatii. All three Curiatii had received wounds by they time they turned on the last Horatius, named Publius, who was as yet unscathed. Publius ran but the wounded Curiatii could not catch him and became strung out. Publius then turned and dispatched the Albans one by one; the last Curiatius had lost so much blood that he could hardly raise his shield when Publius came and thrust his sword through the champion's throat. It was a sacrifice: Publius offered the deaths of the Curiatii to the shades of his brothers.

The tradition followed by Dionysius of Halicarnassus – a contemporary of Livy – is more detailed, which possibly means more inventive, borrowing from ancient literary traditions about single combat, such as those employed by Homer to describe the duels of the Trojan War, as well as details of actual fights from the wars of the later third to first centuries BC, and probably from witnessing gladiatorial combats. Dionysius emphasises the silence and tension of the two armies at the start of the combat, then how the soldiers began to shout encouragement to their champions, but because of the distance between the armies and the champions – presumably beyond the range of missiles and far enough to prevent soldiers from intervening to aid their champions – some had difficulty clearly distinguishing between Roman and Alban. As in Livy's version, the Curiatii drew first blood. The eldest Curiatius got underneath the guard of one of the Horatii, thrust his sword into the Roman's groin and so killed him. The three Curiatii thought it would be easy to dispose of the two remaining Roman brothers, but one of the Horatii rushed at the eldest Curiatius and landed a killing blow. He was in turn cut down by another of the Alban brothers, being stabbed forcefully in the back, but as the Roman fell he lashed out with his sword and seriously wounded the Alban in the thigh. It was now that Publius Horatius began to run from the contest, as if in fright and cowardice:

> The Alban who was not mortally wounded followed at his heels, but the other [the Curiatius with the thigh wound] was unable to keep going and fell behind. The Albans shouted encouragement to their men and the Romans reproached their champion for cowardice, the former singing songs of triumph and crowning themselves with garlands as if the contest were already won, and the latter lamenting as if Fortune would never raise them up again. But the Roman, having carefully waited for his opportunity, turned abruptly and, before the Alban could put himself on his guard, struck a blow on his arm which clove his elbow in two, and when his hand fell to the ground together with his sword, he struck one more blow, a mortal one, and dispatched the Alban. Then, rushing from him to the last of his adversaries, who was half dead and fainting, he slew him also. (Dionysius of Halicarnassus, *Roman Antiquities*, 3.20.2–4)

Publius then stripped the corpses of their arms and armour. Mettius accepted the outcome of the combat and acknowledged Rome's dominance. As for the later *socii* (the Allies), the foreign policy of his city-state would henceforth be directed by Rome and his army would bolster the strength of the legions. However, Mettius soon reneged on the agreement, withdrawing his troops from the line at a crucial moment during a battle against Fidenae and Veii. Yet the Romans won through and Tullus had his centurions seize the treacherous Alban. He was strung between two chariots and torn apart.

The victorious Publius Horatius returned to Rome laden with his triple spoils, and wearing the war cloak (*sagum*) of one of the Curiatii. It is the wearing of the cloak that turns Publius Horatius' tale from one of triumph to tragedy. His sister watched the army entering the city and spying Publius in the distinctive cloak mistook him for the Curiatius to whom she just happened to be engaged; according to the tradition followed by Dionysius, the Horatii and Curiatii were cousins. Horatius was enraged and cut his sister down. Tullus wanted to execute Publius immediately but his father begged the king to let at least one of his children live. So it was Publius' punishment to pass daily under a beam symbolising a yoke (*iugum*). The *iugum* likened a man to a beast, a ploughing ox, to be used and abused as his master saw fit.

The act of passing under the yoke was probably also symbolic of decapitation: note the closely related *iugulum*, meaning neck or throat and also a term for slaughter. Decapitation was a common method of punishment for cowards and soldiers who disobeyed orders in ancient Italy. We have already seen how the Samnites decapitated those aristocratic warriors who refused to join the Linen Legion.

Being forced under the yoke was a particularly shameful punishment and much used by victorious armies across ancient Europe to humiliate the defeated. There are many historic examples of defeated armies being forced under the yoke, and many of them refer to unfortunate Romans. For instance the Samnites famously trapped the Romans in the mountain pass called the Caudine Forks and forced them under the yoke (321 BC), and Jugurtha and the Tigurini humiliated Roman armies by the same means as late as 110 and 107 BC. However, it seems that the legend of Horatius' Beam or Yoke actually developed out of a misunderstanding of the function of an ancient arch or gateway (*ianus*) in the Forum formed by two columns with a wooden crossbar and leading to an altar sacred to double-headed god Janus. Soldiers who passed through the arch were purified of blood guilt after combat. It is important to remember, though, that the Romans believed the tales to be true and took inspiration and moral guidance from them.[3]

The tale of the Horatii and Curiatii probably does have a kernel of truth to it, that is the folk memory passed on through oral tradition that the early Romans fought in battles of champions (the neighbouring Umbrian tribes still fought judicial duels in historic times),[4] but the details must be the invention of annalists of the middle and late Republican periods who were keen to render Roman folk tales into glorious 'fact' and so create a convincing early history for Rome. The writings of the annalists (so-called because their histories followed a strict year by year sequence) were used in turn by the likes of Livy and Dionysius at the beginning of the Imperial era (from 27 BC). They attempted to make sense of legends and reconcile the histories of various annalists who were not above over-emphasising the role of their own clans, as well as making their own additions using the single and one-on-one combats of their own age to supply detail. However, these legendary duels should not be dismissed entirely. Many of the particulars about how single combats were fought, how the victors despoiled the corpses of the defeated and how the spectators reacted, were influenced by contemporary and long established battle practices.

As well as the literary sources considered below, numerous tomb and vase paintings of the fourth and third centuries BC from central and southern Italy depict triumphant Samnite, Campanian and Lucanian warriors with spears hung with the gaudy tunics and bronze belts stripped from their enemies. The belt was an important symbol of manhood and Italic militarism. The tombs of Etruscan aristocrats sometimes had helmets nailed to the walls, not part of the panoply of the deceased but spoils taken from enemies and attached to the walls of tombs as everlasting trophies. Dionysius' account of the Albans singing and garlanding each other in anticipation of the victory of their champions clearly reflects the actual battle practices of Republican and Imperial Roman armies. For example, legionaries sang in the midst of combat at the battles of Pharsalus (48 BC) and

Lugdunum (AD 197), Mark Antony's legionaries left the battlefield of Forum Gallorum singing victory odes and soldiers of the *legio Martia* were crowned with olive-leaf garlands following the battle of Mutina (43 BC).[5]

THE ROMAN ACHILLES

The Romans believed that Lucius Siccius Dentatus was a hero of the plebs (the common people) in their struggle against oligarchs, who engineered Dentatus' assassination in *c.* 450 BC. Dentatus was probably a historical character but by the time his story was first set down in writing in the mid-first century BC, probably by the antiquarian Varro, the original oral tradition of Dentatus' deeds had become tangled with other folk tales and legends, and historic deeds of the second and first centuries BC were perhaps employed to help 'reconstruct' the details his life.

From Dionysius we learn that when aged twenty-seven Dentatus was serving in the ranks as a common legionary. During a battle against the Volscians his legion was defeated and its standards captured but Dentatus single-handedly recaptured the standards and so 'saved the centurions from incurring everlasting disgrace'. This act won his first decoration for valour – a gold crown (*corona aurea*). In a subsequent battle the chief centurion (*primus pilus*) of Dentatus' legion (the Second) was knocked to the ground and the enemy seized the eagle standard (*aquila*) from him. Dentatus rushed forward to save the *primus pilus* and recaptured the eagle, the most sacred of all the legion's standards. The *primus pilus* was ashamed and attempted to pass his command to the heroic legionary. Dentatus refused but the consul promoted him to the rank of *primus pilus* in the First Legion.

During his forty years of military service Dentatus fought in 120 battles. He won 8 or 9 single combats, always having been challenged by an enemy, and stripped the spoils from 34 or 36 warriors. He had 45 scars, all on the front of his body, *none* on the back. Twelve of the scars were sustained in a single fight. For his valour he was the recipient of 18 ceremonial spears; 25 *phalerae* (decorated discs either worn on a harness over the chest or as part of horse trappings); 83 torques (heavy necklaces); 160 bracelets; 14 civic crowns (*corona civica*, a crown of oak leaves awarded for saving the life of a fellow-citizen in battle); eight gold crowns; three mural crowns (*corona muralis*, for being the first man to gain the wall of an enemy fortress), and one siege crown (*corona obsidionalis*, a crown made of grass for relieving a besieged or beleaguered army). He was also presented with a basket full of coin, 10 prisoners, that is as personal slaves, and 20 oxen. The early Imperial writer Valerius Maximus declared that Dentatus had decorations enough for a complete legion. Aulus Gellius, writing in the mid-second century AD, noted that on account of his martial prowess Dentatus was called the Roman Achilles. It may be from his ferocity in battle that the *cognomen* (nickname) Dentatus was derived, for it can mean 'having teeth', in the sense of the fangs of a wild animal, but Roman *cognomina* were often quite derogatory and it could refer to bad or prominent teeth.

In 450 BC Dentatus held the rank of military tribune but was lured into an ambush laid by his political enemies. He sent many of his attackers to the underworld before he himself was finally killed. His body was discovered in the centre of a ring of slaughtered enemies. The news of his assassination caused the army to mutiny and ultimately led to the downfall of the tyrannical board of Decemvirs who had seized power in Rome.[6]

Very little of this, apart from Dentatus' status as an opponent of the Decemvirs, has any factual basis. Dentatus' promotion to centurion for saving the eagle reads like an episode lifted out of Caesar's wars, for example Lucius Petrosidius' desperate efforts to save the *aquila* of the Fourteenth Legion from the Eburones in the winter of 54–53 BC, and Scaeva's promotion to senior centurion for his tenacious defence of one of Caesar's forts at Dyrrhachium in 48 BC (*see* Chapter IV). We saw in Chapter II that the *aquila* did not become the principal standard of the legion until the end of the second century BC and the Roman army might not yet have been divided into two legions in Dentatus' day. However, there is much in the tales of this warrior to illuminate the practice of single combat and Roman concepts of courage and honour.

That Dentatus won at least eight single combats but took the spoils of thirty-four or thirty-six warriors emphasises the distinction, albeit a sometimes slight one, between single combats which were prefaced by challenges and fought in the no-man's land between on-looking opposing armies, and the one-on-one fights between warriors who happened upon each other in the chaos of battle. Two incidents in the career of Pompey the Great can serve by way of illustration.

First, in the civil war between Sulla and Carbo (a Marian), Pompey marched his Sullan army against the combined Marian forces of Carrinas, Coelius and Brutus Damasippus near Ariminum (83 BC). Pompey led his cavalry in a charge against Brutus' Gallic mercenary cavalry. As the Gauls counter-charged, Pompey spurred ahead of his men and speared the Gallic commander. The Gaul was killed and his men broke off their charge. As the Gallic cavalry retreated they collided with the advancing Marian legions; Pompey promptly took advantage of the confusion to win an easy victory. In fact, some of the enemy legionaries were so impressed with Pompey's prowess that they advanced as if in attack but proceeded to change sides. Here then is an example of one-on-one combat, but if a challenge had been shouted and quickly accepted it could quite easily have been considered a single combat because of the separation of the commander from his men.[7]

Second, when fighting against the forces of the Roman rebel Sertorius at the battle of the Sucro (75 BC), Pompey met one of the enemy in more conventional one-on-one combat. Pompey, mounted on his horse, was confronted by a tall enemy infantryman:

> When they came to close quarters and were at grips, the strokes of their swords fell on each other's hands, but not

> with the same result, for Pompey was merely wounded, but he
> had cut the hand from his opponent. (Plutarch, *Pompey*, 19.2)

This fight attracted the attention of large group of Sertorius' Libyan infantry, but Pompey escaped by abandoning his horse. The Libyans gave up their pursuit when they realised the horse's trappings were covered in gold and started to fight among themselves over the spoils.

One-on-one combats normally concluded with the victor pausing to strip the loser of his weapons and perhaps decapitate him. As well as the obvious reason of stripping the dead of valuables for the victor's personal profit, spoils taken from an enemy had to be presented to the general before he would award a military decoration. Sometimes heads were required before a reward was given. The quasi-legionaries hastily recruited from slave volunteers to make good the horrendous casualties suffered in the disaster at Cannae (216 BC), were encouraged to produce the heads of Carthaginian soldiers to secure their freedom. Visitors to Rome can still see sculptures on Trajan's Column, the Great Trajanic Frieze (incorporated into the Arch of Constantine) and the Column of Marcus Aurelius of Roman soldiers presenting heads taken in battle to the emperors. Later emperors like Probus (reigned AD 276–282) offered a bounty in gold for every enemy head taken. One battle scene on Trajan's Column even shows a soldier fighting with the hair of a severed head clenched between his teeth, while another scene depicts a soldier at the top of a siege ladder having just decapitated the defender of a Dacian fortification. The Roman holds on to the hair of his fresh trophy. Following a victory in the Munda campaign (45 BC), Caesar's soldiers stacked the corpses of Pompeian legionaries to form a gruesome parody of a triumphal monument, and decorated it with severed heads impaled on swords and *pila*. The triumphal arch at Orange, probably built to celebrate the suppression of a Gallic revolt during the reign of Tiberius (AD 14–37), is liberally decorated with sculptural representations of severed heads.[8]

A legionary from the time of the Pyrrhic War about to throw his heavy *pilum*. Note his simple pectoral armour and the bronze belt, perhaps plundered from a Sabellian, though the warriors of the *legio Campana* would certainly have worn such belts. *Graham Sumner*

Below: Detail of dead and dying barbarians on the Ludovisi Battle Sarcophagus, recalling the collapse of the Senones when charged by the *devotus* Decius Mus at Sentinum. *Author*

A replica of the statue of the Capestrano Warrior, thought to represent a Picente *devotus* of around 500 BC. Note his pectoral and abdominal armour, armlets and torque or gorget. *Jasper Oorthuys*

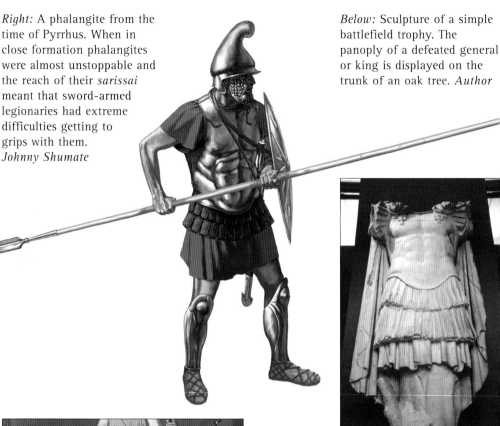

Right: A phalangite from the time of Pyrrhus. When in close formation phalangites were almost unstoppable and the reach of their *sarissai* meant that sword-armed legionaries had extreme difficulties getting to grips with them. *Johnny Shumate*

Below: Sculpture of a simple battlefield trophy. The panoply of a defeated general or king is displayed on the trunk of an oak tree. *Author*

Wall painting from Pompeii of Jupiter being crowned by Victory. He holds a sceptre-like *fulmen* (thunderbolt) and is accompanied by his messenger, the eagle. *RHC Archive*

Detail of the statue of the Dying Gaul illustrating his torque. *Author*

Below: An *aquila* (eagle standard) being carried into battle. Portonaccio Battle Sarcophagus, *c.* AD 180. *Author*

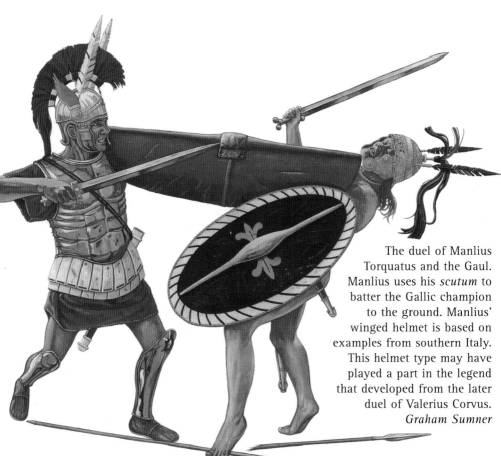

The duel of Manlius Torquatus and the Gaul. Manlius uses his *scutum* to batter the Gallic champion to the ground. Manlius' winged helmet is based on examples from southern Italy. This helmet type may have played a part in the legend that developed from the later duel of Valerius Corvus. *Graham Sumner*

Below: Caesar's Centurion. Funerary relief of Minucius Lorarius, centurion of the *legio Martia*. Minucius may have been killed at Forum Gallorum in 43 BC or during the fateful crossing of the Adriatic in 42 BC.
Steven D. P. Richardson

Below left, main picture: Minucius Lorarius in full battle gear and challenging the enemy to fight. Note the transverse crest, the symbol of the centurion's rank.
Graham Sumner

A Roman general in the thick of battle in the late second century AD, Portonaccio Battle Sarcophagus. Note how the face of the general was never completed. *Author*

The battle of the Milvian Bridge frieze (beneath the roundels) on the Arch of Constantine, Rome. The bridge of boats over the Tiber has collapsed and Maxentius and his praetorian cavalry drown in the river. Constantine's divinely inspired cavalry are unaffected and strike down at their struggling opponents. *Author*

Praetorian standard. In AD 193 Septimius Severus (*bottom portrait*) reformed the Guard as an elite fighting unit and recruited it exclusively from legionaries, reverting to the practice of the late Republic. Note the wall crown (*centre*) awarded for storming an enemy fortification. *Author*

An imaginative nineteenth-century reconstruction of a Roman army storming a city. Note the *testudo* formation in the centre, such as Scipio Barbatus employed to take the gate at Aquilonia. *RHC Archive*

A Roman triumph. The spoils from Titus' siege of Jerusalem are carried by singing legionaries. Arch of Titus, Rome. *Author*

A centurion of the fourth
century AD. Ammianus
Marcellinus watched such
men battle their way into the
Persian camp at Amida.
Graham Sumner

A battle-crazed *bellator* of *legio XXII Primigenia* charges towards the enemy in one of the battles of the later first century AD. Legionaries were not the uniquely disciplined soldiers of popular belief. *Jim Bowers*

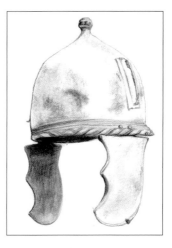

Sabellian warriors as depicted on south Italian pottery of the fourth and third centuries BC. Note the spoils – tunic and belt – carried by one on his spear. *RHC Archive*

Richly decorated helmet of a Senones chieftain from the necropolis at Montefortino, probably contemporary with the battle of Sentinum. The Romans' 'Montefortino' helmet was based on this type. *Not. Scav. 1886*

An early Montefortino helmet. The type was used by Roman and Italic warriors from the late fourth to first centuries BC. Note the holders for plumes which associated the wearer with the war god Mars. *Steven D. P. Richardson*

Sarcophagus of Scipio Barbatus, defeated at Camerinum but instrumental in the great victories at Sentinum and Aquilonia. The second line of the reworked inscription refers to his handsomeness and excellence. *RHC Archive*

The Ludovisi Battle Sarcophagus depicts a Roman commander making a *devotio*-like charge. Note his detached expression while barbarians writhe in agony beneath his horse. The sumptuous sarcophagus probably commemorates the heroic death of a general or imperial prince in one of the many desperate battles of the third quarter of the third century AD. *Author*

Detail of the general or prince on the Ludovisi Battle Sarcophagus. He beckons his soldiers on, but makes no effort to fight or defend himself. Note the small cross chiselled on his forehead. A portrait bust of the same man also features this mark but, like his identity, the symbolism remains a mystery. *Author*

The Lightning Miracle on the Aurelian Column, Rome. Jupiter sends a bolt of lightning to destroy the German siege tower. *Petersen, Die Marcus-Säule, 1896*

Left: The Rain Miracle on the Aurelian Column. The Rain God shelters Roman legionaries while Quadi warriors drown in the flood. *Petersen, Die Marcus-Säule, 1896*

Above: The Emperor Constantius II holds the holy Labarum standard with its Chi-Rho monogram. *RHC Archive*

A Roman warrior (*middle left*) grips the hair of the severed head of a Dacian between his teeth, while above Jupiter hurls a thunderbolt at the Dacians. Battle scene from Trajan's Column, Rome. *RHC Archive*

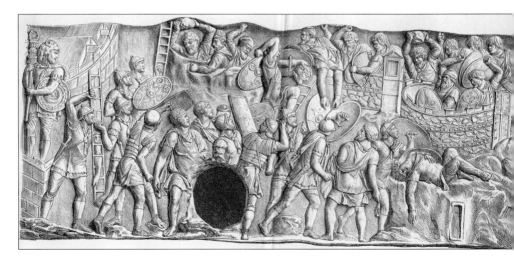

Roman soldiers assault a Dacian fort. In the centre, the Roman at the top of the assault ladder has just decapitated one of the Dacian defenders. Battle scene from Trajan's Column. *RHC Archive*

Inscription of Marcus
Billienus, veteran of
Octavian's Eleventh Legion,
who took the *cognomen*
Actiacus after fighting at
Actium (lines 2–3).
Steven D. P. Richardson

Top: coin depicting
Marcellus carrying the
spolia opima taken from
Viridomarus to the temple
of Jupiter Feretrius.
RHC Archive

Above: Marcus Sergius Silus
brandishes a head taken in
battle. *RHC Archive*

A centurion battles his way
through German warriors on
the Portonaccio Battle
Sarcophagus. *Author*

Scene on the Aurelian Column which may represent
the encounter (single combat?) in battle of Valerius
Maximianus and Valao, chieftain of the Naristae, in AD 173
(*top centre riders*). Petersen, *Die Marcus-Säule, 1896*

Legionary of the first
century BC from the so-
called Altar of Domitius
Ahenobarbus.
He wears a mail shirt and a
Montefortino helmet, and
carries a *scutum*.
Steven D. P. Richardson

Reconstruction of Caesar's inner line of defences at Alesia. The vicious booby traps prevented Vercingetorix from breaking out. *RHC Archive*

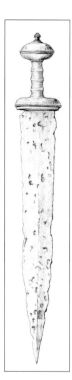

Left: Centurion's *gladius* from Rheingönheim in Germany. The centurion had the hilt plated with silver. *Steven D. P. Richardson*

Right: Marcus Aurelius Lucianus, a praetorian of the third century AD. He was probably the son of a legionary. Note his weighted *pilum* – praetorians continued to use this weapon after the legionaries had largely abandoned it – and the eagle-hilted sword, perhaps a gift from an emperor. *Steven D. P. Richardson*

Right: The centotaph of Marcus Caelius, leading centurion, perhaps *primus pilus*, of *legio XVIII*, killed in the battle of the Teutoburg Forest in AD 9. Like the centurions of the Republic, he is laden with decorations and wears a civic crown for saving the life of a fellow soldier in battle. *RHC Archive*

Below: Imperial praetorians. Drawing of a sculpture, probably from a triumphal monument of Emperor Claudius (AD 41–54), now in the Louvre. Note the eagle standard – a reminder of the legionary origins of the praetorian cohorts. *RHC Archive*

Left: Ninth *Hispana* tile stamps from York, Nijmegen and near Carlisle (*top to bottom*). *After RIB and Bogaers, Studien Militärgrenzen Roms 1967*

Below left: Epitaph of Aelius Asclepiades from Naples. Asclepiades was possibly transferred to the Ninth during the reign of Hadrian. *CIL X 1769*

Right: Sling bullets from the siege of Perusia, 41–40 BC. Number 5 reveals Scaeva as *primus pilus* of Octavian's Twelfth Legion. *Ephemeris Epigraphica 6, 1885*

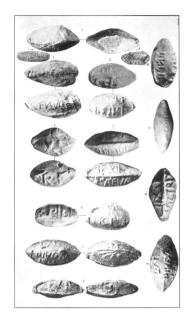

```
   D · AELIVS · ASC  M
   LEPIADES · NATI
 cIL · MIL · LEG · IX
   VIX · ANN · XXXXII
 5 MIL · ANN · VIII
   AELIA · SELERIA
       B · M · F
```

Left: This building inscription from York, dating to AD 108, is the last clear evidence for the Ninth Legion (RIB I 665). *After Keppie 2000*

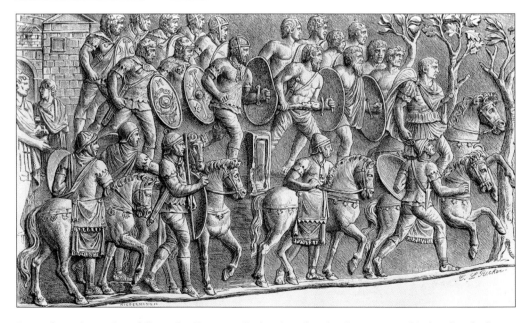

Bare-chested warriors follow the Emperor Trajan into battle. German auxiliaries fought bare-chested at the siege of Placentia in AD 69. Scene from Trajan's Column. *RHC Archive*

As well as the dangers of being attacked while in the act of despoiling a fallen enemy, there were other perils. Despoiling an opponent in civil war could have unexpected results. When a man's helmet had been taken from him and his features could be clearly discerned, more than a few legionaries discovered that they had killed or mortally wounded family members. When Cinna and Marius captured Rome in 87 BC, the formidable army of Pompeius Strabo (father of Pompey the Great) was easily defeated when the general suddenly dropped dead, perhaps having been struck by lightning.

> During this campaign, two brothers, one of Pompeius' army, the other from that of Cinna, unwittingly came to blows. When the victor was stripping his slain rival, he recognised his brother, broke into loud lamentation, and when he had built his brother's pyre, he stabbed himself on it and was consumed in the flames with his victim. (Livy, *Periochae*, 79)

Tacitus tells a similar tale about the second battle of Cremona, the decisive engagement of the civil war of AD 69. A young conscript of the new Seventh Legion (later *Gemina*) easily dispatched a veteran opponent. Pausing to rifle the corpse for valuables, the conscript discovered he had killed his father, Julius Mansuetus, who served in the opposing legion, *XXI Rapax*. The conscript's outpourings of grief led to a general halt in the fighting, with the Flavian and Vitellian legionaries bemoaning the horrors of civil war. However, the fighting and plundering soon resumed.[9]

It was the Roman custom for soldiers of all ranks to display their *spolia* on the doorposts of their houses, on the walls of public rooms and so on. The walls of Siccius Dentatus' house would have been laden with *spolia*. Items were inscribed with brief details of where, when and from whom they had been won. A recently discovered bronze breastplate, evidently taken during the destruction of Falerii in 241 BC, carries the inscription, 'Captured at Falerii, in the consulship of Quintus Lutatius and Aulus Manlius'. Once the arms were fixed they could not be taken down, even if the house was sold to a new owner. Many ancient temples decorated with trophies, some apparently dating from the regal period, and houses belonging to generals of the republican period and still preserving their *spolia*, were destroyed in the great fire of Rome in AD 64. The ship's beaks (rams) taken by Pompey during his campaign against the Cilician pirates (67 BC) and affixed to his town house in Rome were still visible in the third century AD.[10]

Siccius Dentatus' collection of military decorations was exceptional and many of them probably belong to a period long after that in which he lived. The torques and *armillae*, for example, may have been adopted by the Romans from the Celts in the fourth century BC (*see below* for the example of Manlius Torquatus, that is decorations developing from spoils), but one cannot discount that such decorations had older Italic precursors. Jewellery like torques (or similar) and bracelets were hardly unique to the Celts. The statue of the Capestrano Warrior (c. 500 BC) depicts a wealthy Picente warrior, perhaps a king and probably a *devotus*, in his complete panoply of war: distinctive 'pot' helmet, pectoral armour to protect his chest, a plate covering his vulnerable abdomen, a short sword, javelins with throwing thongs and a shield. Most important to our discussion are the armlets and broad neckband he wears. These might just be items of jewellery that emphasised his wealth and rank but it is also likely that they were symbols of valour (although the neckband might actually have been a gorget to protect his throat in combat – remember how in Livy's version of the fight of the Horatii and Curiatii, Publius dispatches the last Alban brother with a thrust to the throat).[11]

Dentatus' many and varied crowns are suspicious. In the mid-second century BC Polybius knew that the gold crown was awarded for various acts of valour, including being the first man to scale an enemy wall. It seems that the specific *corona muralis*, with decorative battlements had yet to develop. Velleius Paterculus, soldier and historian of the early first century AD, asserts that Scipio

Aemilianus won a *corona muralis* in Spain in 151 BC, but he may have been projecting an award of his own age onto Aemilianus. Polybius knew that a civic crown was presented by the soldier whose life had been saved, so it is probable that it was not a gold crown but woven from oak twigs. The *corona obsidionalis* is not mentioned by Polybius. It was presented by ordinary soldiers to the general who had rescued them from a siege or encirclement on the battlefield. It was woven from locally growing grasses and wild flowers and its simplicity could suggest considerable antiquity. Scipio Aemilianus is said to have won this crown at Carthage (146 BC).[12]

Even though most of Dentatus' decorations are anachronistic, as are the *dona militaria* (military decorations) and feats of other early Republican heroes like Manlius Capitolinus, they served as an example to the soldiers of the later Republic and early Empire. In 171 BC the veteran centurion Spurius Ligustinus enumerated his campaigns and decorations to the Senate. As well as promotion from the ranks to centurion, he stated 'thirty-four times I was decorated for courage by my generals and six times awarded the civic crown'. The five gold crowns (indicating five separate acts of valour) won by Statius Marrax, a centurion who fought in Augustus' wars of conquest, were remarkable in an age when the traditional system of awards was being undermined. For example, in 27 BC the Senate voted Augustus a civic crown for 'saving the Republic' and generals and governors became unsure if it was still in their power to grant such awards to ordinary soldiers. (According to Polybius, Republican officers were not actually empowered to grant the award but were supposed to compel the man who had been saved to present a crown. For the Imperial period, *see* the Helvius Rufus incident, *below*.) The epic poets Ennius and Virgil exhorted the Romans to equal or surpass the deeds of their ancestors in battle; Ligustinus and Marrax were clearly men to rival the legendary Dentatus.[13] But the awarding and wearing of such decorations led to high expectations of centurions and other recipients: they could never show fear or back down from a fight, even if it meant certain death. Thus, during the

Munda campaign (45 BC), two centurions stepped forward to stem the collapse of one of Caesar's units:

> When it was observed that our men were giving more ground than was usual, two centurions from the Fifth Legion crossed the river and restored the battle line. They displayed exceptional courage as they drove superior numbers of the enemy back, but one of them succumbed to a heavy volley of missiles discharged from higher ground. His fellow centurion now began an unequal battle, and when he found himself completely surrounded he retreated but lost his footing. As the brave centurion fell many of the enemy rushed forward to strip him of his decorations. (Anonymous, *Spanish War*, 23)

Josephus demonstrates how the passage of more than a century had not diminished the strong character of the centurion. When the troops attempting to capture the Temple at Jerusalem (AD 70) were finally repulsed after a long night of fighting, a Bithynian centurion named Julianus, whom Josephus knew personally, stepped down from his position of safety on the Antonia fortress and ran to hold back the triumphant Jews:

> Single-handedly he drove the victorious Jews back to the corner of the inner temple. The multitude fled in droves before him, regarding such strength and courage as superhuman . . . He ran amok scattering their ranks and killing all in his way, and no spectacle was more splendid to the eyes of Caesar [Titus], or more terrifying to the enemy. But . . . like any other soldier he wore boots thickly studded with hobnails, and while running across the paving stones he slipped and fell on his back with a loud crash of armour, which made the fugitives turn. A cry of concern for the hero went up from the Romans in Antonia, while the Jews crowded round him and attacked him with spears and swords. He blocked many blows with his shield and each time he tried

to rise up the overwhelming number of opponents pushed him back down. Though prostrate, he managed to stab many with his *gladius*, and having his vitals protected by helmet and body armour and by drawing in his neck, he was not easily killed. Eventually, however, when his arms and legs were hacked to pieces and no comrade came to help him, he died. Caesar was greatly moved by the death of such a heroic soldier, butchered before the eyes of so many, and though personally anxious to aid him, he was prohibited by his responsibility, and those who might have done so were held back by terror. (Josephus, *Jewish War*, 6.82–89)

Note how no one came forward to aid Julianus or the centurions at Munda; fear and the dejection resulting from defeat would often immobilise Roman soldiers. Once a centurion embarked on a struggle such as this he was generally on his own. Julianus need not have descended from Antonia to attack the Jews; unlike the centurions at Gergovia (*see* Chapter IV), he was not trapped on the battlefield and compelled to look to the safety of the troops under his command (though troops from his unit may have been involved in the fight). Julianus may well have expected his stand to encourage a Roman counter-attack like that of Baculus at Aduatuca (*see* Chapter IV), but it did not and he was unable to extricate himself. In battle a centurion could only retreat with honour intact if the general sounded the recall or if the enemy fell back before him. The stress of being the focus of heroic leadership must have weighed heavily on these men. A centurion could not show fear and in every battle he was expected to be the first man to charge and the last to break off fighting, or to die covering the retreat of his men.

When a centurion did show fear in battle – and almost every centurion was marked out by decorations because proven valour was one of the requirements for promotion to the rank – he was subject to the most terrible of punishments. In 38 BC a *primus pilus* named Vibillius panicked and fled from a battlefield in Spain. He must have been a brave man to have reached such an exalted rank but clearly this was one battle too many. The governor of the province decided to make an example of him and had the centurion beaten to death by his comrades (*fustuarium*), because his flight from the battlefield had put their lives in danger.[14]

Dentatus' forty-five scars highlight another genuine Roman preoccupation. Scars were a symbol of valour and much flaunted and often used to elicit sympathy or support. Catiline's centurions and *evocati* (veterans who had completed the standard term of service but were asked to re-enlist on account of their quality) died to a man at Pistoria, all with their wounds to the front, something that clearly impressed their opponents (62 BC). The scars of a veteran centurion added authority to his plea that Mark Antony reconsider fighting a sea battle at Actium (31 BC): '*Imperator*, why do you despair of these scars of mine and my sword and put your hopes in miserable planks of wood? Give us land, for that is where we are accustomed to stand, that is where we conquer our enemies or die!' Antony found himself unable to reply. He proceeded to fight at sea and lost. When campaigning for the consulship in 108 BC, Gaius Marius declared that his military decorations (some of which must have been won for a successful single combat at Numantia in 134/3 BC) and scars gave him the right to stand for consul even though he was a self-made man and had no noble ancestors:

> I cannot, to justify your confidence, display family portraits [the wax effigies of accomplished ancestors displayed by nobles] or the triumphs and consulships of my forefathers; but if occasion requires, I can show spears, a banner, horse trappings and other military prizes, as well as scars on my chest. These are my portraits, my patent of nobility, not left to me by inheritance as theirs [the nobles'] were, but won by my own innumerable efforts and perils. (Sallust, *War with Jugurtha*, 85.29–30)

Such an appeal was irresistible to the plebs who duly saw to it that Marius was elected consul for 107 BC, and he repaid their support by abolishing the property requirement for service in the legions, thus allowing the poorest citizens to serve and share in the opportunity for booty and social advancement through military promotion.

Scars might even be displayed to sway the decision of a jury. When Manius Aqulius was standing trial (c. 95 BC) for extortion after his term as governor of Sicily, his defence counsel, Marcus Antonius (grandfather of Mark Antony), suddenly ripped open Aquilius' clothing 'so that his countrymen might see the scars he bore on the *front* of his body'. Antonius also spoke at length about how Aquilius had acquired a serious head wound in single combat with Athenion, leader of a Sicilian slave rebellion (*see below*). This tactic revealed Aquilius to be a hero of Rome and even if he was guilty of extortion – numerous witnesses had proved that beyond doubt – how could such a brave man be condemned? Aquilius was duly acquitted.

The distinction and symbolism of battle scars is fully emphasised by the feelings of Quintus Sertorius. His face was terribly scarred from combat and one of his eye sockets was empty, but he was proud of the permanent 'decoration' for his courage; other brave men had to leave their torques, spears and crowns at home, but his *dona* were always on proud display.[15]

Lack of battle scars was a cause of scorn and could also be exploited in court. When prosecuting the rapacious Verres, also on trial for extortion during a governorship of Sicily (73–71 BC), Cicero amused the court by bidding Verres to bare his torso and display his 'battle' scars, 'Scars made by women's teeth!' When in 167 BC old Servilius Geminus Pulex spoke against the motion to deny Aemilius Paullus a triumph for his defeat of Perseus, king of Macedon, he challenged Servius Sulpicius Galba, a young military tribune and the instigator of the motion, to strip and show his scars. 'I have on twenty-three occasions challenged and fought an enemy,' roared Servilius. 'I brought back the spoils from every man with whom I engaged in combat and I have a body decorated with honourable scars, all of them received in the front!' Servilius then bared his torso. As he pointed to various scars and recounted how he had received them, his toga slipped down a little too far. He was not perturbed:

> While he was displaying his scars he accidentally uncovered what should have been kept concealed, and the swelling in his groin raised a laugh among the nearest spectators but Servilius retorted: 'Yes, you laugh at this. I got this as well by sitting on my horse for days and nights on end, and I have no more shame or regret about this than about these wounds, since it never hindered me from successful service to the state either at home or abroad. I am a veteran soldier, and I have displayed before these young troops [the soldiers supporting Galba] this body of mine which has often been assailed by the sword. Now let Galba lay bare his smooth and unblemished body.' (Livy, 45.39.18–19)

Servilius' display swayed the assembly and Aemilius Paullus was voted his well-deserved triumph. Servilius' single combats were later celebrated on the coins issued by his descendants and show duels on both foot and on horseback.[16]

When acting as a defence counsel, Cicero exploited the tactics of Servilius and Antonius, remarking that juries found it impossible to find against men who bore scars of honour on their faces. The wounds sustained by a veteran of the battle of Munda (45 BC) persuaded Julius Caesar to find in favour of him in a land dispute. The veteran put Caesar in a difficult position. Before the battle he had offered the thirsty general a drink, using his helmet as a cup. Caesar remembered the incident but did not believe the veteran was the same man. The veteran replied, 'I do not blame you for not recognising me, Caesar. When I offered you water I was unwounded but afterwards, at the battle of Munda, my eye was struck out, and the bones of my face crushed. Nor would you recognise that helmet if you saw it, for it was split by a Spanish sword.' Caesar then recognised the man and judged in his favour, granting him the disputed fields and protecting him from further prosecutions. Scars clearly had some advantages in the Roman world.[17]

CORNELIUS COSSUS AND THE SPOLIA OPIMA

It is unfortunate that no details – real or imagined – of the eight or nine single combats attributed to Siccius Dentatus are preserved in the sources. However, in the generation following Dentatus' murder, an Etruscan king and a Roman officer met in a fight of great significance before the walls of Fidenae. Although not actually a single combat, the fight between Lars Tolumnius and Aulus Cornelius Cossus was a genuine historical incident that resulted in the second dedication of the *spolia opima* (spoils of honour) in the temple of Jupiter Feretrius. The story of this deed was kept alive by the proud and noble Cornelii clan, first in song and later in writing, in both cases probably embellished, and the spoils survived for centuries.

In 437 BC (the traditional date) Rome and the Etruscan city of Veii were again at war. Veii was located only ten miles north of Rome and their territories bordered on the north bank of the River Tiber. The bone of contention between the cities was Fidenae, an important bridgehead on the Latin bank of the Tiber and only a few miles upstream from Rome. The town had fallen to Rome in 498 BC but had recently revolted with the support of Veii. The Romans sent four ambassadors to the town but they were killed on the orders of Tolumnius, who then proceeded to advance his forces into Roman territory and fought a hard but inconclusive battle against the legions near the River Anio. A second battle was fought before the walls of Fidenae, the Etruscans and Fidenates reinforced by allies from Falerii. This time the Romans forced back the enemy infantry with relative ease, but Tolumnius was winning the cavalry battle.

Livy relates that Cornelius Cossus, a military tribune, watched how Tolumnius scattered the Roman cavalry formations with every charge he led. Cossus intended to offer Tolumnius in sacrifice to the spirits of the murdered Roman envoys and waited for his opportunity. Cossus spurred his horse forward as Tolumnius came close by at the head of his troop. He unsaddled Tolumnius with his lance, then leapt from the saddle and battered the king with the boss of his shield as he struggled to rise and meet his attacker. Cossus speared the king through the torso and pinned him to the ground. He then tore out the lance and stabbed the king repeatedly until he was dead. Cossus quickly stripped the king of his armour, then hacked off his head and fixed it to the point of his lance and remounted his horse. The Etruscan cavalry panicked at the sight of this bloody warrior charging towards them with the severed head of their king. They fled back to Fidenae and left the Romans in possession of the battlefield. Fidenae was put under siege but did not fall until 435 BC.

Cossus' assault on Tolumnius was clearly not a single combat. No challenge was issued and Cossus appears to have taken the king of Veii unawares, perhaps even charging him side-on, but the brutality of Cossus' assault and the frenzied manner in which he killed Tolumnius must have been typical of single combats of the age. Cossus' use of the shield was certainly typical of later Roman infantry combat.

Dionysius of Halicarnassus' account survives in excerpts and differs from that of Livy, rendering the fight into a regular one-on-one combat. Dionysius' sources or imagination had him make Tolumnius and Cossus charge at each other with levelled lances. Cossus' lance struck the chest of the Etruscan's horse. As it reared up and Tolumnius struggled to control it, Cossus again struck with the lance, ramming it through the king's shield, his linen corselet and into his side. This blow hammered Tolumnius from the saddle. With the lance trapped in the shield, Cossus appears to have dismounted, drawn his sword and stabbed Tolumnius in the groin as he struggled to rise.

Livy's account of an opportune attack has the ring of realism and was conceivably based on a source which itself drew on the original oral tradition. Dionysius' reconstruction was perhaps influenced by an annalist, a member of the Cornelii or someone employed by them, who had elevated the fight into something approaching a formal duel.

Aemilius Mamercus, the Roman commander at Fidenae, was awarded a triumph for the victory, but during the procession all eyes fell on Cossus and his spoils and the soldiers sang verses comparing him to Romulus, the first taker of the spoils of honour. After the triumph Cossus went to the temple of Jupiter Feretrius and dedicated the spoils, setting them beside those believed to have been stripped from Acron by Romulus. The spoils probably included Tolumnius' head – we have seen how later Roman trophies and triumphal monuments were adorned with the heads of the defeated – and Cossus inscribed his deed on the king's mangled linen cuirass.

Some 400 years later, the cuirass was retrieved from the temple by the Emperor Augustus and its faded inscription interpreted to frustrate the attempt of another Roman general to dedicate the *spolia opima* (*see below*).[18]

MANLIUS TORQUATUS

When we move to the fourth century BC we are presented with a series of famous single combats fought by Romans that are grounded in historical fact but which acquired anachronistic and apocryphal elements.

Not long after Rome finally conquered Veii in 396 BC, Roman expansion came to a sudden halt when an army of Gallic Senones led by Brennus marched out of the territory they had conquered in northern Italy, crossed the Apennines and routed the Roman army a little north of Fidenae at the River Allia (390 BC). The Gauls proceeded to sack Rome. It took Rome over thirty years to recover from this disaster and much of the fourth century BC was dominated by warfare against Gallic war bands. In 361 BC a powerful Gallic war band (perhaps operating out of a base in Apulia in southern Italy and possibly in the pay of Dionysius, tyrant of Syracuse) again threatened the city and made camp by the River Anio.

It is worth quoting here the account of the historian Claudius Quadrigarius who wrote his *Annals* around 80 BC and was a principal source of Livy:

In the meantime a Gaul came forward, who was naked except for a shield and two swords and the ornament of a torque and two bracelets [*armillae*]. In strength and size, in youthful vigour and in courage as well, he excelled all the rest. At the very height of the battle, when the two armies with fighting were the utmost ardour, he began to make signs with his hands to both sides to cease fighting. The combat ceased. As soon as silence was secured, he called out in a mighty voice that if anyone wished to engage him in single combat, he should come forward. This no one dared do, because of his size and savage appearance. Then the Gaul began to laugh at them and to stick out his tongue. This immediately roused the great indignation of one Titus Manlius, a youth of the highest birth, that such an insult should be offered to his country, and that no one from so great an army should accept the challenge. He stepped forward, and would not suffer Roman valour [*virtus*] to be shamefully tarnished by a Gaul. Armed with a legionary's shield and a Spanish sword, he confronted the Gaul. Their fight took place on the very bridge [over the Anio], in the presence of both armies, amid great apprehension. Thus they confronted each other: the Gaul, according to his method of fighting, with shield advanced and awaiting an attack; Manlius, relying on courage rather than skill, struck shield against shield and threw the Gaul off balance. While the Gaul was trying to regain the same position, Manlius again struck shield against shield and again forced the man to change his ground. In this fashion he slipped under the Gaul's sword and stabbed him in the chest with his Spanish blade. Then at once with the same mode of attack he struck his adversary's right shoulder, and he did not give ground at all until he overthrew him, without giving the

Gaul a chance to strike a blow. After he had slain him, Manlius
cut off the Gaul's head, tore off his torque and put it, covered
as it was with blood, around his own neck. Because of this act,
he himself and his descendants had the surname [*cognomen*]
Torquatus. (Quadrigarius, fragment 10b (Peter), quoted by Aulus
Gellius, *Attic Nights*, 9.13. 6–19)

Livy adds that Manlius was quite small for a soldier and he
sought the permission of the consul before accepting the challenge.
In Livy's account the Gaul is also richly clothed and armoured but
Manlius ignores these spoils to concentrate on the torque. The
common soldiers then name him Torquatus.

Manlius' victory over the giant shocked the Gauls. They had no
heart for the subsequent battle and quickly retreated. However, they
did not leave Latium. Instead the Gauls pillaged the Alban territory
and were soon employed as mercenaries by the Latin cities of Tibur,
Praeneste and Velitrae, but were defeated before Rome's Colline Gate
in 360 BC. The Latin cities were all forced back into alliance with
Rome by 354 BC.[19]

An anachronistic element in the tale is the Spanish sword, the
famous *gladius Hispaniensis*. The Romans did not adopt this sword
for another century and a half, but they were certainly using cut-
and-thrust weapons in Manlius' day and had developed a fighting
style to counter the terrifying long slashing swords of the Gauls.[20]
Dionysius of Halicarnassus placed the introduction of the new
fighting style in 367 BC. The Gauls mostly used their swords to slash
and cut and blows could be delivered with such force as to cut
through shield and armour, but the Romans took advantage of their
tendency to raise the sword arm high before delivering a blow:

While their enemies were still raising their swords aloft, they
would duck under the Gauls' arms, and holding up their
shields while stooping and crouching down low, would render
impotent the blows of the enemy which were aimed too high.
The Romans, on the other hand, held their swords straight out

and would strike their opponents in the groin, pierce their sides and drive their thrusts through their chests into their vitals. If the Romans saw any of them keeping these parts of their bodies protected, they would cut the tendons of the knees or ankles and topple them to the ground. (Dionysius of Halicarnassus, *Roman Antiquities*, 14.10.2)

Polybius notes that the Romans were using their swords in a similar manner in 225 and 223 BC, not long before the introduction of the *gladius Hispaniensis*. He also relates how the Romans employed tactics to force Gallic warriors to bunch up so that they would not be able to wield their long swords effectively. In such circumstances the legionaries did not have to duck but simply thrust their swords at the faces and chests of their opponents.[21]

It would be surprising if the Roman fighting style did not change in response to the Gallic threat, but one wonders if Dionysius' account of the Roman fighting style in 367 BC was influenced by Rutilius Rufus' legionary training reforms of 105 BC following the disaster at Arausio. According to Valerius Maximus, 'he called in gladiator instructors from the school of Gaius Aurelius Scaurus to instill in the legions a more sophisticated method of avoiding and giving a blow.' It seems that training methods had declined since the middle of the century because Polybius, who was in Roman captivity between 168 and 150 BC, describes legionaries defending themselves not only with their shields but also 'continually moving so as to meet a threatened blow'. Vegetius' statement that the Romans used only the point of the sword is easily refuted. Polybius emphasises that the Romans viewed the sword as a cut and thrust weapon, and Roman cavalry used the *gladius Hispaniensis* to devastating effect in the First Macedonian War (200–196 BC), lopping off heads and limbs with ease.[22]

Hundreds of years later legionaries and auxiliaries were still using shields to barge opponents in the manner of Manlius and thrusting at exposed vitals while an enemy raised up his sword to deliver a cutting blow. 'Continue the chaos and slaughter with shield boss and sword until victory is gained, then think of plunder,' ordered Suetonius Paulinus before his vastly outnumbered force charged Boudicca's horde (AD 61). At the battle of Mons Graupius (AD 84) Batavian and Tungrian auxiliaries treated their Caledonian opponents with contempt. The Caledonians' swords were suited only to slashing and useless in the crush of close-quarter fighting says Tacitus, so the Roman auxiliaries relentlessly punched out with shield bosses and stabbed at their faces. In AD 69 legionary fought legionary at the first battle of Cremona, each trying to batter the other down, shield against shield. Later that year legionaries defending Vetera used their shield bosses as the principal means of battering rebel Batavian auxiliaries off the walls. According to legend, Manlius Capitolinus, a relative of Torquatus, won his *cognomen* by defending the Capitol from the Gauls in 390 BC, cutting the hand from one warrior wielding a battle-axe, and using his shield boss to punch another in the face and shove him over the cliff edge. Valerius Maximus lamented that the deed of Acilius, a soldier of Julius Caesar's Tenth Legion, in capturing a Massilian warship in 49 BC was not widely known. Acilius' right hand was cut off as he clambered aboard the enemy ship but he still battered the crew into submission with his shield boss.[23]

VALERIUS CORVUS

In 349 BC yet another Gallic army marched towards Rome, acting in co-ordination with a fleet of Greek raiders from Syracuse. The recalcitrant Latin cities still hoped to rid themselves of Rome's domination and refused to send their levies of soldiers.

> At that time vast forces of Gauls had encamped in the Pomptine district [marshland south east of Rome], and the Roman army was being drawn up in battle order by the consuls, who were most concerned by the strength and number of the enemy. Meanwhile, the chief of the Gauls, a man of

enormous size and stature, his armour gleaming with gold, advanced with long strides and flourishing his spear, at the same time casting haughty and contemptuous glances in all directions. Filled with scorn for all he saw, he challenged anyone from the entire Roman army to come out and meet him, if he dared. Thereupon, while they were all wavering between fear and shame, the tribune Valerius, first obtaining the consuls' permission, advanced to meet him, boldly yet modestly. They met, they halted, they were already engaging in combat, when a divine power became apparent. A raven [*corvus*], unnoticed beforehand, suddenly flew to the spot, perched on the tribune's helmet and from there began to attack the face and eyes of the Gaul. It flew at the Gaul, harassed him, tore at his head with its claws, obstructed his sight with its wings, and after venting its rage flew back to the tribune's helmet. Thus the tribune, before the eyes of both armies, relying on his own *virtus* and defend by the help of the raven, conquered and killed the arrogant leader of the enemy, and thus won the *cognomen* Corvinus. (Quadrigarius, fragment 12 (Peter), quoted by Aulus Gellius, *Attic Nights*, 9.11.4–9)

Livy and Dionysius add some interesting details, perhaps authentic. The Gallic chief made his challenge through an interpreter. The duel was fought with swords and, notably, the Gaul used his sword in Roman fashion, attempting to dispatch Valerius with a thrust to the side of the torso. After Valerius had killed the Gaul a fight erupted over possession of the corpse, which in turn developed into a full-scale battle won by the Romans. On learning of the Gallic defeat the Greek fleet broke off from ravaging the coast of Latium and sailed for home. Valerius was rewarded with a gold crown and named Corvus in recognition of his feat (Corvinus was a later development). Unlike Quadrigarius, Livy and Zonaras do not identify the Gaul as the commander of the Gallic army; Dionysius identifies him as 'one of the chieftains'. If he was the leader of the Gauls, one would expect Valerius to have claimed the right to dedicate the *spolia opima*, but the customs relating to *spolia opima* may have changed since Cornelius Cossus' day to favour only those of supreme rank.[24]

What are we to make of the intervention of the *corvus*? The pious Romans viewed it as divinely inspired, perhaps even a god in disguise. The raven is depicted on some coins of the Roman Republic as the attendant of the pre-eminent Italic goddess Juno in her guise as Juno Sospita, 'the Saviour', a rather apt deity to intervene on behalf of a Roman in a desperate single combat.[25]

It is not surprising that a carrion bird would be seen on an ancient battlefield but that one landed on Valerius' helmet sounds like fantasy.[26] It has been suggested that the Gallic champion's helmet was adorned with bird wings and that the name Corvus and the legend developed from the taking of the helmet as part of the spoils, that is in the same manner as Torquatus won his *cognomen*. At this time the Italians were adopting a new form of helmet, the so-called Montefortino type, based on Gallic models, the chiefly examples of which were richly decorated and would be prime items of plunder. Gauls certainly wore helmets adorned with real or metallic wings; some of elaborate construction would 'flap' when the wearer moved. The Gunderstrup Cauldron depicts Celtic warriors with crests in the form of a perched bird. (Some southern Italian helmets of this period, especially local variants of Chalcidian and Phrygian types, also featured small wings, made of embossed bronze and positioned just above the ears, and one wonders if such an Italian helmet contributed to the legend.) Perhaps the wings adorning the helmet of Valerius' opponent were cut or somehow came loose during the fight and so obscured his vision. We have seen how the tall feathers worn by Romans on their helmets signalled their devotion to, and intimate connection with, the war god Mars. It may be that the historian Valerius Antias, writing in the early first century BC, cleverly distorted this religious element of helmet crests and plumes to recast the duel to include this divine intervention and so make it surpass the famous deed of Torquatus of the rival Manlii clan. The Manlii never forgot Torquatus' deed and when members of the family attained the magistracy that included control of the mint, they often issued coins featuring a torque.[27]

Cognomina like those of Torquatus and Corvus were frequently adopted by or bestowed on noble Romans. Another *cognomen* deriving from a single combat with a Gaul was the name Drusus. In 302 BC the consul Marcus Livius Denter (later a hero of Sentinum) may have slain a Gallic chieftain called Drausus in a single or one-on-one combat and consequently adopted and Latinised the name in commemoration of the feat. Generals would also adopt suitable *cognomina* derived from the scene of a successful campaign or the name of the defeated tribe or nation, thus the Scipio who conquered Hannibal was named Africanus and the Metellus who defeated Jugurtha was called Numidicus. When Quintus Fabius Maximus defeated the Allobroges in 121 BC he took the name Allobrogicus.

The use of honorific *cognomina* was not limited to Romans of high rank. A deranged legionary veteran settled at Perusia called himself Macedonicus after serving in Macedonia. When the city was about to be sacked by Octavian's forces he set fire to his house and leapt into the flames. The conflagration spread and soon engulfed the whole city (40 BC). A veteran of *legio V Alaudae* took the royal Parthian name Arsaces having survived Mark Antony's harrowing Parthian expedition of 36 BC; this was either an ironic example of humour or commemorated his having defeated a noble warrior called Arsaces (*see* Chapter IV). Legionaries who served as marines on Octavian's warships at the battle of Actium (31 BC) took the name Actiacus to advertise their role in the victory.

The story of how Marcus Helvius Rufus acquired the *cognomen* Civica is in keeping with the heroics of Torquatus and Corvus. In AD 20 the army of the African rebel Tacfarinas assaulted the town of Thala:

> When the forces of Tacfarinas assaulted a stronghold named
> Thala, they were routed by a detachment of legionary

veterans [the *vexillum veteranorum* of *legio III Augusta*], not more than 500 in number. During the battle a common soldier, Helvius Rufus, earned the distinction of saving a fellow citizen and was presented by the governor Apronius with a torque and spear. The civic crown [*corona civica*] was added by the Emperor Tiberius, who regretted, more in sorrow than anger, that Apronius had not exercised his power to award this further honour. (Tacitus, *Annals*, 3.21)

An inscription from Rufus' hometown of Varia in Italy reveals that he adopted the name Civica and had attained the rank of *primus pilus* – one suspects he was promoted to centurion when he received his *dona militaria*.

Civica's contemporary Pontius Pilatus, better known as Pilate of the New Testament, also had a most notable *cognomen*. Pontius was perhaps a former legionary who had progressed through the grades of centurion, attained equestrian rank and eventually became a provincial governor. *Pilatus* is Latin for a soldier armed with a *pilum* and it could be that Pontius won the name for a notable feat with the *pilum* in battle. There is another possibility. Pilatus might be derived from *expilator* meaning someone who plunders, a pillager.[28]

Many *cognomina* were derived from physical and personal attributes. For example Cossus meant 'wormish' (referring to a long neck or spindly limbs?), the semi-legendary Quinctius *Cincinnatus*, who forced the Aequi under the yoke in 458 BC, was named for his curly hair, Scipio *Barbatus* for his beard and Scipio *Nasica* for his big nose. (Scipio was itself a hereditary *cognomen* of a branch of the Cornelii clan, deriving from the name of a staff symbolic of high office.) Fabricius *Luscinus* was 'Fabricius the one-eyed' and Aemilius *Barbula* was 'Aemilius little beard'. It is sometimes suggested that Corvus was a *cognomen* of this type, perhaps indicating a harsh crowing voice, and that the duel with the Gaul was invented as a glorious explanation for the name, but that Valerius took the name from a winged helmet won in a duel seems more convincing.

Considering the number of battles the Romans fought with the Gauls in the fourth century, it would be most surprising if Manlius Torquatus was the only man to engage in single combat. In fact his example probably spurred others to engage in duels with Gauls. Single combat was a key feature of Gallic warfare, whether against other Gauls or foreign peoples:

> It is their custom when formed up for battle, to step out in front of the line and challenge the most valiant men from among their opponents to single combat, brandishing their weapons in front of them to terrify their adversaries. And when any man accepts the challenge to battle, they break forth into a song of praise of the valiant deeds of their ancestors and in boast of their own high achievements, reviling all the while their opponent, and trying, in a word, by such talk to strip him of his bold spirit before the combat. (Diodorus Siculus, 5.29.2–3)

As it was usual for battles to be prefaced by challenges to single combat, instead of doubting the authenticity of the Corvus story, perhaps we should wonder why we hear only of two such fights between Gauls and Romans in the fourth century BC.[29]

One account of Valerius Corvus' single combat maybe suggests another tradition in which the raven had a lesser role:

> The Gaul, enraged and exhausted by loss of blood, pursued Valerius, eager to grapple and fall with him. But, as Valerius kept continuously retiring, the Gaul at last fell headlong. (Appian, *Gallic History*, fragment 10)

Perhaps the complete account was in agreement with the usual tradition, making the Gaul eager to grapple with Valerius like a wrestler because, having been attacked by the raven, he could neither see nor fight with a sword. Valerius thus easily avoided the clumsy lunges of the warrior. However, the raven may have played a less active and more symbolic role in this version, where its simple appearance was taken as a good omen. (Note how the cawing of a raven or crow was interpreted as a sign of divine favour at the battle of Aquilonia in 293 BC, but there was no obvious manifestation of divine intervention.) Valerius then proceeded to wound the Gallic champion, perhaps only with a lucky blow and, rather like Publius Horatius' tactic against the Curiatii, he deliberately exhausted the dangerous warrior before moving in to deliver the killing blow.[30]

Despite being aged only twenty-three, Valerius Corvus' victory was instrumental in securing him a consulship in the following year; Manlius Torquatus did not hold his first consulship until 347 BC, more than a decade after his famous duel.[31]

THE YOUNGER TORQUATUS

We have seen how some *cognomina* became hereditary, passing from father to son and down the family line. Manlius Torquatus gave his *cognomen* to his son, and the younger Torquatus shared his father's passion for single combat. As we have seen, in 340 BC the cities of the Latin League revolted and put their not inconsiderable manpower into the field in Campania, alongside their Sidicini and Campanian allies. The Latins demanded full Roman citizenship and an equal share in government. Their complaint was exactly the same as that of the Italian Allies who revolted in 91 BC: they had supplied much of the manpower that won the Roman Empire but had little share in the profits; they felt like an exploited underclass. The Romans would not countenance such terms and joined forces with the Samnites who had designs on rich Campania.

Before the battle of the Veseris Manlius Torquatus (now in his third consulship) and the *devotus* Decius Mus gave a general order that no soldier should compromise the defence of the camp or integrity of the battle line by leaving his station to attack the enemy, that is no soldier was to engage in dangerous feats of bravado or single combats. However, while out on patrol, the younger Manlius Torquatus led his cavalry *turma* to within a spear cast of a Latin outpost, which just happened to be manned by a troop of cavalry from Tusculum under command of Geminus Maecius, a Latin warrior of great renown. According to Livy Maecius rode out towards the Romans, insulted Torquatus and the Roman army in general and made the inevitable challenge to single combat:

> They caused the rest of the horsemen to stand back, as if it was a spectacle, and spurred their steeds against one another across the vacant space between. With lances levelled they charged, but the lance of Manlius glanced off the helmet of his enemy, and that of Maecius passed over the neck of the other's horse. Then, as they pulled their horses around, Manlius, who was the first to gather himself up for a second thrust, pricked his enemy's charger between the ears. The pain of this wound made the horse rear and toss his head so violently that he threw off his rider. Maecius, raising himself with lance and shield, was struggling to his feet after the heavy fall, when Manlius plunged his lance into Maecius' throat, so that it came out through his ribs and pinned him to the ground. He then gathered up the spoils and rode back to his troopers, who attended him with shouts of triumph to the camp. (Livy, 8.7.9–12)

Being a good, honest Roman, the younger Torquatus progressed to his father's *praetorium* (headquarters tent), half expecting punishment but also anticipating praise for his victory. The consul was not amused; he was furious that his son had explicitly broken an order. He called on a *lictor* (a magistrate's attendant, equipped with rods and an axe to administer corporal and capital punishments) to bind his son to a stake in front of the *praetorium*. The Roman army looked on in disbelief as Manlius Torquatus oversaw the beheading of his son. Chaos followed, with the soldiers hurling abuse at the consul but, luckily for him, their main concern was not a lynching but to gather up young Manlius' remains and his spoils to give him a funeral with military honours outside the camp. The soldiers returned to the camp subdued and ready to obey orders. Extreme instances of Roman military discipline were thereafter referred to as 'Manlian'.

Did Torquatus really execute his own son? The sources make it clear that Manlius and his fellow consul had threatened the ultimate punishment to any soldier who engaged in single combat. Polybius, a witness of the Roman army of the mid-second century BC, noted the summary justice administered by the Romans to those who disobeyed orders, and believed that Torquatus had indeed executed his son. How could the consul expect to maintain discipline if he excluded his son from punishment? We should also consider that the Roman army had mutinied in 342 BC and strenuous efforts were being made to keep it in line. Another element of the tale suggests its essential reliability: the young Manlius was quickly beheaded and spared the usual horrendous scourging (beating) with the *lictor*'s rods. What struck the ancients most about the punishment was the complete contrast it formed to the elder Torquatus' relationship with his own father: as a young man he risked everything in order to save his father from persecution.[32]

The severity of the punishment indicates that unsanctioned skirmishes and duels were becoming a problem. This was nothing new. During the siege of Veii (396 BC) legionaries became fond of indulging in wasteful and unauthorised fights in the no-man's land between the city walls and the siege lines (compare the regular duels fought beneath the walls of Capua, *below*). Once again an edict had to be issued banning unauthorised fighting and the legionaries' energy was redirected into the construction of new siege works. In the aftermath of the elder Torquatus' victory over the Gauls, it was found necessary to threaten soldiers with severe punishments should they be tempted to prove their valour and attack or challenge the enemy without orders (359–358 BC). The continuing tendency of Roman soldiers to leap spontaneously into action is exemplified by the actions of Pullo and Vorenus in 54 BC (*see* Chapter IV).

Titus was presented with same problem when he besieged Jerusalem in AD 70. Individual Roman cavalrymen were charging into bands of Jews and trying to outdo one another by killing as many enemies as possible (compare Pullo and Vorenus), or by dragging back captives to a bemused Titus. The new prince (Titus' father Vespasian had recently seized the imperial throne) rewarded these acts of valour but ordered the soldiers henceforth to restrain themselves from indulging in dangerous and unsanctioned acts of bravado. Of course, in the face of temptation, the command was ignored. A Roman cavalryman (but fighting on foot) named Priscus accepted the challenge of the Jew Jonathon to meet him in single combat. Jonathon killed Priscus when the Roman slipped and thus exposed himself to a mortal blow. The Jewish warrior danced over the corpse (something that Romans were also wont to do) but this behaviour only encouraged a Roman centurion to grab a bow and shoot him down.[33]

It is notable in the accounts of single combats by the elder Torquatus and Valerius Corvus that the enemy always made the challenge. In the duels of the legendary Siccius Dentatus the enemy always issued the challenge. The Roman warrior is also portrayed as being at a disadvantage. He is usually young and inexperienced and smaller than his opponent, who is invariably a giant or veteran fighter with a ready tongue for insults. Livy's account of the battle of the Veseris also includes a (purely symbolic?) one-on-one fight between a young Roman centurion and a mighty veteran *primus pilus* of the Latin cohorts.[34] The Roman wins, naturally.

In contrast to the fury of the enemy, the Roman duellist maintains the traditional discipline by requesting the permission of his commander to fight. The Roman is always made the underdog and the physical and moral aspects of his victory are consequently magnified. It is interesting that this essentially 'David and Goliath' scenario is reversed in the single combat of Priscus and Jonathon at Jerusalem, the Roman being the experienced and formidable Goliath figure but perishing as a result of an unfortunate slip as he charges towards his apparent victim.

One suspects that the actions of the younger Torquatus represent a closer reality than the somewhat idealised and moralising versions of the single combats of the elder Torquatus and Corvus. The young

Torquatus clearly rode out in search of Maecius and one wonders if he actually issued the challenge (the usual term is *provocatio*, *provocare* – to call out, challenge). Aggressive conduct in such a style was exhibited by three Roman envoys sent to Etruscan Clusium in 390 BC. They were merely supposed to discuss the approaching Gallic menace but, unhindered by a strict commander, they threw in their lot with the Etruscans to fight against Brennus' Senones. Like Cossus at Fidenae, Quintus Fabius spurred out from the Clusian battle line to fight an opportune one-on-one combat with a Gallic chief and despoiled him. When Fabius was recognised as a Roman, Brennus turned his attention to Rome and so began the countdown to the disaster at the Allia.

The taunting and arrogant behaviour of Maecius should also be instructive, for Rome was but another Latin city (compare the challenges of the Italic Mamertines and their Campanian brethren). As we have seen, the battle-scarred Servilius Pulex claimed to have challenged twenty-three enemies to single combat, though one wonders whether he included one-on-one combats in this total.[35] When serving as a legate in Spain in 142/1 BC, Quintus Occius Achilles accepted a challenge to single combat (perhaps more accurately described as a challenge to a private duel) without seeking the permission of his commander, though he held the high rank of legate (*see below*). Later Roman warriors, such as the centurions of Julius Caesar, had a tendency to issue challenges in situations where the commander or senior officers were absent or could not intervene (*see below*).

Success in single combats was clearly a way for ambitious young officers to attain fame and authority that could be carried over into the political sphere. Both Torqautus and Corvus progressed to multiple consulships; Corvus' first consulship was held the year after his single combat, and the path to Claudius Marcellus' first consulship was paved by numerous duels. We should again conclude that Romans were not always reticent when it came to issuing challenges to single combat. Asking permission seems a literary convention prominent in the minds of Roman historians when they reconstructed duels.

HISTORICAL DUELS
MARCELLUS AND THE SPOILS OF HONOUR

Just a few years before the wrath of Hannibal swept over the Alps, the Romans were engaged in their last great struggle with the Gauls on Italian soil. In 225 BC an immense Gallic army of 50,000 infantry and 20,000 cavalry and charioteers, marched into peninsular Italy. It was composed of the warriors of the great Gallic nations: the Boii, Taurisci, Lingones and Insubres of the Po valley, and even Gaesati from beyond the Alps. The Gallic army was not a huge raiding expedition like those of the fourth century BC. It was a pre-emptive strike by the Gauls against Rome's expansion towards the Po valley; the Gauls were fighting in defence of the lands they had conquered two centuries before.

The Gallic host crossed the Apennines, neatly avoided the army of a praetor sent to bar its way (and also completely avoided the consular army of Aemilius Papus which had rushed to the Adriatic coast in the expectation that the Gauls would strike first at Ariminum), and then plundered its way south through Etruria. When only three days' march from Rome, it was discovered that the praetor's army was on the trail of the Gauls, so the host turned north again; the decision was probably also influenced by Rome being defended by a garrison of over 50,000 men. In the vicinity of Faesulae, the Gauls successfully drew the praetor's army of Etruscan and Sabine levies into an ambush and killed 6,000 of them, but finding that Aemilius Papus had crossed the Apennines and was hot on their heels, the Gauls continued their northern march along the coast of Etruria. Papus' consular army was composed of two reinforced legions, each of 5,200 men, as well as 30,000 infantry and 2,000 cavalry from the Allies. Even when reinforced with the remnants of the praetor's army, he decided not to offer battle to the Gauls but harried their march.

The Gallic army was presented with a most unpleasant surprise as it approached the sanctuary of Telamon. The army of the other consul, Gaius Atilius Regulus, had been campaigning in Sardinia but sailed for Italy on hearing of the emergency. Atilius' vanguard was on the road from Pisa when Gallic foragers stumbled into it. The consul formed his army into line and barred the way. The Gauls also deployed, but into two lines, the warriors back to back, one line facing Atilius, the other facing the approaching army of Papus. Outnumbered almost two-to-one and caught between the vice of two Roman armies, the Gauls fought heroically but the outcome was inevitable. The great host was destroyed. Three-quarters of the foot warriors were killed and the rest taken prisoner; the surviving cavalry fled. The Romans also suffered substantial casualties, the consul Atilius among them.

The Romans then carried the war into the territory of the enemy. The Boii were conquered in 224 BC, and in the following year Flaminius won a great victory over the Cenomani. However, his tactics were questionable. He deliberately placed his army with a river at its back and cut the bridges, so that the legionaries and Allies would not be tempted to retreat. In 222 BC Roman attention turned to the Insubres. The new consuls, Gnaeus Cornelius Scipio and Marcus Claudius Marcellus, rejected peace proposals offered by the Insubres and assaulted their stronghold at Acerrae. In anticipation of this, Insubres had enlisted the services of 30,000 Gaesati mercenaries, and attacked the Roman supply base at Clastidium. The consuls had to divide their forces, Marcellus rushing to Clastidium with two-thirds of the cavalry (3,000–3,500?) and only 600 light infantry, while Scipio pressed on with the siege of Acerrae.

It was the aspiration of the generation of Claudius Marcellus to be like the heroes of old. In order to progress to the great magistracies and military commands, the first concern of Lucius Caecilius Metellus was to prove himself 'a warrior [*bellator*] of the first rank'. Marcellus had the same ambition. While still a junior officer he won numerous military decorations, one of which must have been the *corona civica* for he saved the life of his wounded half-brother in Sicily during the First Punic War, 'covering him with his shield and killing those who were setting upon him'. Plutarch states that Marcellus was an accomplished duellist and, while the number of his single combats is unknown, they were clearly numerous: 'he never refused a challenge and always killed his challengers.' As we have seen, Marcus Servilius Geminus Pulex, another contemporary of Marcellus, won twenty-three single combats. According to the elder Pliny, Marcellus fought in thirty-nine formal pitched battles as well as lesser actions, giving him ample opportunity to engage in single combats.[36]

Marcellus covered the distance to Clastidium in record time but his tired force appears to have been surprised by the Gauls just outside the town. The Gauls, Gaesati numbering 10,000, were commanded by their king, Viridomarus, a typically towering and muscular figure. Plutarch says that Viridomarus immediately led his superior force of cavalry against the Romans and Marcellus hastily gave the command for the column to extend into a long line so that his horsemen would not be surrounded and might even threaten the flank of the enemy. This tactic could have persuaded Viridomarus to break off his charge but Frontinus, a successful Roman general and contemporary of Plutarch, wrote in his *Stratagems* that Marcellus was actually contemplating retreat when Viridomarus recognised him and issued the challenge.[37] Plutarch takes up the tale:

> The king of the Gauls spotted Marcellus and, judging from his insignia that he was the commander of the Romans, rode far out in front of his army and confronted Marcellus, shouting challenges and brandishing his spear. His stature exceeded that of the other Gauls and he was conspicuous for his armour which was decorated with silver and gold: it flashed like lightning. Accordingly, as Marcellus surveyed the ranks of the enemy, this seemed to him to be the most beautiful armour, and he concluded it was this which he had vowed to

the god. Marcellus therefore charged at the king, and by a thrust of his lance which pierced his adversary's cuirass, and by the impact of his horse at the gallop, threw him, still living, upon the ground, where, with a second and a third blow, he promptly killed him. (Plutarch, *Marcellus*, 7.1–3)

In his poem about the dedicators of the *spolia opima*, the Augustan poet Propertius wrote that Viridomarus challenged Marcellus from a war chariot and declared he was a descendant of Brennus, victor of the Allia and sacker of Rome. In contrast to the account of Plutarch, Marcellus is not merely concerned with capturing Viridomarus' rich armour, but appears to have cut off the king's head and taken the royal torque as his prize. As with Cossus' decapitation of Lars Tolumnius, it seems that the head of the defeated king may well have formed a key part of the spoils dedicated to Jupiter Feretrius.[38] Plutarch's account ends with Marcellus calling up to Jupiter and offering the spoils:

Then, leaping from his horse and laying his hands on the armour of the dead man, Marcellus looked towards heaven and cried: 'O Jupiter Feretrius, who witnesses the great deeds and exploits of generals and commanders in wars and combat, I call you to witness that I have overpowered and slain this man with my own hand, being the third Roman ruler and general so to slay a ruler and king, and that I dedicate to you the first and most beautiful of the spoils. You therefore grant us a like fortune as we prosecute the rest of the war.' (Plutarch, *Marcellus*, 7.3)

The speech is suitably dramatic and has two notable elements. First, Marcellus specifies that only a general or ruler could win the *spolia opima* from a like opponent. How then was Cornelius Cossus, a mere military tribune, allowed to dedicate the *spolia opima*? Had Marcellus just changed the rules to make his deed too difficult for others to replicate? Second, Marcellus' dedication to the god is not made entirely freely; Jupiter should help the Romans in return for the gift of the spoils. Although in awe of the gods and thoroughly superstitious, the Romans conceived religion in terms of obligation and favour in return for the sacrifices they offered. And perhaps Jupiter did intervene for, despite being massively outnumbered, Marcellus' cavalry attacked almost as soon as he had killed the king, and scattered the presumably stunned Gallic cavalry and infantry.

Meanwhile, Scipio's legions had taken Acerrae and advanced on the Insubrian capital, Mediolanum (Milan), but the Insubres and Gaesati defended the town stubbornly and even forced Scipio's troops back into their camp: according to Plutarch, 'Cornelius was less besieger than besieged.' Marcellus arrived in the nick of time with his triumphant cavalry and saved the day. The Gaesati mercenaries deserted when they learned of the death of their king and the Insubres were forced to surrender. Thus, only three years after the Gauls' pre-emptive strike into the peninsula, the Romans had overrun the Gallic states of northern Italy.

Marcellus was voted a triumph by the Senate. He led the procession of captives and spoils through Rome from a chariot, perhaps that of Viridomarus. Strapped to the side of the chariot was the armour (and head?) of Viridomarus arranged by Marcellus himself as a trophy on a slender oak sapling. The victorious army followed, the legionaries and troopers in their most splendid armour, singing hymns to Jupiter Feretrius and victory paeans for Marcellus. He carried the trophy into the temple himself and set it up beside the spoils taken by Romulus and Cossus, the third Roman to do so and the last, but another would try. Marcellus choreographed the whole event. It had been 200 years since Cossus entered the temple with the spoils taken from Tolumnius and we might wonder if Marcellus conceived the idea of dedicating the *spolia opima* after his single combat with Viridomarus. Although he was clearly a devout man – Marcellus also vowed to build a temple to his protective deities Honos (Honour) and Virtus (Courage) in thanks for his victory – the political advantages of being a national hero and being recognised as the man who achieved the same feat as Romulus, cannot have escaped him. He may also have restored the inscription on Tolumnius' corselet, now surely faded, in contemporary Latin.[39]

SINGLE COMBAT IN THE WAR WITH HANNIBAL

The war with the Carthaginian general Hannibal, known as the Second Punic War, broke out in 218 BC. Hannibal won a string of crushing victories over the Romans: the Trebia (218 BC), Lake Trasimene (217 BC) and infamous Cannae (216 BC). Flaminius, conqueror of the Cenomani, was lured to destruction at Trasimene. Silius Italicus, a consul and epic poet of the first century AD, imagined Flaminius riding to his doom wearing a bronze helmet covered with the skin (the scalp?) of a Gallic chief he had killed in single combat, and crested with the long hair of another barbarian warrior. According to Livy, Flaminius was killed in a one-on-one combat with Ducarius, an Insubrian Gaul in Hannibal's service. Much in the way that Cornelius Cossus offered the life of Lars Tolumnius to the shades of the murdered Roman envoys, Ducarius offered the life of the general to the Gauls killed in the Roman conquest of northern Italy, but he was prevented from stripping the corpse by the intervention of a handful of legionary veterans. After the battle Hannibal ordered a search for Flaminius' body so that it could be given an honourable funeral, but it could not be found. Ten thousand Roman and Allied troops did escape the ambush at Trasimene; perhaps the veterans managed to spirit the corpse away and bury or cremate it somewhere in Etruria.[40]

At Cannae the Romans mustered the largest army yet and impatient legionaries and Italian Allies demanded that the consuls lead them out so that the slaughters at the Trebia and Trasimene could be avenged. Hannibal banked on this impatience, anticipating that the legionaries would drive their way forward, so that, as his army in crescent formation fell back, it would gradually surround the Romans. Indeed the Romans charged with so much force, deploying the maniples as columns, that they almost smashed through. Almost. Hannibal tied the knot around the Roman army and there was no escape. Perhaps as many as 70,000 Romans and Italians were killed. Hannibal hoped that the Italian Allies would now defect *en masse* and, deprived of their manpower, Rome would surrender. A considerable number of cities and tribes did defect but hardly on the scale Hannibal wished; Rome did not contemplate surrender and the great Marcellus now plotted the defeat of Hannibal. We should also note here that when the Senate considered the matter of replacing the huge number of senators killed at Cannae, it favoured men (presumably of suitable class) who had won civic crowns or taken spoils from the enemy, the usual result of single and one-on-one combats.[41]

Marcellus repulsed Hannibal from the walls of Nola in Campania in 216 and 214 BC, and with Fabius Maximus Cunctator ('Delayer', the famous consul who devised 'Fabian' scorched-earth tactics) took Casilinum, another important Campanian town from Hannibal in 214 BC. The following year Marcellus opened a second front against Carthage in Sicily and captured Syracuse, Carthage's powerful ally on the island, in 212 BC. Archimedes, the famous inventor, was killed by Roman troops during the sack. Marcellus then returned to the Italian mainland and attempted to draw Hannibal into a decisive battle. Hannibal had destroyed another Roman army at Herdonea in Apulia and moved into Lucania.

At Numistro the armies of Hannibal and Marcellus met in what was apparently a monumental but ultimately indecisive struggle, though, interestingly, Frontinus considered that Hannibal emerged victorious (210 BC). In the following year Marcellus confronted Hannibal at Canusium. On the first day Marcellus was defeated, losing several standards. He publicly shamed the defeated maniples, making a particular example of the centurions who should have died trying to retrieve the sacred standards, by parading them in front of the rest of the army without swords or military belts. Further punishment is not specified but, for a Roman or any Italic warrior, being stripped of his distinctive military belt was a most shameful humiliation: it was another form of spoliation. This made the soldiers fight all the harder the next day but Hannibal quickly withdrew. Marcellus' force was again mauled in a subsequent encounter and had to retire to Venusia. Still, Marcellus' persistence was causing Hannibal considerable aggravation and he acknowledged the Roman as a worthy adversary.[42]

In 208 BC Marcellus was sixty years old and elected to his fifth consulship. He joined his consular army with that of Quinctius Crispinus in the vicinity of Venusia. Hannibal followed; like the Romans he sought a decisive encounter, but the consuls were ambushed while reconnoitring the enemy positions. Marcellus, the 'sword of Rome' was killed, run through with a lance, and his body was taken to Hannibal. The Carthaginian treated it with the greatest respect. Meanwhile the surviving consul withdrew the Roman forces. He later died as a result of his wounds. A funeral games was held for Marcellus in Rome. It may have been then that Naevius' *Clastidium*, the poem celebrating the taking of the *spolia opima*, was first performed.[43]

It fell to a Scipio to defeat Hannibal in battle. Hannibal was forced to abandon Italy in 203 BC when attempts to send reinforcements to him failed and, most importantly, because Publius Cornelius Scipio had routed successive Carthaginian armies in Spain (208–206 BC) and crossed over into Africa in 204 BC and threatened Carthage itself. Hannibal was finally defeated at Zama in 202 BC.

In his epic poem *Punica*, Silius Italicus invented a single combat for Scipio's father. Although this was imaginary, Silius was clearly influenced by the conduct of men like Marcellus, Servilius Geminus Pulex, and perhaps Marcus Sergius (*see below*), believing that it would be entirely fitting for a Scipio to be presented at the battle of the Ticinus (218 BC) as offering a challenge to single combat (yes, a Roman issuing a challenge!) to Crixus, a Gallic chief in the service of Hannibal. Young Publius proved his mettle in the subsequent battle of Placentia, saving the life of his father. It was deeds like this that led to the apocryphal tradition that he and Hannibal agreed to fight it out as champions to decide the battle of Zama. However, many actual combats were fought during the Second Punic War, especially between Romans and the Italians who had sided with Hannibal.[44]

In 215 BC a Campanian cavalry officer named Cerrinus Vibellius Taurea rode up to the Roman cavalry lines around Capua and enquired after Claudius Asellus, the most renowned of all Roman cavalrymen. Before the war Taurea and Asellus had served together. Capua had been a Roman Ally for over a century and Taurea had even won Roman citizenship for his brave service. However, Capua sided with Hannibal after Cannae, and now Taurea wanted to fight things out with his old rival. Implying that Asellus was a coward, he asked the silent Roman troopers why did Asellus not come out fight and so to settle their rivalry? Was he afraid to take or capture the *spolia opima*? This reference to the spoils of honour emphasises Taurea's hubris.

Word of the challenge sped back to the Roman camp and Asellus sought the permission of the consul to fight it out with Taurea. He then sent a message to Taurea asking, 'Where and when?' Taurea came to regret his challenge. When the duellists met on the open ground before the walls of Capua they exchanged the usual insults and charged at each other, but neither made contact, the expert riders wheeling and dodging as if on the training ground. Taurea accused Asellus of deliberating trying to wear out the horses: 'What of the fight? This will be a test of horses, not of men!' He pointed to a nearby sunken lane or ditch and dared Asellus to fight within its confines; there would be no room to wheel or dodge. Incensed at the charge of cowardice, Asellus immediately spurred his horse down into the lane. Boastful Taurea did not follow. He was heard to mutter something about the lane being a likely place to put down a useless horse, and fled back to Capua. Asellus eventually emerged from the lane to find the Capuan gone and 'pouring scorn on his antagonist's cowardice, returned victoriously to the camp amidst the joy and congratulations of his friends.' Taurea seems to have regained his nerve and is later found in a one-on-one fight or single combat with a Roman named Artorius. Its result is not known.

At first sight it would appear that Asellus and Taurea were of relatively low rank, perhaps only commanders of small squadrons, and have therefore been cited as a rare examples of non-aristocratic duellists. However, Asellus was a member of the Claudii, one of the most ancient and noble Roman clans, and is probably identical with the Tiberius Claudius Asellus who was praetor (the second highest magistracy) in 206 BC. That he and Taurea are presented as relative equals suggests the Campanian was also an aristocrat.[45]

Appian notes that many single combats were fought at Capua. One day in 211 BC an aristocrat named Badius rode out of Capua and abused Quinctius Crispinus, then commanding one of the besieging legions, and challenged him to single combat. This was a rather tragic fight. Badius was a *hospes* (guest-friend) of Crispinus. *Hospitium* (guest-friendship) was an almost sacred bond made between friends of the highest social rank from different nations. The friendship was supposed to be perpetual and usually assumed by the sons of the original friends. It was as much a political as a personal friendship, thus Rome secured the co-operation and loyalty of many Italian and foreign aristocrats, and placed the friends under stringent terms of reciprocal obligation. The obligations of *hospitium* were considered as weighty as duties to blood relatives, sometimes even more so because of the political and international aspect. Before the war Badius had been a guest in Crispinus' house in Rome and was nursed there when ill – a classic example of the duties of guest-friendship. Crispinus did not want to fight but Badius renounced their guest-friendship and continued his tirade of abuse. Crispinus mounted up to meet him, charged and neatly slipped his lance over the rim of his opponent's shield and ran the point through his left shoulder. Badius was knocked from the saddle and staggered back to his companions; it seems that Crispinus desisted from inflicting a killing blow and allowed Badius to get away, but he nevertheless died of his wound. Crispinus took Badius' shield and horse as spoils and he must have done so with considerable sadness, but the Roman troopers who escorted him back to camp were exultant.[46]

, Another Roman who can be suspected of having indulged in single combat is Marcus Sergius Silus, great-grandfather of the infamous Catiline. He fought in the war against Hannibal; he was twice captured by Hannibal but successfully escaped both times. In the subsequent wars against the Gallic peoples that had sided with the Carthaginians, he earned more scars than Siccius Dentatus. The Elder Pliny tells us that

> In his second campaign he lost his right hand, and in two campaigns he was wounded twenty-three times, so much so that he could scarcely use either his hands or his feet. (Pliny, *Natural History*, 7.104)

Sergius was not deterred by missing hands or numerous wounds:

> On four occasions he fought with his left hand alone, and two horses were killed under him. He had a right hand made out of iron and attached to the stump, after which he fought a battle, and raised the siege of Cremona, defended Placentia and captured twelve of the enemy's camps in Gaul [Gallic north Italy]. (Pliny, *Natural History*, 7.104–5)

Sergius' grandson later issued coins celebrating his exploits. He is depicted on a charger, and with his left hand he brandishes a sword and the long hair of a severed head. As we have seen, taking an opponent's head was often the final act of single or one-on-one combats and it would not be surprising if some of Sergius Silus' many wounds were sustained in duels against Gauls in northern Italy.

As we saw above, honourable scars could have advantages in the Roman world. Marcus Sergius was covered in them, but in 197 BC his political opponents attempted to have him barred from the office of city praetor on the grounds that such a mutilated man was unfit to perform the religious rites associated with the praetorship. They failed.[47]

SINGLE COMBAT IN THE SECOND CENTURY BC

The next recorded single combat involving a Roman does not occur until 151 BC. Scipio Aemilianus, son of Aemilius Paullus, conqueror of Macedon, and grandson by adoption of Scipio Africanus, was then serving as a military tribune in the army of Licinius Lucullus and defeated a Celtiberian chief at the siege of Intercatia. The most extensive account survives in Appian's history of the Iberian Wars. It is a familiar story:

> There was a certain barbarian distinguished by his splendid armour, who frequently rode into the space between the armies and challenged the Romans to single combat. When nobody accepted the challenge he jeered at them, performed a triumphal dance and rode back to his army. After he had done this several times, Scipio, who was still a youth [he was about thirty-three years old], felt very much aggrieved, and springing forward accepted the challenge. Fortunately he won the victory, although he was small and his opponent big.
> (Appian, *Spanish Wars*, 53)

Aemilianus' victory has the usual result of lifting the spirits of a demoralised Roman force and he soon leads the attack on the Spanish stronghold. From other sources we learn that Aemilianus was the first Roman to storm the walls of Intercatia and was awarded a coveted *corona muralis*.[48] The parallels with the single combats of Manlius Torquatus and Valerius Corvus are obvious. The arrogant barbarian, identified as a noble by his rich armour, issues the challenge. No Roman dares accept until an invariably young and small officer can no longer bear the shame and vanquishes the barbarian in typical David versus Goliath style.

It is unfortunate that Polybius' account of this single combat survives only in a few short fragments. Polybius was a close friend of Aemilianus and probably witnessed the fight. The fragments of his account make it clear that it was not an easy fight for the Roman.

Aemilianus was in two minds whether he should accept the challenge: 'He was simultaneously assailed by an eager impulse to meet the barbarian in single combat and by doubt whether he should do so.' Even when personally challenged to a duel a Roman officer could decline (probably a better term than 'refuse') or nominate a substitute. When challenged by a German warrior before the battle of Aquae Sextiae (102 BC), the crafty Marius called forth one his bodyguards – a gladiator – and told the German if he could defeat the gladiator he would then fight him. Such tactics may have been more common than our sources allow. The challenger would be faced with the unwelcome prospect of two single combats and, more often than not, probably retreat back to his own lines followed by the jeers of the other side. Aemilianus was not challenged by name at Intercatia but his personality made it inevitable that he would accept the challenge. As a youth he was considered effete and un-Roman and was often depressed by the heavy expectation that he equal or surpass the glorious deeds of his ancestors. Even though he had proved his valour in battle since the age of sixteen or seventeen (he fought at Pydna in 168 BC), he was clearly driven to perform suicidal acts of bravery, for example the subsequent storming of the wall at Intercatia, and when he later attained the rank of general he still exposed himself unnecessarily in action. Aemilianus' doubts about accepting the challenge will therefore have been influenced not only by regular human emotions but also the practical consideration that if he accepted but was killed, the Roman army would become dejected.[49]

Appian's account – presumably derived from Polybius – makes it appear that Aemilianus impetuously spurred out from the Roman line without seeking the permission of his commander. The other surviving fragment of Polybius' account demonstrates that Aemilianus' Celtiberian opponent was no mean fighter. The warriors charged at each other and collided, the Spaniard seriously injured Aemilianus' horse and the Roman was forced to scramble out of the saddle as it collapsed. Somehow he managed to land on his feet. This was not an easy thing to do from the four-horned Roman saddle, which offered almost a good a fighting platform as stirrups but also tightly gripped the thighs of the rider so that dismounting in a hurry was not easy. Unfortunately we have no idea how Aemilianus managed to defeat his still mounted opponent. Florus, who probably wrote his epitome of Roman military history in the second century AD, elevated the duel, erroneously identifying the Celtiberian as a king and declared that Aemilianus stripped from him the *spolia opima*. Still, Florus' glorified notice should allow us to expect that Aemilianus performed the customary stripping of his enemy's armour and weapons and that he went back to the Roman lines, probably on the Spaniard's horse and brandishing his other trophies.[50]

Although sixty years separate the duels of Quinctius Crispinus at Capua and Scipio Aemilianus at Intercatia, Polybius indicates that single combats were common during the intervening period. When discussing contemporary Roman political and military practices, Polybius notes the precedence accorded to men who had won single combats. Noble Romans were therefore keen to advertise their individual prowess in battle. Scipio Nasica, who played an important part in the victory at Pydna, wrote an account of the battle and emphasised his defeat of a Thracian mercenary in one-on-one combat, 'spearing him through the chest with his javelin'.[51]

Spain remained the principal theatre of Roman warfare in the latter half of the second century BC and single combats between Roman officers and native aristocrats were a periodic occurrence. In 143 BC the aptly named Quintus Occius Achilles was serving as legate under the stern disciplinarian Caecillius Metellus Macedonicus. Metellus was the kind of general who did not accept failure; his men were in the habit of making wills on the battlefield because after any retreat Metellus would send them straight back at the enemy, even if it meant certain death.[52]

One day, as Occius was about to sit down to a meal, he received a message that a Celtiberian had challenged him to single combat and was waiting beyond the ramparts of the Roman camp. Aware that Metellus would not sanction the duel, Occius had his arms and horse led out of the camp in secret. Occius then slipped out, donned his fighting gear and rode out to meet the Celtiberian (one wonders if he had done this before; as a high-ranking legate he could probably expect to get away with it).The Spanish warrior charged as soon as he saw Occius but was quickly dispatched. Exultant in his swift victory, Occius stripped the Spaniard and, in contrast to his stealthy exit, re-entered the Roman camp in triumph. Metellus' reaction is not recorded.

It is interesting that this duel occurred outside of a battle. The *cognomen* Achilles – the name of the legendary Greek monomachist of the Trojan War and ancestor of king Pyrrhus – could be explained by frequent duelling. Perhaps Occius' Celtiberian challenger was the blood relative or friend of a previous victim of a single or one-on-one combat and therefore obliged to challenge the Roman, though it may be that he simply challenged Occius on account of his reputation for valour and wished to make a name for himself.

Probably as a result of this victory, Occius was subsequently challenged by Pyresus, 'who surpassed all the Celtiberians in nobility and courage' (he is called Tyresius in another source). Once again the Roman was victorious but he spared the life of the young Spanish noble. Occius was evidently impressed by Pyresus' courage and spirit and entered into *hospitium* (guest-friendship) with him. This lessened the disgrace of Pyresus' defeat and survival. To secure their bond the two exchanged gifts. Occius gave the Spaniard his sword and received in return a fine cloak, and then they clasped hands in friendship.

The chivalrous Occius was killed in 140 BC. A summary of one of Livy's lost books states he was ambushed in Lusitania and, as would be expected, he died hard. If Occius did die in Lusitania he would have been serving in the war against the wily chief Viriathus. However, Appian reports that a military tribune called Oppius, serving under the proconsul Quintus Pompeius, died that year in the disastrous fighting further north at Celtiberian Numantia:

Pompeius, coming back to the siege of Numantia, endeavoured to turn the course of a certain river into the plain in order to reduce the city by famine. But the inhabitants harassed him while he was doing this work. They rushed out in crowds without any trumpet signal, and assaulted those who were working on the river, and even hurled missiles at those who came to their assistance from the camp and finally shut the Romans up in their own fortification. The Numantines also attacked some foragers and killed many, among them Oppius, a military tribune. (Appian, *Spanish Wars*, 78)

Oppius could be a copyist's error for Occius. Whatever the case, it is possible that Occius' heroic death and duels were used by later Roman historians to flesh out the legend of Siccius Dentatus, who is also given the name Achilles in sources of the Imperial period. Roman historians were keen on 'historical reconstruction' rather than invention and had few qualms about using genuine historical events and personalities as models for the battles of early Rome and her heroes.[53]

Our next single combat was fought at Numantia in 134 or 133 BC, when Scipio Aemilianus was entrusted with the reduction of the small Spanish city which had humbled every army Rome sent to take it. Gaius Marius was a young officer in the Roman army, aged about twenty-four, and he 'encountered and cut down an enemy before the eyes of his general'. There are no other details of the fight but that it seems to have been fought in isolation suggests it was a single combat. Marius was duly decorated (*see above* for his *dona militaria*) and promoted. Marius was invited to dine with Aemilianus. According to legend, when the after-dinner conversation turned to Rome's great leaders and generals Marius sought to flatter Aemilianus, asking him, 'Where will the Roman people find such a commander to replace you?' Aemilianus returned the flattery by tapping Marius on the shoulder and saying, 'Perhaps here.'[54]

By 133 BC the proud Numantines were starving and finally

surrendered, though many preferred to take their own lives rather than hand themselves over to the Romans. Numantia was razed and the survivors sold into slavery. Scipio Aemilianus died in somewhat suspicious circumstances in 129 BC and it was not until 107 BC that Marius' star really began to shine. In that year he was elected to the first of his seven consulships, a rare accomplishment for a *novus homo* (new man) from outside the usual noble clique. He revived Roman fortunes in North Africa, defeating and ultimately capturing (through the agency of his later enemy Sulla) the rebel Numidian prince Jugurtha, who incidentally had served alongside Marius at Numantia. As we have seen Marius avoided a duel before Aquae Sextiae (102 BC); however, he did not shy away from hand-to-hand combat in the actual battle or the subsequent fight at Vercellae (101 BC).

Marius was too canny to accept a challenge to a single combat which he might lose and thereby shatter the fragile morale of a Roman army awed by the fearsome reputation of the Germans. But at least one Roman officer did engage in single combat during the campaigns against the Germans. Lucius Opimius defeated a Cimbric warrior during Lutatius Catulus' attempt to bottle up the Cimbri Thermopylae-style in the narrow Adige river valley in northern Italy in 102–101 BC. The attempt was of course disastrous and the ignominy of the Roman failure was lessened only by Opimius' victory and perhaps Gnaeus Petreius' extrication of his legion when it was surrounded by the Cimbri (*see* Chapter V). Catulus' army finally got a taste of victory when it was united with Marius' force at Vercellae. Opimius may well have been the son of a disgraced consul of the same name. It is possible that he sought out a German champion in order to restore the family reputation.[55]

Opimius' single combat has survived only in the form of a brief notice in the weird and wonderful miscellany compiled by the late Roman writer Ampelius. It is unfortunate that the source Ampelius used, perhaps stemming from the campaign memoirs known to have been written by Catulus or Sulla (sent to Catulus by Marius after the

Adige debacle in order to give him a competent military advisor), but it demonstrates that the tradition of single combat was alive and well and we might wonder if Opimius' duel was as unique as the lack of references to single combat in the extant written sources makes it appear. In fact another single combat fought at the end of the second century BC has already been mentioned, although it is not universally accepted as such. The problem, as ever, with Manius Aquilius' fight against the slave leader Athenion in Sicily in 101 BC, is that no detailed account survives and our best source, a fragment of Diodorus, does not allow us to determine whether it was a formal single combat or an opportune one-on-one encounter in the midst of battle:

> Meeting Athenion, the king of the rebels, face to face, he put up a heroic struggle. He slew Athenion but was himself wounded in the head and recovered after treatment. (Diodorus Siculus, 36.10.1)

It is attractive to imagine Athenion challenging Aquilius. The Cilician slave was a remarkable man and evidently charismatic, having raised his own small army and led it with success against Roman forces. Now, however, his army was starving and facing a new consul fresh from success in the Cimbric Wars (Aquilius was Marius' senior legate) and a full army of legionary veterans rather than the scratch levies that he and his recently expired partner in rebellion, 'King' Tryphon, had previously defeated. Challenging Aquilius to single combat would serve to level the field somewhat, reducing the conflict to a battle of champions. The morale of ancient armies, even veteran ones, was often fickle; if Athenion slew the consul the legions might be too shocked to fight. We should also consider that a few Roman commanders, for example Metellus Pius (*see below*), were starting to act more like generals and less like individual warriors. Roman soldiers liked to see their general in the front rank or charging with the cavalry but it was also his responsibility to hang back and oversee the battle, issuing orders to the various battle lines and sending in reserves as necessary. To have Athenion and Aquilius engaging hand-to-hand suggests that one sought the other out, and perhaps it was Aquilius who searched the battlefield for the rebel leader. His subsequent conduct in Asia Minor (90–88 BC) demonstrates his aggressive nature: when sent to Asia Minor as a peace envoy he stirred up a war with Mithridates of Pontus. It would be the crowning achievement of the suppression of a dangerous slave rebellion to kill its leader in combat 'with his own hands'. It must remain speculative, but there is a good chance that the fight of Aquilius and Athenion was a formal single combat.[56] Aquilius met his end in 88 BC. He was defeated in battle by Mithridates and captured, publicly humiliated and because Mithridates despised him as a greedy Roman, was eventually executed by having molten gold poured down his throat.

The captives taken after the defeat of Athenion were sent to Rome and sentenced to fight beasts in the arena. However, the captives decided among themselves to fight each other to the death. The last captive, having no one left to fight, fell on his own blade. This spectacle met with great approval from the Roman spectators for it was like a gladiatorial fight, that is a ritualised form of single combat. As we have seen, to die well in Roman society, whatever your station, was of paramount importance, and valiant death in combat, albeit within the confines of a stinking arena, was always glorious and redemptive. It is ironic that the Sicilian rebels died better deaths than Aquilius.[57]

SINGLE COMBAT IN THE FIRST CENTURY

As we move into first century BC we are quickly presented with a single combat of the classic type, where an enemy champion advances into the space between armies to make a challenge. It is accepted by a small Roman soldier and the big, arrogant challenger is inevitably vanquished and his army panics at his defeat. However, the single combat at Nola in 89 BC is notable because the Roman victor was not actually Roman or even Italian.

In 91 BC the Italian Allies revolted. They supplied half or two-thirds of the manpower of every Roman army but since the middle of the second century BC had received a lesser proportion of the spoils of successful wars, and were consistently denied Roman citizenship and therefore a say in the running of the empire they had shed so much blood to build. The Romans suffered numerous setbacks in the early stages of this war, known to them as the Italian War but now usually called the Social War because it was fought against the *socii* ('Allies'). Cornelius Sulla emerged as Rome's most able general and he was charged with bringing Campania and Samnium back under Roman sway. In 90 BC the redoubtable Samnites had inflicted a series of defeats on the Romans, and Gallic auxiliaries serving alongside the legions had defected to them. In 89 BC Sulla quickly shifted the balance back to Rome and, by placing the important rebel stronghold of Pompeii under siege, forced the Samnite general Cluentius into a set-piece battle. Cluentius had to defeat Sulla's field army before he could make any move to relieve Pompeii. The ensuing battle was the decisive engagement in the Campanian theatre and the Roman victory was brought about by a single combat.

Cluentius actually had the better of the fighting to start with. He advanced to within 700 yards of Sulla's camp near Pompeii. Sulla responded immediately to the provocation but his hasty attack was beaten back and only the appearance of his numerous camp followers dissuaded Cluentius from pressing an assault on the camp. Sulla then withdrew to a new camp near Nola:

> Having received certain Gallic reinforcements he [Cluentius] again drew near to Sulla and, just as the two armies were coming to an engagement, a Gaul of enormous size advanced and challenged any Roman to single combat. A Mauretanian of short stature accepted the challenge and killed him, whereupon the Gauls became panic-stricken and fled. Cluentius' line of battle was thus broken and the remainder of

his troops did not stand their ground, but fled in disorder to Nola. Sulla followed them and killed 3,000 in the pursuit, and as the inhabitants of Nola received them by one gate, lest the enemy should rush in with them, he killed about 20,000 more outside the walls and among them Cluentius himself, who fell fighting bravely. (Appian, *Civil Wars*, 1.50)

Here an African auxiliary, rather than a Roman officer, accepts the challenge. He is typically small whereas the Gaul is huge but, nevertheless, is quickly vanquished. The flight of the Gallic contingent wrecks the cohesion of Cluentius' battle line and his disordered and demoralised troops are easily defeated.

It is a pity that the Mauretanian is not more clearly identified. Was he just a common soldier who rushed forward to meet the Gaul? All the duels detailed above were fought by officers, usually of noble blood. However, the fighting at Jerusalem in AD 70 demonstrates that ordinary Roman soldiers were often unable to resist the temptation of opportune fights, even if there were clear orders against doing so. The general orders of 360 BC and 340 BC against breaking ranks and fighting duels applied to ordinary legionaries as well as officers. Yet when such opportune fighting was sanctioned, perhaps in the hope of provoking the enemy into a formal engagement (as occurred at Sentinum), Polybius tells us that common soldiers might receive special rewards:

> ... [if] during a skirmish or some similar situation in which there is no necessity to engage in single combat, [they] have voluntarily and deliberately exposed themselves to danger. (Polybius, 6.39.4)

But was the African's acceptance of the single combat really as spontaneous as Appian's account makes it appear? Perhaps he did seek the permission of Sulla to fight. If he was a senior officer, conceivably the commander of the African troops, he could freely approach the general. An ordinary ranker could not leave his place in the battle line without being reprimanded. We should perhaps also wonder if Sulla called for a volunteer to fight the Gaul.

Another remarkable single combat was fought some time between the late 80s and early 40s BC: the victor served under Pompey Magnus, whose campaigns were nearly continuous between 83 and 62 BC, and resumed again in 49 BC when he commanded the Senatorial armies against Julius Caesar. According to the Elder Pliny:

> Varro, speaking of persons remarkable for their strength, gives us an account of Tributanus, a celebrated gladiator, and skilled in the use of the Samnite arms; he was a man of meagre person, but possessed of extraordinary strength. Varro makes mention of his son also, who served in the army of Pompeius Magnus. He says that, in all parts of his body, even in the arms and hands, there was a network of sinews, extending across and across. The latter of these men, having been challenged by an enemy, with a single finger of his right hand, and that unarmed, vanquished him, and then seized him and dragged him back to the camp. (Pliny, *Natural History*, 7.81)

Some of Pompey's hardest campaigns were fought in Spain against the renegade Sertorius (77–71 BC). As a Roman of equestrian origin and senatorial rank Sertorius was fond of issuing challenges to single combat, especially to Pompey's fellow commander Caecilius Metellus Pius. Metellus' legionaries were very keen on the suggestion but he refused, declaring that a general should die like a general and not like a common soldier. This only made Metellus' troops jeer him. Sertorius derided him as an 'old woman' and liked to refer to Pompey as 'the boy'. One wonders if the son of Tributanus was employed by Pompey as a bodyguard to protect him from the inevitable challenges of Sertorius' Spanish and North African warriors.[58]

The final single combat to be considered here is one of the most interesting. In 45 BC Julius Caesar confronted his Pompeian enemies for the last time at the battle of Munda in Spain. While the rival Roman armies were building their camps and forming battle lines, one of the Pompeians came forth:

> The Pompeians were too timid to come down on to level ground and join battle [some of Caesar's legionaries had left their half-built camp and were taunting them and challenging them to fight], except for one man, Antistius Turpio. Confident in his strength, he began to proclaim that none of his opponents was his equal. At this point, as in the duel of Achilles and Memnon, Quintus Pompeius Niger, a man of equestrian rank from Italica, advanced from our ranks to meet him. Because Antistius' ferocity had made everyone watch instead of concentrate on their task [constructing fortified camps], the battle lines were set out: for it was unclear which of the warring principals would be victorious, so that it seemed that the duel would bring the war to an end. Thus eager and intent, each man favoured his own side and willed it to win. Alert and courageous, they came down to the flat ground to fight, and their shields and battle decorations shone . . . (Anonymous, *Spanish War*, 25)

Unfortunately the text breaks off at this point – it seems that the duel was interrupted by a running cavalry skirmish – but the narrative is of great importance. Its anonymous author was a soldier in Caesar's army, variously identified as a centurion or cavalry trooper. It is generally agreed that the author's Latin was not of a high standard – it is full of colloquialisms and is translated with difficulty. The passage also demonstrates a school-boyish fascination with epic poetry, hence various allusions to duels of the Trojan War, yet he was probably an eyewitness to the duel. His is a rare first-hand account of a Roman single combat.[59]

Turpio and Niger have been described as junior members of their respective armies, not men of high rank like the Roman duellists of the third and second centuries BC. It is tempting to view the men as centurions. We hear of centurions challenging the Gallic warriors to fight during the Nervii's siege of Quintus Cicero's camp in 54–53 BC. At one stage the centurions of cohort IV (the legion is not identified) fell back from the rampart at the approach of a siege tower, making room for the Gauls and challenged them to come down and fight it out, hand-to-hand. The Gauls refused and the tower was ultimately destroyed by fire. However, the names of the Munda duellists tell a different story. The Antistii were an important Patrician family: Turpio will have served at the very least as a military tribune or maybe as a legate. Some upper class men in the Caesarian army did accept 'lower' ranks. For example Valerius Flaccus, son of a former governor of Asia, was killed at Dyrrhachium with the rank of senior centurion. There could only be so many tribunes in an army (six to each legion) and while waiting for a vacancy one wonders if Flaccus chose to serve as a centurion in order to make a reputation for himself? The way in which Antistius Turpio descended from the Pompeian camp and made his challenge suggests a man who did not have to worry over much about reproaches from higher authority. One could cite the actions of Pullo and Vorenus, leaping from the ramparts of their besieged fort into a group of Gallic warriors (a way for them to fight one-on-one combats with Gauls instead of a duel between themselves), or the unsanctioned assault on Gergovia, as examples of centurions acting on their own initiative, but these episodes occurred during chaotic fighting, not the relative calm before a battle. It is inconceivable that centurions did not fight single combats but it is unlikely that Turpio and Niger were centurions.[60]

Pompeius Niger was a native Spaniard, and his name demonstrates that Pompeius Magnus gave him the Roman citizenship. He was of equestrian rank, that is a man of some wealth and probably belonging to the local aristocracy, and was therefore a prominent defector to Caesar's camp. Both Turpio and Niger were conspicuous for their military decorations. This suggests long military service; perhaps Niger fought under Pompey during the Sertorian War? The high status of both men shows this duel to have been of the classic type, fought between noble champions, and puts paid to the notion that single combats were no longer fought by aristocrats in the first century BC.[61]

MARCUS LICINIUS CRASSUS AND THE SPOLIA OPIMA

The most notable feature of Marcus Licinius Crassus' campaigns in Moesia (29–28 BC) was not his centurion Cornidius terrifying the enemy by wearing a helmet surmounted with a small brazier of coals that made his head appear to be on fire, but that Crassus slew a barbarian king and claimed the right to dedicate the *spolia opima*.[62]

Crassus was the grandson of Marcus Licinius Crassus, the famous triumvir and richest man in Rome. The elder was an effective commander – he was the conqueror of Spartacus – but his defeat and death at Carrhae in 53 BC has irretrievably blackened his reputation as a soldier. According to one tradition the general was killed by one of his own soldiers so that he could not be humiliated by the Parthians.[63] Crassus' father, called Publius, was also killed at Carrhae. Before this he had been one of Caesar's most effective officers in Gaul and was instrumental in the defeat of the Helvetii in 58 BC. Crassus inherited their military skill.

Some time before the battle of Actium (31 BC) he shrewdly defected from Mark Antony to Octavian. In 30 BC he shared the consulship with the victorious Octavian and was soon made proconsul of the troubled frontier province of Macedonia. In 29 BC a force of Bastarnae invaded a friendly Thracian kingdom neighbouring Macedonia. More out of concern for the Roman province than the Thracian allies, Crassus led his legions against the Bastarnae and pursued them into Moesia. Near the River Cebrus (somewhere in Bulgaria), he hid his army in a wood and lured the Bastarnae towards it by placing some scouts as bait on the clear ground before the trees. The Bastarnae could not resist such an easy target and chased the scouts into the trees and Crassus' trap. Crassus found their king, Deldo, amid the confusion and killed him. After the victory over Deldo Crassus proceeded to defeat the Bastarnae and

Moesians (whom Cornidius so terrified), as well as subdue remnants of the Bastarnae and rebellious Thracian tribes. He also recaptured the Roman standards lost by Gaius Antonius Hybrida to the Bastarnae in 59 BC.

No specific details of Crassus' fight with Deldo survive. It may have been an opportune one-on-one combat, and the idea to dedicate to Jupiter Feretrius the arms taken from the king might not have occurred to Crassus until after the battle, but his intention to do so caused Octavian great anxiety. The ruler may have unwittingly put the idea of *spolia opima* into the mind of Crassus by starting the restoration of the ruinous temple of Jupiter Feretrius in 32 BC, but Octavian could not countenance a new dedicator of the spoils of honour. He had only recently defeated Antony, brought peace and reunified the Roman world. He was promoting himself as a new Romulus and the ancient magisterial powers were being concentrated in his person. He was effectively emperor – something that was confirmed in January 27 BC when he became Augustus. Generals fought under his auspices. He was the supreme commander; their victories were his. Crassus was not playing the game. Crassus returned to Rome early in 27 BC and was voted a justly deserved triumph but Augustus determined to scupper his plan to dedicate the spoils.[64]

The linen corselet Cornelius Cossus took from Tolumnius had been discovered during the restoration of the temple of Jupiter Feretrius. It was presumably much decayed but Augustus claimed to have been able to read the inscription on it. He declared that it stated Cossus had killed Tolumnius while he was consul in 428 BC, not when he was military tribune nine years before. This meant that, like Romulus and Marcellus, Cossus had won the spoils when he was supreme magistrate or 'ruler'. Crassus, on the other hand, was merely a governor fighting under Augustus' auspices.

No other person saw the corselet, which has prompted the suggestion that it was never found but had probably rotted away. However, as suggested above, Marcellus may have restored the inscription in such a way as to make it difficult for other Romans to claim the *spolia opima* (now that Marcellus had reminded them of its existence) and diminish his glory. It would have been easy for Marcellus to restore the inscription to declare that Cossus took the spoils as consul. Alternatively, Augustus could have misunderstood (perhaps deliberately) an abbreviated form of Cossus for consul – usually abbreviated as 'COS'; abbreviations were common on such inscriptions. Whatever the truth, Livy was suspicious. Augustus told him about the inscription a few years after its rediscovery, and Livy duly noted it in his history, but he also states that all the other sources he had consulted were emphatic in placing Cossus' killing of Tolumnius during his military tribunate in 437 BC.

The men who took the *spolia opima* were emulating the feat of Romulus and were reckoned his true heirs. As late as the mid-first century BC the antiquarian Varro, who had fought against Caesar at Pharsalus and was therefore not an armchair warrior, believed that *any* Roman soldier could claim the *spolia opima* if he killed an enemy king or commander – but few common soldiers found themselves in hand-to-hand combat with kings. Kings did not always engage in combat, were surrounded by bodyguards and often had champions who took care of challenges. Like Marcellus, Augustus was ensuring that his status as the heir of Romulus could not be usurped: he was posing as the restorer of Rome after a generation of civil war. If Crassus was permitted to dedicate the spoils he might easily become a figurehead for those powerful men discontented with the regime of Augustus, and cause a coup or new civil war. No more is heard of Crassus after his triumphal procession through Rome in July 27 BC. Augustus did not have him killed; suspicion would inevitably have fallen on the new emperor and discredited his programme of reconciliation with former Pompeians and Antonians. Crassus was somehow silenced and sidelined and the warrior-general simply fades from view.[65] By the time Valerius Maximus wrote his book of maxims during the reign of Tiberius (AD 14–37), Augustus' assertion about those eligible to dedicate *spolia opima* was firmly established:

> Titus Manlius Torquatus, Valerius Corvinus, and Scipio
> Aemilianus showed the same valour in single combat. They
> also slew enemy leaders whom they had challenged, but since
> they had acted under other men's auspices, they did not place
> the spoils to be consecrated to Jupiter Feretrius. (Valerius
> Maximus, *Memorable Deeds and Sayings*, 3.2.6)

Another man did strive to win the *spolia opima*. His attempts
were permitted because he was Nero Claudius Drusus, descendant of
Marcellus and son of Augustus by adoption. The imperial prince was
an effective general, over-running vast swathes of Germany
(12–9 BC), and he was in the habit of searching battlefields for
German chiefs so that he might challenge them to single combat and
despoil them. He was unsuccessful in these endeavours and died an
unfulfilled duellist following a bad fall from his horse in 9 BC.[66]

* * *

The single combats fought by Romans between the fourth and first
centuries BC were not the decisive battles of champions, such as the
legendary fight between the Horatii and Curiatii, but successful
single combats (except for Priscus at Jerusalem in AD 70, we never
hear of unsuccessful Roman duellists) which frequently inspired
Roman armies and demoralised their enemies. Sometimes the defeat
of a champion even caused an army to panic or retreat. The fights
between Taurea and Asellus or Badius and Crispinus at Capua were
little more than trials of strength and honour, although still
important to Roman morale, but the victory of the little Moor over
the giant Gaul at Nola is singled out as the reason for the collapse
of the Samnite army. Even if a battle did not feature a single combat,
a general was likely to refer to Torquatus and Corvus in his
exhortation in order to inspire the troops. The idea of a decisive
battle of champions never went away. Sertorius challenged Metellus
Pius to settle the war in Spain by single combat, and Mark Antony
twice challenged Octavian to single combat, in 31 and 30 BC, to

decide the mastery of the Roman world. The sickly Octavian was wise to refuse.[67]

Marcus Crassus held his defeat of Deldo, king of the Bastarnae, in hand-to-hand combat to be his highest martial accomplishment. For Roman generals the desire to engage in combat always hovered below the surface, and even the most rational commanders like Julius Caesar could not resist its temptation indefinitely. His personal interventions in combat at the Sabis (57 BC) and Munda (45 BC) were necessary to restore collapsing battle lines, but his leading the opening cavalry charge at Thapsus (46 BC) was hardly as essential. The emperors who succeeded Caesar desisted from combat for more than two and a half centuries, but when the generals seized power in the third century AD the emperor took his place in the front rank. In AD 251 the Emperor Decius appears to have died in a *devotio*-like charge against the Goths. Maybe he was actually attempting to engage the Gothic king, Kniva, in single combat?[68]

There are many single combats in Procopius' account of the wars of the sixth century AD. Roman champions dazzle enemies with their skill at arms, not with sword and lance as before, but lance and bow. Two examples will suffice. Althias, commander of Hunnic auxiliaries in Libya, challenged the Moorish chief Iaudas to single combat in AD 535. Spurring his horse forward, Iaudas hurled his spear at the Roman commander, but with lightning speed Althias caught the missile with his right hand!

> This filled Iaudas and the enemy with consternation. With his left hand Althias instantly drew his bow, for he was ambidextrous, and [presumably having ditched the spear] hit and killed Iaudas' horse. As he fell the Moors brought up another horse for their commander, upon which Iaudas leaped and straightaway fled. The Moorish army followed him in complete disorder. (Procopius, *History of the Wars*, 4.13.15–16)

Single combat of the earlier classic type is represented by the fights of Andreas at the battle of Daras in AD 530. During a lull in the fighting a haughty young Persian rode into the space between the Persian and Roman armies, challenging anyone who dared to single combat. No Roman soldier would accept his challenge, but Andreas, the bath attendant of the general Bouzes, rode out to meet him, notably, says Procopius, without being ordered by the general to do so. Andreas was not a soldier but was a skilled wrestler and strong. He knocked the young Persian from the saddle with his spear, leaped down from his horse and used a small knife to 'slay him like a sacrificial animal as he lay on his back'. Another Persian rode out to avenge his comrade. This warrior was a veteran with grey in his beard. The Persian and Roman knocked each other from their mounts, but scrambled to their feet. Then Andreas, employing his skill as a wrestler, 'smote the Persian as he was rising on his knee, and as he fell again to the ground killed him.' Andreas' double victory was enough to persuade the Persian army to withdraw.[69]

We hear little of single combat in the preceding centuries. Yet the prefect Valerius Maximianus 'killed Valao, chief of the Naristae, with his own hand', perhaps meaning in single combat (AD 173), and the fighting at Jerusalem in AD 70 demonstrates that ordinary Roman soldiers indulged in single combat with relish. It seems unlikely that they lost this habit only to rediscover it in the sixth century.[70]

Chapter IV

WARLORDS AND
THEIR WARRIORS

'Caesar had the Seventh, Eighth and Ninth, real veteran legions of incomparable courage, and also the Eleventh, a promising legion of picked young men. It was now in its eighth year of campaigning, but when compared with the others had yet to win a similar reputation for mature courage.' (Hirtius, *Gallic War*, 8.8)

In the wars of the late Republic a number of legions and cohorts, and indeed some individual soldiers, became almost as famous as the great generals who led them to victory. The army was by now almost professionalised. For many Roman citizens, especially those who sought social advancement, or those who could find no other employment, soldiering had become a full-time occupation; it was no longer an obligation to be performed when the consuls went to war and enrolled new legions. The needs of the Roman state to garrison and extend its empire made huge demands on manpower.

Moreover, the legions were evolving into permanent formations with fixed numerals and titles, a process catalysed by the retention and re-formation of Julius Caesar's veteran legions by Antony and Octavian and finalised by the latter when he re-established the army in the aftermath of his victory at Actium.

Here we will consider Caesar's favourite legions and centurions; the rise of the praetorian cohort under Antony and Octavian; and trace the history and disappearance of perhaps the most famous legion of all – the Ninth.

Full-time soldiering and long wars of conquest bound legionaries and their generals closer together than ever before. This added a new and very dangerous element to the traditional competition between Roman nobles. The loyalty of legionaries was primarily to their generals (so long as they were successful), rather than to the Roman state. If a noble like Caesar wanted to be the leading man in Rome, what was to stop him using his army against his enemies in the city?

CAESAR'S SOLDIERS
THE GALLIC WAR

The opening years of Gaius Julius Caesar's Gallic command were characterised by glory, profit and atrocity.

In 58 BC, near modern Autun, Caesar held the migrating nation of the Helvetii with only four veteran legions, the Seventh, Eighth, Ninth and Tenth (c. 20,000 men in all if at full strength, but probably far below this). The newly recruited legions, the Eleventh and Twelfth, and all the auxiliaries, were positioned on a hill behind the battle line and guarded the baggage.[1] When a sudden attack by the Boii and Tulingi, the reserve of the Helvetian army, threatened to engulf the right flank of the Romans, Caesar coolly detached the third line of cohorts from each veteran legion, wheeled them to face the new threat and so fought two battles at once. Both Helvetian contingents were routed. Out of the 92,000 warriors and 276,000 other men, women and children migrating with the Helvetii, Caesar claims to have slaughtered 258,000. This was considered justifiable revenge against a people that had once forced a defeated Roman army under the yoke.

Later that year Caesar drove the feared Suebians of the arrogant German king Ariovistus, who had conquered a large portion of eastern Gaul, back across the Rhine. Huge numbers drowned in the river. Ariovistus managed to escape in a small boat but died soon after. His two wives and a daughter were killed in the pursuit. Another daughter was captured. Like the daughter of the chief of the Helvetii, this Barbarian princess would decorate Caesar's triumphs.[2]

In 57 BC the Belgae, the most fearsome of the Gallic peoples being an admixture of Celts and Germans, were defeated, but only after hard fighting, particularly on the River Sabis (usually identified as the Sambre but this has been challenged), where they ambushed Caesar's army while part of it was constructing camp, and another part was still on the march. Many of the Twelfth Legion's centurions and standard-bearers were killed and, despite the efforts of the *primus pilus* Sextius Baculus (*see below*), a few panicking legionaries began to peel away from the back of the line. Caesar himself took to the front of the battle line and prevented the collapse of the legion:

> Taking a shield from one of the soldiers at the rear, Caesar made his way to the front rank. There he called upon the centurions by name and encouraged the men, ordering them to advance and open up the maniples,[3] so they could use their swords more easily. His coming gave the men fresh hope and rallied their spirits: each one was eager to do well before his commander's eyes, even at great personal risk – and the enemy assault was checked. (Caesar, *Gallic War*, 2.26)

This kind of heroic leadership engendered in the legionaries the fiercest loyalty to Caesar. Time and again his personal magnetism spurred his men to superhuman efforts; it was a great thing to fight before the eyes of Caesar.[4] Pride overcame terror and the men of the Twelfth linked with the Seventh Legion to drive forward. The Tenth and Ninth Legions overcame the Belgae on the left and the eventual arrival of two fresh legions, separated on the march from the others, turned the tide in the Romans' favour. Few Belgic warriors escaped. 'They were wiped out,' reports Caesar, but he was greatly impressed by their *virtus*.

After this victory Caesar turned on the Aduatuci who had supported the Nervii, the main Belgic tribe at the Sabis. The Aduatuci fortified themselves in their main town and, in order to avoid a lengthy siege, Caesar offered to spare them if they surrendered and disarmed. The Aduatuci agreed but secretly kept a third of their arms, then made a surprise attack on Caesar's siege lines. This was repulsed and the Aduatuci lost 4,000 men and the Romans easily forced their way into the town. The 53,000 refugees inside were sold into slavery. The profit to Caesar must have been immense and added to the tribute already received from defeated tribes and plunder taken on the battlefield, particularly from the royal baggage of Ariovistus.[5]

Amid the numerous campaigns fought by Caesar and his legates between 56 and 54 BC, those that caught public attention most in Rome were his crossing of the Rhine and forays across the ocean to mysterious Britannia.

The defeat of Ariovistus had delighted the Roman populace. The Germans replaced the Gauls – who had sacked Rome in 390 BC – as the bogeymen of Roman nightmares when, in the final decades of the second century BC, wandering Germanic tribes routed successive Roman armies and eventually invaded Italy. At Arausio (modern Orange) in 105 BC the Romans suffered a defeat as catastrophic as infamous Cannae. Only in 101 BC did Gaius Marius (Caesar's uncle) defeat the German menace at Vercellae in north Italy. In 55 BC Caesar administered the final revenge the Romans longed for. He first found an excuse to massacre the Usipetes and Tencteri who had crossed the Rhine into the vicinity of Xanten to escape depredations by the Suebi. This he followed up by bridging the Rhine and leading the legions into Germania proper, where he terrorised the Sugambri and laid waste their territory for eighteen days.

Then followed the first invasion of Britain. Caesar had no intention of occupying southern Britain. He sailed with a relatively small force of two legions (the Seventh and Tenth) and while he campaigned on land lost most of his fleet to a storm (an episode repeated in his second invasion in 54 BC), but Rome was enthralled by the audacity of a general who dared to campaign on the fringe of the known world. The euphoria spread even to the conservative senators who, having declared an unprecedented fifteen days of thanksgiving for Caesar's victories in 57 BC, now announced twenty days of celebration. Not all were happy, though. The dedicated republican Marcus Porcius Cato (great-grandson of the famous censor) viewed Caesar's ambitions as a grave threat to the state; he had been imprisoned for his opposition when Caesar was consul in 59 BC. Cato was praetor in 54 BC and proposed to the Senate that, on account of his atrocities, Caesar should be handed over to the Germans.

Caesar's subsequent invasion of Britain in 54 BC distracted his attention from Gaul. He had overrun the country but its many tribes were not fully conquered and the thinly spread Roman garrisons encouraged them to think of revolt.[6]

THE GALLIC REVOLT

In the winter of 54–53 BC Caesar was forced by a poor harvest to disperse his legions widely across Gaul. The isolation of the legions made them vulnerable to attack; despite attempts to locate the legions with a few days' march of each other, some were almost 100 miles apart.

Ambiorix, chief of the Eburones, tricked the legate Titurius Sabinus and lured his Fourteenth Legion, and five other cohorts, out of winter quarters in north-east Gaul, surrounded and eventually destroyed it. Some legionaries fought their way back to the fort and the *aquilifer*, Lucius Petrosidius, saved the sacred eagle standard of the legion by throwing it over the rampart into the fort. It is worth noting that Petrosidius is the only legionary below the rank of centurion to be named by Caesar in his *Commentaries*, and his name is Sabellian; his ancestors probably fought against the Romans.[7] Those legionaries who managed to get back into the fort and close the gates behind them fought until darkness fell, then despaired and took their own lives. This shock defeat spurred the remnants of the Nervii to attack another wintering legion. This time, however, the legion's commander, Quintus Cicero (brother of the famous orator), would not be tricked into leaving the security of the fort. The Nervii laid siege to the camp in Roman fashion but the legionaries, in particular the centurions, threw back the enemy assaults with contempt. It was during this siege that the rival centurions Pullo and Vorenus, now familiar to many because of the television series *Rome*, leapt from the ramparts in a bizarre competition to see how many warriors they could kill. (In the television series Pullo has been recast as a common legionary with Vorenus as his superior.)

There were two courageous centurions, Titus Pullo and Lucius Vorenus. They quarrelled continually about who came first [in seniority] and every year fiercely contested the most important posts. When the fighting by the ramparts was intense, Pullo said, 'Why hesitate, Vorenus? What chance of proving your bravery are you waiting for? This day will decide our contest.' So speaking, he left the defences and charged where the Gauls were thickest. Neither did Vorenus remain within the rampart, following Pullo for fear of what men would think. Then, at close range, Pullo threw his *pilum* at the enemy, skewering one Gaul who had run forward from the multitude. [But Pullo was soon] knocked senseless and the enemy sought to cover him with their shields and they all threw their missiles at him, giving him no chance of retreat. Pullo's shield was pierced and a javelin was lodged in his belt. Vorenus, his rival, ran to him and helped him out of trouble. Vorenus fought with his *gladius* at close quarters, killing one and drove the others back a little. But he pressed on too eagerly and fell into a hollow. He was surrounded in turn, but Pullo came to his aid. They killed several men and retired to the ramparts with the utmost glory. In the eagerness of their rivalry Fortune so handled them that, despite their hostility, each helped and saved the other, and it was impossible to decide which should be considered the braver man. (Caesar, *Gallic War*, 5.44)

The legion (its numeral is not reported) held out until Caesar arrived with a relieving force. The force of Nervii was destroyed. Revenge was then administered on the Eburones by devastating their territory in 53 and again in 51 BC, but Ambiorix escaped and was never captured. Caesar had won the first round, but the resentment of the Gauls still simmered and soon they were unified under the leadership of Vercingetorix, a charismatic nobleman of the Arverni.[8]

Caesar was performing duties as governor in Gallia Cisalpina (northern Italy) when he learned that the tribes of central Gaul had united under Vercingetorix. Caesar rushed northwards to reach his main concentration of legions in central Gaul. With typical daring he rode through rebel territory with a few bodyguards. He was aided by the wintry conditions: it was early 52 BC and the Gauls never expected him to travel through the snowdrifts or with so few men.

It is a mark of Vercingetorix's powers of leadership that he was able to unite the rival Gallic tribes so quickly and, in particular, that he persuaded them to embark on a scorched-earth policy to deny Caesar supplies. The Gauls devastated their lands and stockpiled their supplies at the fortress of Avaricum (modern Bourges); Caesar's army would either starve or fail before its ramparts. They were wrong. Come the spring Caesar stormed the stronghold, but only after a desperate fight, and the legionaries killed everyone within. Caesar's supply problem was temporarily solved but then northern Gaul rebelled. Caesar decided to split his army: his trusted legate Titus Labienus would confront the northern rebels, the Senones (descendants of those driven from Italy by Curius Dentatus) and the

Parisii (after whom Paris is named), while he pursued Vercingetorix who had hastily struck his camp, located close to Avaricum, when the town fell.[9]

The hill town of Gergovia (between Lyon and Clermont) was the capital of the Arverni and it was here that Vercingetorix determined to encourage Caesar to wear out his legionaries on its formidable slopes – the hill rises over 900 feet – and slaughter them as they reached its heavily defended ramparts.

The hill was too big to surround effectively with siege lines so Caesar planned to make his initial assault up the less steep southern slopes, and seize the hill bit by bit. He made camp to the south-east, but also constructed a double rampart leading to a much smaller camp on another hill facing the southern slopes of the plateau. Batches of legionaries were transferred between the ramparts to mass in the small camp unseen by the Gauls. Caesar then launched a diversionary attack from his main camp. Aeduan Gallic cavalry, still loyal to him, made a long circuitous ascent of the slopes of Gergovia. The attention of the rebels diverted, Caesar's legions erupted from the small camp. Their objective was not the town itself but the camps of the Gallic tribal levies before it. However, the legionaries did not stop there. Confident that they would be victorious as usual, they went on to assault the walls of Gergovia. Disaster ensued. Those few who made it on to the ramparts were surrounded and cut down; then the Romans panicked. The Aedui had completed their march and appeared on the Roman flank, but the legionaries took them for an attacking rebel column and fled down the slopes. Vercingetorix's warriors poured after them and killed 700 legionaries. The most notable Roman casualties, however, were the forty-six centurions who stood their ground and covered the flight of the legionaries. Caesar gives a dramatic account of a centurion of the Eighth Legion sacrificing himself in order to save his men:

> The centurion Lucius Fabius and those who had climbed the
> wall with him were surrounded, cut down, and hurled from the

wall. Marcus Petronius, a centurion of the same legion, had tried to break down a gate, but was overpowered by superior numbers and in a desperate situation. He had already suffered many wounds, and he cried to his *manipulares* [comrades] who had followed him: 'I cannot save myself with you, but I will at any rate provide for your lives. It was my desire for glory that brought you to this danger. When the chance is given you look after yourselves.' With this he burst into the midst of the enemy, and by killing two pushed the other Gauls back a little from the gate. When his men tried to help him he said, 'Your efforts to save me are in vain, for blood and strength are failing me. Get away while you still have a chance and make your way to the legion.' A moment later he fell fighting, and so saved his men. (Caesar, *Gallic War,* 7.50)

A total rout was averted when Caesar brought up the Tenth and Thirteenth Legions to block the Gallic pursuit, but he was still forced to retreat south towards Roman provincial territory. The Aedui, who had unwittingly triggered the Roman defeat at Gergovia, now went over to the rebels. Caesar's supply depot at Noviodunum, where the hard-won supplies from Avaricum were stored, was destroyed. Vercingetorix was elated and hoped to annihilate Caesar's dismayed army as it retreated. But then Caesar's famous luck returned. Labienus arrived victorious from the north, his confident legionaries greatly increasing the morale of Caesar's army.[10]

Vercingetorix now launched one of the greatest cavalry attacks in history on Caesar's marching army. Some 15,000 mounted warriors in three divisions bore down upon it, but Caesar was not daunted. In the early stages of the campaign he had recruited large numbers of German mercenary cavalry, of whom the Gauls had an almost irrational fear. Vercingetorix's final hammer blow made hardly a dent as Caesar formed the legions into a hollow square (*agmen quadratum*) with the baggage in the centre, then let loose the Germans who routed the Gallic cavalry. Thus Caesar's retreat halted abruptly. His army turned about and eagerly pursued Vercingetorix.[11]

The Arvernian leader fled to Alesia (to the north-west of Dijon), another great hill-town like Gergovia, and sent out for a Gallic relief army. Caesar quickly surrounded the hill with a double line of entrenchments. The inner circuit of almost eleven miles was to keep Vercingetorix trapped on Alesia, and the outer of fourteen miles to protect the legions from the approaching Gallic relief force, estimated by Caesar at 250,000 men. Vercingetorix's attempts to break out faltered as his warriors fell victim to the 'mine field' Caesar had placed facing Alesia:

> Trunks or very stout branches of trees were cut, and the tops trimmed and sharpened. Continuous trenches five feet deep were then dug and the stumps were sunk and fastened at the bottom so they could not be torn up. The boughs were left projecting. They were in rows of five and entangled together, and anyone who pushed into them must impale himself on the sharpest of stakes. In front of these, arranged like a figure of five, pits three feet deep were dug, sloping slightly inwards towards the bottom. In these tapering stakes as thick as a man's thigh, sharpened at the top and fire-hardened, were sunk so as to project no more than four fingers' breadth from the ground. The pits were covered with twigs and brushwood to conceal the trap. Eight rows of this kind were dug. In front of all these, logs a foot long, with iron hooks firmly attached, were buried in the ground and scattered at brief intervals. (Caesar, *Gallic War*, 7.73)

From the high vantage point of Alesia, Vercingetorix managed to co-ordinate his attacks on the inner Roman line with the assaults of the Gallic relief army on the outer. Fighting was particularly desperate at the north-west of the Roman lines: a huge deposit of human and horse bones and broken Gallic and Roman weaponry was excavated at Mont Réa in the 1860s and attests to the furious fighting there. However, the Gallic relief army was too unwieldy to be used in co-ordinated assaults along the complete length of Caesar's lines. Vercingetorix's attempts to break through the inner line were fought off and Roman cavalry, making a sortie from one of the camps of the outer line, fell on the rear of the Gallic attackers at Mont Réa. The huge Gallic relief army was utterly dismayed. Lacking leadership and direction, it dispersed overnight. Vercingetorix surrendered to Caesar the following day. The valiant patriot was not executed immediately; he had to wait six long years. He was paraded through the streets of Rome during Caesar's triumphal procession of 46 BC, and then strangled.[12]

CIVIL WAR: CAESAR VERSUS POMPEY

Resistance did not end at Alesia. Some northern rebels still had to be dealt with. The final battle was fought at the fortress of Uxellodunum in 51 BC. As a warning to other aspiring rebels, the hands were cut from the surviving defenders.[13] Yet still conflict loomed. Caesar's tenure in Gaul was coming to an end. His political enemies in Rome were plotting his ruin and lobbying for his impeachment on various charges, but if Caesar could continue to hold his provincial command until 48 BC he would have immunity from such an attack, then he could reassume the consulship – the re-election of such a popular general by ordinary citizens would be assured. The Senate, dominated by Caesar's political enemies and others who were simply jealous of his military success and wealth, would not acquiesce. Waiting with a single legion, the Thirteenth, on the frontier of his Gallic province with peninsular Italy, Caesar learned of the Senate's decision: he must lay down his command or be declared an enemy of the state. To defend his honour he decided on war.

On 10 January 49 BC the die was famously cast and he crossed the River Rubicon. Reinforcements in the form of the Twelfth and Eighth Legions, and twenty-two cohorts of recruits yet to be formed into legions soon followed and in little more than two months Caesar held all Italy. (Ten of the twenty-two cohorts were almost certainly the *Alaudae* –'the Larks' from the side plumes on their helmets – native Gauls recruited in 52 BC and trained and organised as a legion, but its members were perhaps not yet enrolled as Roman citizens and therefore not legally legionaries.)

The Senate had entrusted the defence of the state to Gnaeus Pompey. He was called Magnus – 'the Great' – for his many victories and conquests, especially in the Near East, and was the foremost general of his generation. By the late 60s BC he was the leading man in Rome but when his political schemes faltered he was forced to form, via the medium of Marcus Licinius Crassus, an alliance with Caesar. Caesar needed Pompey's influence and Crassus' wealth to win him the consulship in 59 BC. As consul Caesar would be a position to implement the policies of Pompey and Crassus, but their rival ambitions meant it was never an easy alliance and Caesar's subsequent success in Gaul made Pompey's resentment soar and prompted Crassus to embark on an disastrous invasion of Parthia.

Most of Pompey's levies in Italy deserted in the face of the Caesarian *Blitzkrieg*, but he was able to stall Caesar (now with six legions) in negotiations at Brundisium (Brindisi) as his few veteran troops boarded transports and set sail for Greece. Here Pompey rallied the Senatorial forces (really Pompeian, like Caesar's troops the loyalty of the legionaries was primarily to the charismatic general, not the state) and build an impressive army of legions and allied forces from Rome's eastern client kingdoms – the kingdoms he had subdued by force of arms in the 60s BC. Moreover, he had control of the Senatorial fleets. Caesar had to deal first with the Pompeian opposition in Spain (marching by the land route through south Gaul), before he could muster a fleet and follow Pompey across the Adriatic.[14]

It was not until early 48 BC that Caesar could muster sufficient transports to carry his army across the Adriatic. Even then he did not have enough to carry his full army. Caesar crossed successfully but many transports were sunk on the return journey by the Pompeian fleet, and Mark Antony was blockaded for a time at Brundisium with the rest of the army. Pompey marched from Greece into what is now Albania to halt Caesar's advance. He would not, however, force a pitched battle with Caesar's veterans. He was content to let Caesar's supplies dwindle and the morale of his army falter, but he was soon forced on to the defensive when Mark Antony managed to slip past the Pompeian blockade and join Caesar. Pompey retreated to a strong position on the coastal heights below the city of Dyrrhachium (Dürres in Albania). Caesar surged after him and, despite still being inferior in troop numbers, began to encircle Pompey's position with entrenchments. Pompey simply reacted by matching Caesar trench for trench and camp for camp, until Caesar's lines lengthened to an unwieldy seventeen miles. Pompey was well supplied from the sea while Caesar's troops slowly grew hungry, and Pompey kept on applying the pressure by mounting increasingly significant assaults on the thinly manned Caesarian lines. Caesar's legionaries held on but only just. As usual, the centurions formed the backbone of Caesarian resistance. At one fort particularly hard-pressed by Pompeian assaults:

> There was not one man who was not unwounded, and four centurions from a single cohort lost eyes. When they wanted to provide proof of their efforts and the extent of the danger they had faced, they counted out for Caesar about 30,000 arrows which had been loosed into the fort, and when he was presented with the shield of the centurion Scaeva 120 arrow holes were counted in it. Caesar gave Scaeva 200,000 sesterces for his services to him and declared that he was promoting him from centurion in the eighth cohort to leading centurion of the legion. It was agreed that it was largely due to his efforts that the fort was saved. Afterwards Caesar generously rewarded Scaeva's cohort with double pay, grain, clothing and rations, and with military decorations. (Caesar, *Civil War*, 3.53)

Later Roman sources claim that Scaeva's helmet was shattered in the fighting and at one point he used a rock to crush the skull of a

Pompeian legionary (*see below*). More certainly he became one of Caesar's favourites and was noted by Cicero as a dangerous man. He later served Caesar's heir, Octavian, at the siege of Perusia (41 BC). But even the valour of Scaeva could not hold back Pompey indefinitely.

Using one of his favourite tactics, Pompey mounted a surprise night attack, sending his legionaries by boat to land a little south of Caesar's lines, from where they made an assault on the unfinished entrenchments. Pompey made a simultaneous assault on the inside of the line. For a time, as at Alesia, Caesar's troops held their own and the fighting raged well into the morning, but they faced a master soldier who threw his reserves into action at the critical point. Part of Caesar's defences collapsed and panic flared through the legionaries in that sector. In their rush to escape the confines of the trenches they trampled the centurions who attempted to stem the flight. Most of the thirty-two Caesarian centurions killed that day were victims of this panic. The legionaries threw away their standards – the ultimate disgrace – and would not halt even when Caesar himself appeared. The Pompeians captured many of the fugitives. 'They were asked in the most insulting fashion,' laments Caesar, 'if it was usual for veteran soldiers to run away, and publicly executed.'

While Pompey savoured his victory, Caesar decided to cut his losses and abandon the entrenchments: at least 960 legionaries had died that day and his supply situation was critical. He gathered his army together and encouraged it with a speech. Notably, he reminded the legionaries of the defeat at Gergovia. Was it not the prelude to a great victory, he asked? Typically, the centurions demanded to be led back into battle, but Caesar knew that the legionaries were too demoralised. He marched the army so rapidly into the interior that Pompey quickly gave up pursuit. On reaching Thessaly in northern Greece Caesar allowed his troops to sack the town of Gomphi, which had declared for Pompey. The legionaries vented their rage on the unfortunate citizens and the plunder and foodstuffs seized raised their spirits no end. Caesar then marched to the plain of Pharsalus where he made camp and awaited Pompey.[15]

By now the senators in Pompey's army believed victory was certain, but their general had become indecisive. He camped opposite Caesar but day after day refused the offer of battle. Finally, when Caesar was about to strike camp and march on, Pompey arrayed his army for battle. He did not, however, place hopes of victory in his eleven legions, reinforced by tested veterans whom he had personally recalled to service. Caesar only had eight legions, all greatly under strength, but Pompey decided to deploy his legions in a static line to halt the running charge of the Caesarians. Then he would let loose his massive force of cavalry on their exposed right flank. Caesar immediately realised Pompey's intentions and detached cohorts from his third battle line. When the Pompeian cavalry attacked it easily dislodged the thin screen of Caesarian cavalry and charged at the exposed right flank, but then Caesar sent in his reserve cohorts at the run at the unsuspecting cavalry. Those cavalrymen who were unengaged fled, while the others, trapped between Caesar's reserve and the right flank of his army, were massacred. Pompey's strategy was then turned on him and the Caesarian right rolled up the exposed left flank of his army. Pompey fled the battlefield and eventually took ship for Ptolemaic Egypt where he hoped to regroup, but before reaching land he was assassinated by a former centurion in the service of the Ptolemies. The killer, Lucius Septimius, had served under Pompey during the campaign to clear the Mediterranean of pirates in 67 BC. Like Antigonus on learning of the death of Pyrrhus, Caesar wept when Pompey's severed head and signet ring were presented to him.[16]

Caesar is often criticised by modern historians and soldiers for relying too much on his luck, yet for Caesar Fortune was the fundamental element in war. 'He could so easily have suffered total defeat!' they cry. But he did not. During the long war in Gaul Caesar had forged an army like no other. It was entirely loyal to him. When Caesar considered lifting the siege of Avaricum because the legionaries were on starvation rations, they declared it would be dishonourable to give up what they had started; they had never failed him before. When Caesar embarked on civil war they followed simply to defend his dignity, though a timely increase in pay may also have helped. Caesar boasted that his legionaries would pull down the heavens if he asked it of them, and when they occasionally suffered defeat, they were so ashamed that they lusted for revenge. Gergovia and Dyrrhachium were Caesar's only defeats. Both were relatively minor and each time he was able to withdraw before defeat turned into rout and regroup his forces. He followed up both setbacks with stunning victories. At Alesia he defeated two armies at once. At Pharsalus he routed a huge Roman army led by one of the greatest soldiers of the age. Setbacks only stimulated Caesar and his men, especially the proud centurions, to greater triumphs.[17]

CAESAR'S CENTURIONS

When soldiers of one of Caesar's legions fled in the face of a determined Pompeian assault on their earth and timber fort at Dyrrhachium, the centurion Scaeva single-handedly defended the gate. Initially holding the gate, then fighting on the slope of the rampart, Scaeva's helmet was shattered by repeated blows and the jagged metal cut his brow; an arrow blinded him in the left eye and his face was awash with blood. He was wounded in all his limbs by a hail of javelins and arrows and his shield was pierced 120 times. Yet Scaeva turned on his opponents, crushing one man's skull with a rock and cutting the hand off another with his sword. In fact, he forced his way into the ranks of the enemy legionaries, hacking and stabbing with berserk rage until his sword was blunt. His opponents fell back, content to let him collapse from loss of blood. Having fallen to his knees, Scaeva called weakly to his opponents, apparently surrendering himself, but when two soldiers came forward to lift him from the ground Scaeva suddenly stabbed one in the throat and, as the second soldier panicked, Scaeva reared up and hacked off his arm at the shoulder. Only then did some of Scaeva's legionaries, who had paused in their flight to watch his defiant stand, come forward to aid their centurion. Their opponents did not attack but stood in awed dismay as Scaeva was carried from the field and the gate of the fort was again barred. Scaeva was the epitome of what made the Romans successful in war: brutal and unrelenting and not knowing when to admit defeat. Caesar relied upon this sort of bravery and rewarded it well. As we saw above, Scaeva was promoted from the eighth cohort to the *primi ordines* (centurions of the first cohort, senior to those in cohorts II–X).[18]

Caesar and his continuators (especially the anonymous authors of the *African War* and the *Spanish War*, who were perhaps themselves centurions) viewed centurions as supplying the crucial factor on which battles hinged. These men were models of *virtus* and their actions bolstered the *animus* (spirit) of the legionaries. Caesar's dramatic description of the battle against the Nervii on the Sabis (57 BC) reaches its initial climax when Sextius Baculus, *primus pilus* of the Twelfth Legion, collapses on account of his many wounds. Baculus' collapse marks Caesar's entry into the fray, taking the shield from a rear ranker, he goes to the front, encourages the men and they resume the fight with vigour, but it is because of Baculus' refusal to fall back and hold his post whatever may come,[19] that the otherwise leaderless legionaries – most of the centurions and standard-bearers are dead or seriously wounded – do not panic and run, but hold their post long enough for Caesar to take charge.

Baculus reappears in other episodes of crisis. When Sulpicius Galba's camp at Octodurus was on the point of being stormed by the Seduni and Veragri (56 BC), it was Baculus who came forward and suggested to the legate that the only hope for the Twelfth Legion, under-strength because only eight of its ten cohorts were present, was to make a sortie and to tackle the enemy on open ground before the continual assaults completely exhausted the legionaries. The camp was too big for the cohorts, which had been fighting continually for six hours, to defend effectively. Every man had to stay at his post on the ramparts and there were no reserves to relieve them. The Gauls, on the other hand, apparently 30,000 in number, had ample warriors to make repeated assaults with fresh men. Supported by the experienced military tribune Volusenus Quadratus, Galba acted on Baculus' suggestion and ordered the men to fall back gradually from the ramparts to the four gates. Then, 'with their only hope of safety in *virtus'* (this is typically Caesarian, the legionary functions best when the danger is greatest and the heroic centurion provides the stimulus for him to act), they stormed out of the gates, burst through the unsuspecting Gauls who were bunched up against the ramparts, turned to surround them and killed more than 10,000.

The final appearance of Baculus is his most heroic. When the Germanic Sugambri attacked the starving Roman garrison at Aduatuca (the new Fourteenth Legion which replaced that destroyed by the Eburones), Baculus was ill and had not eaten for five days, but when the cohort on guard duty was about to break he emerged from his tent and took the situation in hand at the point of greatest danger:

> He took weapons from the nearest men and stationed himself in the gate. He was followed by all the centurions of the cohort on guard, and together for a short time they bore the brunt of the battle. Sextius collapsed after receiving several severe wounds and with difficulty he was dragged by hand to hand to safety. In the respite thus given the common soldiers found the strength to venture back to their posts on the defences. (Caesar, *Gallic War*, 6.38)

We do not know if Baculus survived his wounds.[20]

On occasions in Caesar's *Commentaries* it is the centurion, not the tribune or legate, who acts decisively or is the primary influence on the decisions made by a commander that leads to victory. The legate disregarded the centurion at his peril, for example when Titurius Sabinus foolishly chose to ignore the advice of his senior centurions and led his cohorts to destruction at the hands of Ambiorix's Eburones (54 BC). Even the desperate bravery of the former *primus pilus* Titus Balventius and the senior centurion Quintus Lucanius, who died trying to save his son, could not save the beleaguered army. However, Caesar presents their courage as a stimulus for the heroic leadership of the other legate, Aurunculeius Cotta, Sabinus' junior colleague. Like the centurions, Cotta died fighting. Sabinus, a previously valiant commander, was ignominiously killed as he attempted to surrender to Ambiorix. His disgrace was compounded because the senior centurions in his party were also slaughtered. Honour-bound to follow their commander, they were denied the chance to die gloriously in battle. Sabinus of course hoped to save the lives of his men, but the very notion of surrender was despised by most Romans.[21]

Like Baculus at the battle of the Sabis, the former *primus pilus* Crastinus is the only soldier named in Caesar's account of Pharsalus. With 120 picked men from his former *manipulares* (his old comrades in the Tenth Legion), he called to Caesar from his position of honour on the right wing: 'I will do things today, *imperator*, that you will thank me for, whether I live or die.' With that he charged forward with his men, opening the battle, and cleaving deep into the ranks of the Pompeian legionaries. Crastinus' action does more than set the battle in motion: it serves to emphasise the justice of Caesar's cause despite the fact that he is fighting fellow Romans. Such a battle actually posed a serious dilemma to men like Crastinus. When Baculus fought Gauls and Germans he met warrior opponents of unsullied and great *virtus*, but Crastinus could not claim entirely legitimate glory for slaying his fellow-citizens.[22] The later Roman poet Lucan was a staunch anti-Caesarian and scathing about Crastinus' role in the battle:

> Heaven punish Crastinus, and not with death alone . . . the
> *pilum* brandished in his hand began the battle and first stained
> Pharsalus with Roman blood. (Lucan, *Civil War*, 7.471–472)

Crastinus was prepared to shed Roman blood in order to maintain the reputation and dignity of Caesar, and thereby protect the reputation he had won under the auspices of Caesar. Honour would not allow the centurion to do otherwise. The Crastinus episode was not entirely spontaneous but to some extent staged, a kind of volunteer forlorn hope intended to create a gap in the strong left wing of Pompey's line which was composed of hardened veterans and *evocati*, yet that does not detract from the value of Crastinus' demonstration. Crastinus, having charged with his men at the run and cut down the leading ranks of the enemy, was finally killed when a Pompeian legionary thrust a *gladius* full into his mouth with such force that the point of the blade emerged at the back of his neck. Presumably most of Crastinus' volunteers were killed along-side him. The fact that Crastinus (and his *manipulares*) was prepared to die for a point of honour reinforces the picture of the centurion as a heroic martyr. And Caesar was grateful. He believed victory stemmed directly from Crastinus' courage, and when the centurion's body was finally discovered among the corpses and debris of battle, Caesar honoured him with *dona militaria* (such a posthumous grant of military decorations was highly unusual), and a hero's tomb on the battlefield.

As well as being honourable in the extreme and utterly devoted to Caesar, Crastinus may seem worryingly unhinged to the modern reader (compare Lucan and Florus who spoke of Crastinus' 'mad rage', *rabies* from which derives rabid), but perhaps the charge of Crastinus and his men is best viewed as an act of *devotio*, made with the same intention as the devotions of the Decii at the Veseris and Sentinum – to send the legions of the enemy to the gods of the Underworld.[23]

Caesar had a talent for getting the best out of his centurions. He inspired them with his charisma and confidence, powers of endurance, tactical genius and generosity. A deep understanding of, and belief in, Roman concepts of courage, reputation and honour, and their effect on the outcome of battles further strengthened his authority. When his inexperienced tribunes (whom he admits were essentially hangers-on hopeful for plunder and prestige when they returned to Rome) panicked at the prospect of being ambushed by the German king Ariovistus, their alarm ultimately infected even the veteran legionaries and centurions. Caesar was disgusted and ordered all the centurions to parade before him. 'Why have you despaired of your *virtus*?' he asked them contemptuously. He shamed them further by declaring that his favourite *legio X* would act as his bodyguard (*see below*), and if necessary he would confront the Germans with it alone: 'He had no doubts about its loyalty.' This rankled so greatly that the senior centurions of the other legions needed little or no convincing from their men to go and make amends with Caesar.

Dio presents the episode as a serious mutiny, and scholars have questioned Caesar's famous method of shaming soldiers back to obedience, especially the episode in 47 BC when mutinous veteran legionaries were shocked to be addressed as *Quirites*, that is civilians rather than *milites* (soldiers). Yet we have seen how easily Appius Claudius Caecus shamed aristocratic senators when they contemplated coming to terms with Pyrrhus in 280 BC. When Caesar called his men *Quirites*, it may not have had the effect of making the troops abandon their mutiny immediately, but as *Romans* and especially as *Roman soldiers* it certainly shamed the legionaries and made them think hard about their prized honour. Thus the fury with which the legions fought the Germans in the battle against Ariovistus – some soldiers literally threw themselves at the enemy – was stimulated by their need to erase the shame of their recent episode of cowardice and restore their reputation for *virtus*. The centurions would have been at the forefront.[24]

Shame was a powerful motivator in the Roman world. The heroic warrior culture of the Romans demanded that soldiers attempt to duplicate or exceed the glories of the past, and especially the brave deeds of their own fathers (again, recall Caecus' speech); it was shameful to do otherwise. The thoughts of the future Emperor Vespasian when he was on the verge of being cut-off in Gamala (AD 67) surely echo those of the Caesarian centurion: it was dishonourable to turn and flee; he must be mindful of the many hardships he had endured and overcome and not stain his reputation for valour. Thus fear of shame, coupled with hunger for fame and glory, led to valour. Polybius emphasised that 'the Roman state produces men who will do anything to win a reputation for courage.' And also anything to preserve it. When caught on open ground in 53 BC a number of centurions, who had been promoted to more senior positions by Caesar on account of their courage, chose to fight the Sugambri and die rather than run for the safety of their camp. Caesar states with admiration that they did not wish to sully their reputations, but their stand also had a selfless quality because it protected their centuries from being cut down by the Sugambric cavalry as they fled towards the camp. As we saw above, more centurions sacrificed themselves at Gergovia in 52 BC and at Munda in 45 BC.[25]

The unnamed author of the *African War* was one of Caesar's junior officers, perhaps a centurion, and recalled with pride what was in effect the martyrdom of a loyal centurion of the Fourteenth Legion, whose transport ship had been intercepted by the Pompeians (47–46 BC). When asked by Metellus Scipio, the malicious Pompeian general, to transfer his allegiance the defiant centurion replied:

> For your great kindness, Scipio – I refrain from calling you *imperator* – I thank you, so far as you promise me, by rights a prisoner of war, my life and safety; and maybe now I should avail myself of that kind offer, but for the utterly iniquitous condition attached to it. Am I to range myself in armed opposition to Caesar, my *imperator*, under whom I have held my command, and against his army, to sustain the victorious reputation for which I have fought for thirty-six years. No, I am not likely to do that, and I strongly advise you to give up the attempt. For you now have the chance of appreciating – if you have not previously found it sufficiently by experience – whose troops that you are fighting. Choose from your men

one cohort, the one you regard as your most reliable, and array it over here against me: I for my part will take no more than ten men from among my fellow soldiers whom you now hold in your power. Then from our prowess you will realise what you should expect from your own forces. (Anonymous, *African War*, 45)

Scipio had the man executed on the spot and his comrades were tortured to death. Here again we might wonder if the centurion hoped to perform a *devotio* by leading a small band against Scipio's cohort.[26]

OCTAVIAN, ANTONY AND THEIR PRAETORIANS

Caesar put his faith in legions and legionary centurions. So too did his successors Octavian and Mark Antony, but they also had recourse to a new form of elite unit, the praetorian cohort.

PISTORIA, 62 BC

Lucius Sergius Catiline had two under-strength legions, and three-quarters of the men – recruited from peasants, herdsmen and the dispossessed – were equipped only with javelins and sharpened stakes. The real strength of his small army lay in 2,000 or so fully armed old centurions and legionary veterans known as the Sullani.[27]

These men had fought for Cornelius Sulla in the civil wars of 88 and 83–82 BC, marching with him on Rome itself and driving the Marians from the city. Between the civil wars they followed Sulla to Greece and Asia Minor, routing the great phalanxes of Mithridates of Pontus at Chaeronea and Orchomenus, and retaking Athens and the Piraeus by storm (87–86 BC). The Pontic general who opposed them later said that the legionaries had 'fought like maniacs'. Yet they were not without humour. When an ineffectual charge by Pontic chariots was easily beaten off at Chaeronea (86 BC), 'the legionaries laughed and clapped for more, as if they were attending a chariot race in the Circus at Rome,' says Plutarch. It was during

Sulla's second civil war that the legionaries first met Catiline. He served for a time as one of Sulla's executioners, hunting down those declared public enemies, and personally torturing and decapitating his own brother-in-law at Sulla's request. Yet, for all his cruelty, Catiline was also a charismatic and capable soldier and acknowledged an expert in military affairs by his enemies.[28]

Catiline's crowning military achievement was the capture of Aesernia. In 91 BC the Italian Allies had rebelled, demanding that they be given Roman citizenship and a full share in the empire they helped to conquer. It took three years to quell the revolt, called the Social or Italian War, and Catiline saw his first military service during it at the siege of Asculum (in Picenum, not the site of the battle with Pyrrhus in Apulia), but Aesernia, capital of the insurgents, was never recaptured. In 80 BC Catiline was sent by Sulla to retake the defiant fortress city. He encircled it with siege works and it finally fell.[29]

Sulla rewarded his loyal legionaries with rich plunder. Some senior centurions even became senators, but honourable discharge and lands to farm was the norm at the completion of service. However, few of the Sullani were cut out to be farmers. They squandered their wealth and antagonised the peasants on whose confiscated land they had been settled. Many abandoned their farms and re-enlisted in the legions. By 63 BC these hard and embittered men lusted for a return to the glory days and Gaius Manlius, a former centurion, easily persuaded some 2,000 of the surviving veterans to join the revolt of Catiline. To ensure the loyalty of his chief conspirators, Catiline forced them swear an oath to succeed or die. The oath was washed down with cups of human blood mixed with wine; the implication of this is that Catiline deliberately sacrificed a man to ensure the success of his plot.[30]

Sulla the dictator died in 78 BC. The stars of his senior lieutenants Pompey and Crassus soared as they stepped into the power vacuum, but Catiline's subsequent military and political career was erratic and dogged by controversy. A scion of the ancient and patrician

Sergii clan (he was the great-grandson of iron-fisted Sergius Silus), Catiline craved election to the consulship. From this almost regal office a man could direct the fortunes of Rome for a year. There were two consuls, of course, one consul was supposed to restrain the ambitions of the other, but a man like Catiline would have no trouble cowing a colleague. He was barred from standing for the consulship in 65 and 64 BC because of charges of corruption during his governorship of the province of Africa (67–66 BC).

In 63 BC Catiline finally stood for election but, despite championing the poor and Sulla's veterans, was defeated at the polls by Marcus Tullius Cicero. It enraged the aristocratic Catiline to be beaten by a *novus homo* like Cicero from outside the Roman nobility. It was then that Catiline plotted to assassinate the new consuls and seize Rome by force. Manlius and other lieutenants, quickly raised a small army, building it on the cadre of the Sullani, but the planned coup was exposed and Catiline was forced to retreat towards Gaul.

The route of his army was blocked by a powerful consular army near Pistoria in Etruria in early January 62 BC. The senatorial force was commanded by the praetor Marcus Petreius. He was the son of a centurion and a veteran of thirty years' service. His legions were composed mainly of picked veteran troops; he had numerous reserves and even an elite praetorian cohort to call upon. (The cohort belonged to the other consul, Antonius Hybrida, but he was an old compatriot of Catiline's and used his gout as an excuse to avoid the battle.) Yet Catiline and his few Sullani were not easily intimidated. They formed up, eight cohorts in close order, in a valley where their small numbers would not be such a disadvantage and they could not be outflanked. The rest of the army was held in reserve, while Catiline led a small mobile force of skirmishers. The battle that ensued became famous for the stubborn resistance of the Sullani and the decisive intervention of the praetorian cohort.[31] Gaius Sallust, legionary commander of Julius Caesar and historian, takes up the tale:

Petreius gave the signal with the trumpet and ordered his cohorts to advance slowly. Catiline's army followed this example. When the soldiers reached a point where battle could be joined by the skirmishers, they charged at each other with loud war cries, then threw their *pila* and took to the sword. Petreius' veterans, remembering their old-time prowess, advanced bravely to close quarters; the enemy, no less courageous, stood their ground and there was a tremendous struggle. Meanwhile Catiline, with his light-armed troops, was busy in the van. He aided those who were hard pressed, ordered fresh troops to replace the wounded, and had an eye to everything. At the same time he fought hard himself, often striking down the enemy, and so performing both the duties of a valiant soldier and a skilful general. (Sallust, *The War with Catiline*, 60.1–4)

Catiline's heroic leadership (his ability to fight while at the same time directing his troops recalls the description of Pyrrhus at Heraclea) and the stubborn defiance of his small army took Petreius by surprise. He had expected Catiline to make a desperate last stand but the rebel was coming close to snatching victory. Petreius summoned his praetorian cohort from the reserve, recalled the legionary cohorts from the fighting and formed a new battle line: the praetorians formed the centre, flanked by the legionaries. The praetorians were to charge the centre of Catiline's army while the legionary cohorts simultaneously assaulted its left and right wings. With Petreius leading them, the praetorians collided with the centre of Catiline's battle line and the Sullani were finally pushed back. Manlius and Catiline's other commanders were cut down in the co-ordinated assaults by Petreius' legionaries at the wings. With the centre of its battle line shattered, Catiline's army finally succumbed to the greater numbers of the enemy. The recruits to the rear scattered into the hills but the Sullani stood their ground until they were all cut down. 'A few in the centre,' wrote Sallust, 'whom the praetorian cohort had scattered, lay a little apart from the rest, but their wounds were all to the front.' Unlike the Linen Legion at Aquilonia, these desperate warriors stood their ground to the very end. Seeing his army collapse Catiline charged into the midst of Petreius' troops. His body was found 'far in advance of his men amid a heap of slain foemen'. Catiline's maddened charge to the death is in fact evocative of a *devotus*. Perhaps it was a conscious act of *devotio* and maybe even successful, for his principal enemies, Cicero and Petreius, eventually met grim ends. Cicero was proscribed (declared a public enemy) on the order of Mark Antony; the executioner sent to decapitate Cicero was an officer he had once defended in court against a charge of patricide (43 BC). The demise of Petreius is related in the next chapter.[32]

WHAT WAS A PRAETORIAN COHORT?

When Catiline's conspiracy was exposed, Cicero derided the rebel's principal associates as 'a praetorian cohort of pimps'. Catiline was styling himself as an *imperator* (general) and as such would normally be accompanied by a *cohors praetoria* (staff and companions, hence the term *cohors amicorum*, 'cohort of friends', was sometimes used). The praetorian cohort took its name from the *praetorium*, the general's headquarters tent. Catiline, Cicero and Pompey, who served together on the staff of Pompeius Strabo at the siege of Ausculum (90–89 BC), might be described as forming Strabo's praetorian cohort, but a general's bodyguards could also be called a praetorian cohort. In some praetorian cohorts the functions of a staff and bodyguard may have been combined, but while governor of Cilicia in Asia Minor (52 BC), Cicero had two distinct praetorian cohorts: his headquarters staff, and an elite fighting unit, like that of Petreius at Pistoria, which garrisoned the city of Epiphanaea. Cicero reports with some pride that, despite being outnumbered, the cohort with the support of some *turmae* of cavalry 'cut to pieces' an invading force of Parthian and Arabian cavalry. However, it was not the norm for all commanders to have a praetorian cohort of this sort. Most generals maintained corps of guardsmen but did not form them into praetorian cohorts. When Julius Caesar parleyed with the German king Ariovistus (58 BC), he selected the Tenth Legion to act as his praetorian cohort – clearly in the capacity of a guard. Because Caesar mounted the legionaries on horses, the soldiers joked that they were both a praetorian cohort and *equites*, the aristocratic class of Roman 'knights' who in earlier times had supplied the cavalry arm of the legions. The legion proudly recalled this episode by adopting the title *Equestris* but not *Praetoria*.[33]

Fighting praetorian cohorts, distinct from the similarly titled groups of staff officers, were essentially *ad hoc* units, recruited at the start of a campaign. The bodyguards of Scipio Africanus in the war with Hannibal and Scipio Aemilianus at Numantia were of this type and are usually cited as the precursors of the praetorian cohorts of the first century BC. The general would select the most experienced soldiers from his legions, men of the best physique, highly decorated and often *evocati*. As praetorians they could expect twice as much pay as ordinary legionaries received and doubtless a proportionately greater share of booty, exemption from mundane duties and probably better chances of promotion. Although they would perform actual and ceremonial guard duties at the *praetorium* and when the army was on the march, praetorians were expected to do more in battle than merely form a protective screen around the general. As Petreius' use of the praetorian cohort at Pistoria demonstrates, praetorians were employed as shock troops.[34]

None of the great Roman generals of the late Republic, not Marius, Sulla or Pompey, employed praetorian cohorts. As we have seen, Caesar was well aware of the guard function of a praetorian cohort, and on one occasion used his favourite legion to fulfil that role, but he never enrolled a formal praetorian cohort from the Tenth or his other legions. It was not until the civil war following Caesar's assassination that praetorian cohorts became a standard feature of Roman armies. (Caesar reports that when Marcus Petreius fought against him in Spain in 49 BC, Petreius had a 'praetorian cohort of shield men'. These shield men were native Spaniards and not Roman citizens and it is questionable if Petreius actually called this bodyguard unit a praetorian cohort.[35])

PRAETORIAN VERSUS PRAETORIAN

Soon after Caesar's murder (15 March 44 BC) Mark Antony, his chief lieutenant, and Octavian, his adopted son and heir, recruited 'bodyguards' from Caesar's legionary veteran colonies across Italy. These units comprised thousands of men and resembled small armies, organised in classic Roman fashion and officered by tribunes and centurions. However, these corps of 'bodyguards' were not praetorian cohorts. Octavian used his veteran legionaries as cadres for the restoration of the famous legions with which Caesar had conquered Gaul and triumphed in the civil war of 49–45 BC.

Antony can be presumed to have done the same with his 6,000-strong bodyguard; he was competing with Octavian to be viewed as Caesar's true heir and the easiest way to do that was to have the backing of Caesar's legions. It was not until October 44 BC that Antony recruited a praetorian cohort from legions recently transferred back to Italy from Macedonia. The size of this cohort is unknown. In the battle in the marsh and scrubland at Forum Gallorum (April 43 BC), Antony's cohort was joined by the praetorian cohort of his ally, the proconsul Marcus Lepidus, but commanded by Junius Silanus, and together they fought Octavian's single cohort of praetorians until it was destroyed.[36] It was a grim fight and left a profound impression on the young legionary recruits who witnessed it:

> Being veterans they raised no war cry, since they could not
> expect to terrify each other, nor did they utter a sound during
> the fighting, either as victors or vanquished. As there could
> be neither flanking movements nor charges amid the marshes
> and ditches, they met together in close order, and since

neither could dislodge the other they locked together with their swords as if in a wrestling match. No blow missed its mark. There were wounds and slaughter but no cries, only groans, and when one fell he was immediately carried away and another took his place. They needed neither admonition nor encouragement, since experience made each man his own general. When they were overcome by fatigue, they drew apart for a brief time to recover, as if they were involved in training exercises, and then grappled with each other again. (Appian, *Civil Wars*, 3.68)

However, the praetorian cohort of the consul Aulus Hirtius, formerly a commander of Julius Caesar and under whom Octavian ostensibly served, gave a fine account of itself. Reinforced by two cohorts of Octavian's *legio Martia* ('Legion of Mars'), the praetorians held back Antony's complete Second Legion and only retreated when Antony's cavalry threatened to surround them. The praetorians and legionaries made it back to camp with only slight casualties.

Antony and Octavian were reconciled not long after the fight at Forum Gallorum and the subsequent battle at Mutina, in which Hirtius was killed. As well as dividing the Roman world between themselves, they belatedly determined to punish Brutus and Cassius, the principal murderers of Caesar. Two engagements were fought against the 'Liberators' at Philippi in Greece in 42 BC. (Octavian, generally called Caesar on account of his adoption, was ill throughout the campaign. However, Julius Caesar was deified by the Senate on 1 January 42 BC, so as well as the magic of his new name, Octavian was regarded as the son of a god, and his proud legionaries were instrumental in the defeat of Brutus.)

The first battle was a draw, but Antony's victory in the second engagement was total. His praetorians, probably now organised in several cohorts, can be presumed to have fought in both battles and to have sustained heavy losses. After the battle 8,000 time-served legionaries volunteered to re-enlist and 4,000 of them were gladly accepted by Antony into his praetorian cohorts. The other 4,000 replaced Octavian's praetorian cohort. Octavian had enrolled a new cohort of 2,000 men after Forum Gallorum, but it did not reach the fight at Philippi. The transports of the praetorians and the doughty *legio Martia* were attacked and sunk by Brutus' navy as they crossed the Adriatic.[37]

Octavian's new praetorians served him admirably at the siege of Perusia (winter 41–40 BC), preventing the breakout of Lucius Antonius' forces. Octavian's war with Mark Antony's brother almost brought the heavyweights to blows again, but their praetorians were instrumental in arranging reconciliation between the two. Antony took his praetorians east. Besotted with Cleopatra, the Ptolemaic queen of Egypt and former lover of Caesar, he dallied in his new Egyptian power base for several years before embarking on the long-delayed invasion of Parthia.[38]

THE PARTHIAN WAR AND ACTIUM

When he was murdered, Caesar was about to embark on an invasion of the great Parthian Empire, which dominated the Middle East; the 'Macedonian' legions from which Antony and Octavian raised their praetorian cohorts had been earmarked for the campaign. In 53 BC Crassus, jealous of Caesar's victories in Gaul, had led a Roman army into Parthia hoping to emulate the successes of Alexander the Great, but Crassus' poor generalship allowed a Parthian army of cataphracts (heavily armoured cavalry) and horse archers to surround his legions at Carrhae. The Roman army was mauled and there followed an ignominious retreat in which the army dissolved. Only Cassius Longinus (the murderer of Caesar) emerged from the debacle with credit: he led a small force back to Syria in good order, and oversaw the successful defence of the Roman province from the Parthian counter-invasion. It was not until 36 BC that Antony roused himself to exact revenge on Parthia. His invasion force included at least three praetorian cohorts, perhaps new formations, again selected from the best veteran legionaries.

The Parthian War was a disaster. Antony successfully invaded Media, at the heart of the Parthian empire, via Armenia, but he foolishly divided his forces and the two legions guarding his siege train and food wagons were surrounded and destroyed by the complete Parthian field army. Without his siege machinery and with few supplies, Antony was forced to retreat and he was harried every step of the way by Parthian arrows. He lost at least 22,000 of his veteran Italian legionaries, but many of these casualties resulted from starvation and exposure on the Armenian highlands. When the Parthians did occasionally break from their hit-and-run tactics and fight a formal battle, the Romans had the better of close combat. In one battle there was the novel spectacle of legionaries and the praetorian infantry bellowing war cries and clashing their weapons as they pursued terrified Parthian cavalry! But the soldiers soon discovered that this was an empty victory:

> Antony pursued the Parthians hard because he had high hopes of ending the whole war, more or less, with that one battle. But after the infantry had given chase for 50 *stades* [c. 6 miles], and the cavalry for 150 *stades*, they counted the enemy dead and captives and found only 30 prisoners and 80 corpses. This made everyone both puzzled and depressed. On reflection it seemed a grim prospect if in victory they should kill so few of the enemy, but in defeat they should lose as many as they did in the battle over the transport wagons.
> (Plutarch, *Antony*, 39.5)

Octavian revelled in Antony's defeat. He refused to supply recruits from Italy to replenish Antony's legions, but was persuaded by his sister Octavia to send Antony a token number of soldiers. Octavia had married Antony in 40 BC, a gesture intended to seal the reconciliation of the warring heirs of Caesar, but Antony was already besotted with Cleopatra (she bore him twins that year) and left Octavia in Italy. Somewhat surprisingly, she remained fiercely loyal to him and in 37 BC arranged for the transfer of 1,000 praetorians. In 35 BC Octavia travelled east with 2,000 more praetorians, equipped with the best weapons and armour, and a great amount of military matériel as well. When she reached Athens she was greeted by a cold missive from Antony instructing her to send the troops and supplies on but for her to return to Italy. This insult played right into the hands of Octavian, whose propaganda now presented Antony as a faithless adulterer and the tool of Cleopatra, which, to a certain extent, he was. By early 32 BC (by which time Antony had divorced Octavia) Octavian had forced Antony's most influential senatorial supporters from Rome, then he declared war, not on Roman Antony but foreign Cleopatra, whose anti-Roman policies gave Octavian the excuse he needed; she aimed at the restoration of Ptolemaic power in the Near East. Antony was placed in an impossible position. He supported Cleopatra, which allowed Octavian to denigrate him as a traitor and an enemy of Rome.[39]

The war was played out in north-western Greece, Antony's most westerly territory, and tantalisingly close to the great prize of Italy and Rome. Antony marshalled twenty-three legions, nineteen to serve on land, and four to man his war fleet (*legiones classicae*). Antony issued a special series of silver coins to pay his army. The coins identify each legion by numeral and title, for example *legio XII Antiqua*, Caesar's 'ancient' Twelfth Legion – the legion of the mighty Baculus. The coins also reveal that Antony had at least two praetorian cohorts and a *cohors speculatorum* ('cohort of scouts'), the latter providing close protection to Antony and carrying out reconnaissance duties. It perhaps also carried out his dirty work: later *speculatores* were also employed as spies and executioners. The *speculatores* were subsequently integrated into the Imperial praetorian cohorts. Octavian had a total of twenty-four legions with which to confront Antony but a smaller fleet, *c.* 400 ships to Antony's 500, but it was far superior having emerged victorious in the naval campaign against Sextus Pompeius. Vipsanius Agrippa, Octavian's friend since childhood and an accomplished admiral, commanded the fleet. As well as eight legions, Octavian gave

Agrippa five praetorian cohorts to serve as marines. It is probable that Octavian had more praetorians with him on land.

Agrippa negated Antony's superior number of ships by bottling up part of his fleet at the promontory of Actium in the mouth of the Gulf of Ambracia, and cut his supply lines to Egypt. Antony has been criticised for not using his fleet to attack Octavian's transports as they crossed the Adriatic and for not engaging Agrippa's smaller fleet until it was too late, but it seems that Antony desired a decisive victory over Octavian on land, a pitched battle like Philippi. Octavian moved his army south on learning of Agrippa's success and established a camp on the opposite side of the Gulf. This was what Antony wanted. He bridged the Gulf with boats, advanced on Octavian's camp, and sent a large cavalry force to outflank the camp and so cut it off, but the cavalry were defeated. Antony personally led the next attempt but he was again fought off and some 2,000 of his auxiliary cavalry deserted to Octavian. Antony was unwilling to suffer more desertions and Octavian was happy to keep his enemy pinned down. There would be no great land battle. Antony crossed back to Actium and made ready to fight it out at sea. Stormy weather prevented the fleets from engaging until 2 September 31 BC. By this time Agrippa had whittled down Antony's fleet to about 400 ships, and Agrippa's ships were mostly faster and more manoeuvrable. Antony may now have summoned another 20,000 legionaries from the land army to fight as marines.

As we saw in Chapter III, just before battle was joined Antony was confronted by a grizzled centurion on his flagship, his floating *praetorium,* which suggests that the centurion was a praetorian. '*Imperator,* why do you despair of these scars of mine and my sword and put your hopes in miserable planks of wood? Give us land,' demanded the centurion, 'for that is where we are accustomed to stand, that is where we conquer our enemies or die!' Antony found himself unable to reply.

Actium is a difficult battle to reconstruct. Agrippa (whose fleet lay out to sea) and Antony (at the entrance of the Gulf) had to wait a long time for the wind to change, then both attempted to turn each other's line, much as in a land battle. Agrippa was successful, sinking ten, maybe fifteen, ships at the extreme right of Antony's line, and even capturing his flagship. The rest of Antony's squadrons believed their commander was taken or dead and backed water or surrendered. Antony had in fact escaped to another vessel and attempted to recapture his flagship, but to no avail. Cleopatra had already escaped with her squadron of sixty ships through a gap in Agrippa's line; Antony followed with about forty vessels and they made their way back to Egypt. Thus the bulk of their fleet and complete field army fell into the hands of Octavian. Eleven months later Antony and Cleopatra were abandoned by their remaining troops. They committed suicide when Octavian led his army into Alexandria (August 30 BC).[40]

THE IMPERIAL PRAETORIAN GUARD

Actium was a scrappy battle but it was certainly decisive. Octavian was the undisputed master of the Roman world. What did the conqueror do with Antony's leaderless and dejected army? Octavian aimed for reconciliation, not retribution. Those famous legions which had fought for Caesar and been reconstituted by Antony were enrolled into Octavian's army – Tenth *Equestris*, Fifth *Alaudae*, Twelfth *Antiqua* (soon renamed *Fulminata*), and so on. The praetorians and *speculatores*, chosen from the best soldiers of these legions, were also welcomed: the nine-cohort establishment of Augustus' Praetorian Guard (a convenient modern title, it was never used by the Romans) possibly reflects the combined number of cohorts in 31/30 BC.[41]

In 27 BC Octavian was recognised as the first Roman emperor and was consequently known as Augustus. It would not be until AD 23 that all of the praetorian cohorts were quartered together in a single fortress in Rome, but soon their function changed. Some cohorts certainly followed members of the imperial family on campaign, but other cohorts were becoming bound to Italy and performing ceremonial and policing duties. The praetorians who accompanied the imperial family in Rome even wore togas. No longer were praetorians recruited exclusively from the bravest legionaries; any seventeen-year-old Italian of good family, and with the right connections, could enlist. He was guaranteed a shorter period of service than a legionary (ultimately sixteen years to the legionary's twenty-five years), three times as much pay, a comfy billet with little prospect of active service, and a considerable pension at the completion of service. In his middle thirties the praetorian veteran was a man of status and wealth. His miserable legionary counterpart would still have many years to serve, faced annual campaigns, and a poor pension. When Augustus died in AD 14 the legionaries on the German and Pannonian frontiers mutinied and demanded parity of service with the praetorians. They never got it, but the legionaries had the last laugh.[42]

In AD 69 the short-lived Emperor Vitellius disbanded the Praetorian Guard and enrolled sixteen new cohorts, each 1,000 strong, from his German legions. The number of cohorts was whittled down to nine by Flavius Vespasian, the ultimate victor of the civil war of AD 69, then increased to ten by his son Domitian. Under these emperors the Guard reverted to its now traditional Italian recruiting grounds, but the Flavians were fighting emperors and their successors continued the trend. The reconstituted Guard regularly saw active service on and beyond the frontiers. In AD 193 the praetorians, who had the nasty habit of lynching weak and stingy emperors, murdered Pertinax and were soon disbanded by Septimius Severus. He re-formed the Guard from the best of his legionaries (who were now recruited in the frontier provinces). Italians were effectively excluded from the Guard and only legionaries and their sons could enter it. The new Guard prided itself as an elite fighting unit. It formed the core of the imperial field armies of the third century AD; the gravestone of Aelius Maximinus of the fifth praetorian cohort declares, 'He served in all the expeditions.' The Emperors Diocletian and Maximian (co-rulers AD 286–305) made their capitals away from Rome and stripped the Guard of its manpower, but in AD 306 the remaining praetorians proclaimed their own emperor, Maxentius, and went down fighting for him in a last battle against Constantine the Great at the Milvian Bridge in 312. Constantine disbanded the survivors and the praetorian cohorts were no more.[43]

THE LOST LEGION

The demise of the Praetorian Guard is well attested but the fate of another famous unit of the Imperial army, which also had its origins in the civil wars of the late Republic, is less clear. The Ninth Legion has become the stuff of legend. Its disappearance from the pages of history has exercised the minds of scholars and romantics for centuries. The mystery has spawned a million-selling novel and prompted sightings of ghostly legionaries on the Yorkshire Moors, but what really happened to the Ninth Legion? Was it destroyed in a bloody battle beyond the northern frontier of Roman Britain, or did it meet its fate in the dust and heat of the Middle East?

THE MISSING LEGIONS

To paraphrase a saying of the Emperor Hadrian (AD 117–138), you do not argue with a man who has thirty legions. But it seems someone did. A generation later the mighty Roman army was reduced to twenty-eight legions. A pair of inscribed columns in Rome, set up early in the reign of the Emperor Marcus Aurelius, probably in AD 162, list the legions according to their geographical location. From the Twentieth Valiant and Victorious Legion in Britannia to the Sixth Ironclad Legion in Judaea, the power of the Roman army and the vast extent of the empire it held under sway is made clear, but the columns name only twenty-eight legions. Two legions are missing: the Twenty-Second *Deiotariana* and the Ninth Spanish Legion.[44]

Unlike today, when army regiments are readily disbanded to meet defence cuts, the Imperial Roman Army held on to all its men and units for as long as possible. Contrary to popular belief, legions that lost their sacred eagle standards to the enemy or displayed cowardice in battle were not disbanded. *Legio V Alaudae* was defeated and lost its eagle when the Sugambri raided Gaul in 17 BC and the *aquila* of *XII Fulminata* was captured by the Jews during Cestius Gallus' retreat from Jerusalem in AD 66, yet neither unit was disbanded. The legions of the permanent, professional army of the Empire were too valuable; it took too long and was too expensive to recruit and train new legions from scratch.

A disgraced legion could expect extreme punishment, decimation for instance (*see below*), but a legion only disappeared from the army list if it was destroyed in battle (a fairly rare occurrence) or disbanded in disgrace for fighting on the losing side in a civil war. In fact, few legions were actually disbanded for rebellion and most were reconstituted after a suitable punishment period. The Third Gallic Legion was perhaps disbanded in AD 218 for supporting a rival claimant to the throne, but was back in favour by 222 BC. However, the Third Augustan Legion spent fifteen years in limbo before it was pardoned for backing the wrong emperor (Maximinus) in AD 238.[45]

It is often proposed that the Twenty-Second *Deiotariana*, based just outside Alexandria in Egypt and last attested in AD 119, was destroyed during the Bar Kochba revolt in Judaea (c. AD 132). However, a more likely scenario is that the legion met its end during an uprising in Alexandria or elsewhere in Egypt some time between AD 119 and 132. The frequent clashes between Greek and Jewish sectarian factions, or those between the Roman authorities and the Jews in the city, could be catastrophic. In AD 116 one such riot developed into a full-scale battle between the Romans and Jews, and in the following year Jewish rebels in Egypt defeated a legion. The Alexandrian disturbances of AD 121/122 – this time the rioters were opposing Egyptian religious factions – were of considerable scale, and the legion, almost certainly weakened from the fighting of AD 115–118 (the revolt of the Jews of Cyrenaica which spread to

Egypt and coincided with the revolt of the Mesopotamian Jews) and well under-strength was perhaps unable to endure.[46]

The only early imperial legions definitely destroyed in battle were the unfortunate Seventeenth, Eighteenth and Nineteenth Legions, along with nine auxiliary units, in the three-day battle of the Teutoburg Forest in the autumn of AD 9. The Roman commander Quinctilius Varus, acting on the information of Arminius, a trusted former auxiliary officer and war chief of the Cherusci, led a Roman army into partially subdued German territory to put down a rebellion. Expecting to rendezvous with Cheruscan levies, Varus unwittingly led the Roman army into a huge ambush prepared by Arminius. Constrained by forested hills and specially constructed turf walls, the Roman army was penned in and gradually massacred. The site of the battle has been located at Kalkriese near Osnabrück. Stories of other destroyed legions are less conclusive. The case for the destruction of *legio V Alaudae* in battle in AD 85/86 is not proven; it may have been disbanded for its role in the revolt of Civilis in AD 70. But *legio XXI Rapax* was most probably wiped out in a battle against the Sarmatians in AD 92.[47]

What happened to the Ninth? There is no evidence to suggest that it was disbanded for rebelling against an emperor, so it seems possible that the legion was destroyed in battle or sustained such high casualties that it could not be reconstituted.

THE NINTH LEGION, 49 BC–AD 108

The Ninth Legion came close to destruction on several occasions. When Caesar's army unexpectedly panicked in the face of unfamiliar tactics at Ilerda and retreated (49 BC), the Ninth valiantly charged forward alone and drove the Pompeians off the field, but it pursued the broken troops too far and found itself surrounded. It took Caesar more than five hours to extract the beleaguered legion.[48] Later in 49 BC the legion mutinied in its camp at Placentia in Italy. The legionaries had expected their discharge and rewards for having fought through the long Gallic War, but Caesar now expected them to fight against fellow legionaries in the civil war against Pompey. Caesar shamed the legion, accusing it of disloyalty and greed, and threatened it with decimation, the practice by which every tenth soldier was selected by lot and executed:

> A cry went up from the whole legion, and its officers threw themselves at Caesar's feet to beg for mercy. Caesar yielded little by little and gradually remitted the punishment as to designate only 120, thought to have been the ringleaders, and chose twelve of these by lot for execution. One of the twelve proved that he was absent when the mutiny occurred, and Caesar put to death the centurion who had accused him. (Appian, *Civil Wars*, 2.47)

The legion almost destroyed itself in the process of regaining its honour. At Dyrrhachium the Ninth was commanded by Mark Antony and proved tenacious in the defence of its entrenchments. At one point the legionaries even made a successful uphill charge against Pompeian troops who were bombarding them with missiles. (Antony also led a successful uphill charge at the first battle of Philippi.) However, by the end of the campaign almost all of the legion's centurions had been killed and at the subsequent battle of Pharsalus, by which time Caesar's legions were vastly reduced in strength (on average 2,750 men), the Ninth and the Eighth Legions were so depleted that they had to be combined to make a single unit approaching the strength of the other weakened legions. The legion took up its customary place on the left of the battle line, a place of honour because it would oppose the enemy right; elite units were traditionally placed on the right in ancient armies.[49]

The Ninth, presumably replenished with new recruits, fought through the African War (47–46 BC). At Uzitta and the battle of Thapsus it again held the left of Caesar's battle line. The legion was discharged soon after and its veterans settled in Italy, but the assassination of Caesar in 44 BC and the resumption of the civil wars led to the re-formation of the legion by Ventidius Bassus, the lieutenant of Mark Antony. Octavian soon gathered the remaining veterans to form an experienced cadre for his own Ninth. The Ninth Legion of the Empire was perhaps formed by amalgamating these two legions; after Octavian's victory at Actium in 31 BC, the legion was known for a time as *Gemella*, meaning 'Twin'.[50]

The legion's brushes with disaster continued in the first century AD. The historian Tacitus appears to report that the complete legion was wiped out when its rash commander, Petilius Cerialis, led it against Boudicca's British rebels in an attempt to relieve Colchester, but the Britons had already stormed the town and Cerialis probably marched into an ambush:

> Turning to meet Petilius Cerialis, commander of the Ninth Legion, who was marching to the rescue, the victorious Britons routed the legion and killed the infantry to a man. Cerialis escaped with the cavalry to the camp [at Lincoln], and found shelter behind its fortifications. (Tacitus, *Annals*, 14.32)

However, it seems that about half of the legion survived the disaster, for the transfer of 2,000 solders from the legions in Germany was considered enough to bring the Ninth back up to strength.[51]

In the civil war of AD 69 a strong detachment from the legion formed part of the elite British guard of the Emperor Vitellius. The British legionary detachments were at the centre of the Vitellian line at the second battle of Cremona, holding back the Flavian legions in a grim combat which lasted from dusk until dawn. The Vitellians lost the fight when they misunderstood a custom of an opposing legion. At dawn, the legionaries of the Third *Gallica*, who until recently had been serving in Syria and had adopted its customs, turned to salute the rising sun. The exhausted Vitellians thought the Third was greeting reinforcements and their resolve crumbled.[52]

During Agricola's conquest of Scotland, a weakened Ninth was almost overwhelmed when the Caledonians made a surprise night attack and broke into the legion's marching camp, located somewhere north of the River Forth (AD 82). (The legion was under-strength because a detachment of 1,000 men was at the same time fighting successfully against the Chatti in Germany; the tribune in command was decorated for his bravery.) Luckily, another Roman battle-group was close by and marched to the aid of the legion. The Caledonians were then trapped between the two Roman forces:

> The Britons were panic-stricken to find themselves between two evils, while the Romans [*i.e.* the Ninth] regained their courage and, no longer concerned for their safety, fought for distinction. They even sallied out of the camp and there was desperate fighting in its narrow gateway until the enemy gave way before the efforts of the two Roman armies. (Tacitus, *Agricola*, 26)

Tacitus goes on to explain that the legionaries of the Ninth fought all the harder because they could not bear the shame of having to admit that they needed rescuing.[53]

Despite these setbacks the Ninth established a reputation as a tough fighting legion. In the closing decades of the first century BC it won the titles *Triumphalis* ('Triumphal'), and *Macedonica* and by 19 BC *Hispaniensis* or *Hispana* for conquests in the Balkans and Spain. The latter title stuck and the legion was known as 'Spanish' until its disappearance. In AD 20 it marched from its base in Pannonia via Rome to quell Tacfarinas' revolt in Africa. It was the first legion to approach the imperial city for years, but whether the legionaries (who had again mutinied a mere six years before) were actually allowed into the capital is another matter.

In AD 43 the Ninth was specially selected as part of the army to invade Britain and eventually found itself based at York, the most northerly legionary garrison in the empire, from where, once more under the command of the impetuous Petilius Cerialis, it spear-headed the conquest of northern England and southern Scotland (AD 71–73/74). The last clear record of the legion's existence is a building inscription from its fortress at York dating to AD 108.[54]

THE EAGLE OF THE NINTH

In AD 122 the Sixth Victorious Legion moved into the fortress at York. Modern scholars once believed that the Ninth had been destroyed in the war that flared up in AD 117 in what is now southern Scotland and northern England. The war was perhaps caused by the Romans' brutal conscription methods and dragged on until AD 119. In a letter written to Marcus Aurelius in AD 162, on the theme of the recent Roman disaster at Elegeia (*see below*), Fronto reminds the emperor of the many Roman soldiers slaughtered in this British war but how the situation was soon recovered. The arrival of the Sixth would seem neatly to plug a gap left by a recently annihilated Ninth.

The destruction theory gained popular credence after a Roman bronze eagle was excavated at Silchester in the later nineteenth century. This bronze ornament was originally interpreted as the *aquila* of a rebellious legion in the service of the British usurper Allectus and buried just prior to a glorious last stand against the forces of Constantius (father of Constantine) in AD 296. It later inspired Rosemary Sutcliff's classic 1954 novel, *The Eagle of the Ninth*, which is most responsible for establishing the destruction of the legion in c. AD 117 as a 'fact' in the popular imagination. In the novel the Silchester eagle was cast as the *aquila* standard of the Ninth, taken as a trophy from the legion by avenging Britons. However, no Roman source mentions a legion, let alone specifically the Ninth, as having been defeated or destroyed in battle against the Britons. The famous bronze eagle is not a military standard but part of a statue, probably of Jupiter, whose symbol was the eagle. Finally, epigraphic evidence demonstrates a legate (the title of legionary commanders in the imperial period) and a number of senatorial tribunes of the Ninth who cannot have served in the legion before AD 120, and in two cases perhaps no earlier than AD 135–140. The legion thus survived beyond AD 117/119.[55]

It is worth adding here that if the legion was disbanded in disgrace, either for suffering a heavy defeat or rebelling against an emperor, these men, some of whom later became consuls, are unlikely to have proudly recorded their service in the Ninth. Also, a legion disbanded in disgrace would have suffered *damnatio memoriae*, whereby its name and numeral were erased from all monuments. As far as is known, this did not happen to any monument of the Ninth Legion.

In the 1930s–1960s archaeological excavations at Nijmegen in the Netherlands brought to light evidence for the presence of the Ninth Legion, but despite subsequent research the material (tiles and pottery stamped with the legion's mark) cannot be dated more precisely than c. AD 100–130 and does not reveal whether the full legion or only a detachment was present. (Two inscriptions indicate the presence of the Ninth in Lower Germany, one attesting a tribune, the other a prefect, but the latter inscription probably dates to before AD 43, prior to the invasion of Britain.) Still, the Nijmegen material can be used to build a most interesting scenario to explain the disappearance of the Ninth.

DESTRUCTION AT ELEGEIA?

The Ninth Legion material at Nijmegen could suggest that the unit was transferred to what was the province of Lower Germany, to fill a gap left in the defence of the Rhine frontier by a legion (*X Gemina*) sent east to fight in the Parthian War of AD 114–117, in which Trajan briefly extended the Empire to the Persian Gulf. The Ninth's absence from York would have encouraged the Britons to revolt. It may seem odd that the Roman high command decided to transfer the most northerly legion in Britain, the closest to the troublesome frontier, but the Ninth had a long record of sending detachments to fight abroad and it may have been considered the most experienced unit for the job. Detachments from the other British legions and auxiliary regiments could have taken over its duties in the north.

Now we have to ask whether the Ninth returned to Britain to fight in the war of AD 117–119? Detachments from the legions of Germany and Spain were sent to the trouble spot and it would make sense for the Ninth, with its long experience of fighting in Britain, to have crossed back to the province. Tiles stamped with the legion's mark have been discovered near Carlisle, so after the quelling of the revolt it is possible that the legion constructed a new fortress at Carlisle to keep an eye on the subdued natives. The Carlisle tile stamps are similar to those from Nijmegen with the numeral form *VIIII Hisp*, rather than those from York, *IX Hisp*. Some of the Roman barracks excavated in Carlisle could be assigned to Ninth *Hispana*, but continuing excavations have brought no conclusive evidence for the presence of the Ninth at this time.

Hadrian now decided to build his famous Wall and the Sixth Legion was transferred to Britain, not to replace the Ninth but to add to the work force necessary for such a massive construction project. If so, why is there no evidence for the involvement of the Ninth in the construction, such as the numerous building inscriptions left by the other three legions (*II Augusta*, *VI Victrix* and *XX Valeria Victrix*)? The far western portion of Hadrian's Wall was constructed of turf – rather like the later Antonine Wall in central Scotland – and not stone. No building inscriptions survive from this section of the wall, possibly indicating that they were made of ultimately perishable wood. If the Ninth was based at Carlisle it would have carried out this work.

We could continue to postulate the presence of the Ninth in north-west England until the early AD 130s. In AD 132 the Jews rebelled (the Bar Kochba revolt) and seized control of much of Judaea. Hadrian decided that the best general to win back the province was Sextus Julius Severus, then governing Britain. Did he take the Ninth Legion with him to the Near East? Now that Hadrian's Wall was finished and heavily garrisoned, a Ninth Legion based at Carlisle might be viewed as surplus to requirements and thus free to serve elsewhere.[56]

An inscription from the vicinity of Naples has been interpreted to show that marines from the Misene Fleet were transferred into the Ninth Legion during the reign of Hadrian. The text reveals that

Aelius Asclepiades from Cilicia (southern Turkey) joined the legion aged thirty-four and served for eight years. The imperial name Aelius suggests he received his grant of citizenship from Hadrian, whose full name was Publius Aelius Hadrianus. Most legionary recruits joined between the ages of seventeen and twenty-three Therefore it is conceivable that Asclepliades was a marine based at Misenum near Naples (his Cilician birth supports this as the Italian fleets recruited in the eastern provinces), who had at least ten years' fleet service before transferring to the Ninth. Mass transfers of fleet personnel were usually made when a legion had to be brought up to strength rapidly for war-fighting duties, or to make good battle casualties. In fact *legio I Adiutrix*, formed by Nero in AD 68, was recruited entirely from Misene marines. It is attractive to date Asclepiades' transfer in response to the Bar Kochba revolt. A transfer of marines would quickly bolster the ranks of the Ninth with trained and experienced men. Such a transfer of Misene marines was received by *X Fretensis*, a legion definitely involved in the suppression of the Jewish revolt.[57]

Julius Severus did not reach Judaea until late AD 133 or early 134, by which time the fighting was focussed on the defensive cave and tunnel complexes employed by the Jews to deny the Romans the superiority they normally in enjoyed in open battle, but he crushed the rebels by AD 135. The Romans carried out vicious reprisals and 580,000 Jewish males are said to have perished. Jerusalem was renamed Aelia Capitolina, garrisoned by *legio X Fretensis* and the Jews were barred from their Holy City.[58]

At the same time, the nearby province of Cappadocia (eastern Turkey) came under pressure from a migration of Alani nomads, renowned for their heavily armoured lancers. The governor Arrian succeeded in repulsing the Alani army but it may have been considered prudent to add a third legion to the garrison of the province. The Ninth Legion, having no base in the East, would be an obvious choice. An objection to this move is that the governors of Cappadocia were not of a seniority to be entrusted with three legions;

emperors were always wary of giving ambitious men too many soldiers. However, in AD 161 Sedatius Severianus, governor of Cappadocia, marched into Armenia with a legion to confront a Parthian incursion into the Roman protectorate. Severianus is ridiculed as a 'silly Celt' by the contemporary Roman author Lucian, and he succeeded in being surrounded by the Parthian army at a place called Elegeia. With their massive superiority in archers the Parthians pinned the Romans down for three days. Severianus despaired and committed suicide, as did his chief centurion. Lucian claims a survivor of the disaster reported that the centurion cut his own throat having performed a spontaneous funeral elegy for Severianus. The now leaderless legion was destroyed. Cappadocia's regular legions, *XII Fulminata* and *XV Apollinaris*, are known to have survived long after AD 161, so can the destroyed legion be identified as the Ninth?

Unfortunately our source for this disaster, the third century AD senator and historian Cassius Dio, does not name the legion, though that might be the result of the epitomised form in which his history has come down to us. This has led to the suggestion that a newly raised legion, yet to win a title, was destroyed. But an eminent scholar of the Roman army insists that Dio's Greek text (*stratopedon Rhomaikon*) does not refer to a 'Roman legion' but to a 'Roman camp and the army in it', and the army need not have contained a full legion.[59]

To recap, the last precisely dated evidence for the Ninth Legion locates it at York in AD 108. It was not there in AD 122 when *legio VI Victrix* arrived to occupy an empty fortress. The career inscriptions of a few officers indicate that the legion was still in existence in the mid–late AD 120s and possibly as late as AD 140, but this latter date cannot be pressed too far. That the legion built a new fortress at Carlisle and was transferred to the East remains purely speculative until some unambiguous epigraphic or archaeological evidence for these moves is discovered. To place the destruction of the Ninth at Elegeia in AD 161 is perhaps too convenient. Even if the legion was surplus to requirements in Britain, or indeed Lower

Germany, in the early AD 130s, other legions based in eastern Europe or the Middle East could have been transferred far more easily and quickly to quell the rebellion in Judaea. Why send the far-off Ninth?

Are we trying too hard to crowbar the fate of the Ninth Legion into wars and battles recorded by the surviving Roman literary sources? Several battles that were fought by the Romans but which became lost to the historical record, have only recently been discovered by archaeology: the great siege sites of Burnswark in Scotland (second century AD) and Dura-Europos in Syria (AD 256/257), and the skeleton-strewn battle sites at Krefeld-Gellep in Germany (mid–later third century AD). An inscription from the legionary fortress of Lambaesis in North Africa reveals that the Third Augustan Legion sent emergency reinforcements to the Eastern frontier in AD 125, but no written source records a war necessitating such a transfer. Papyri from Egypt record several serious Roman military defeats in the second and third centuries AD. Again, these setbacks are not recorded in the surviving histories. Small frontier wars and internal rebellions were endemic to the Roman Empire, and in an age before mass media they were not readily recorded.[60] A letter written by an army doctor in Egypt in the third century AD is a snapshot of the one these small wars:

> Marcus to Antonia, Sarapion and Cassianos, my parents, many greetings. I make obeisance for you in the presence of the gods sharing the temple. For no one can go up-river to make obeisance, because of the battle which has taken place between the Anoteritae and the soldiers. Fifteen soldiers of the *singulares* [guardsmen] have died, apart from the legionaries, *evocati*, the wounded, and those suffering from battle fatigue. (*P. Ross. Georg.* III, 1.1–7, after Davies 1969, 94)

The last few words are a rare admission that even Roman soldiers could become 'shell shocked'.

The Ninth Legion might have met its end in a conflict for which we (as yet) possess no evidence. The Asclepiades inscription points to the transfer of marines to the legion during the reign of Hadrian, which could have made good casualties sustained in a battle fought somewhere in Europe. However, the authenticity of this inscription is disputed. The actual inscription does not survive; we possess a note of its text made in 1714. One of the problems with the authenticity, or accuracy, of the text is that the form is suggestive of an inscription of the later second or third century AD, clearly too late for Ninth *Hispana*. If the text is genuine, it is possible that the numeral of the legion (no title is given) was copied incorrectly and that it does not refer to the Ninth.

AMALGAMATION?

What other scenarios could explain the disappearance of the legion? It was suggested by Ritterling that the legion met its end in a second (unrecorded) British revolt in the late AD 120s.[61] It is even possible that the legion was in Britain in AD 117 but suffered such heavy causalities that it had to be replaced by the Sixth Legion, was sent to Nijmegen to recuperate, and never returned to Britain. The archaeological evidence for the Ninth at Nijmegen might point to its demise in Germany at the hands of one of the Germanic nations which went on to cause such chaos in the later AD 160s and 170s. But what if the Ninth was not destroyed to a man in battle? As we have seen, the early imperial legion was possibly an amalgamation of Antony's and Octavian's respective Ninth Legions. Perhaps the legion, having suffered a heavy defeat, or even a costly victory, in Britain or Germany, was amalgamated with another depleted legion. If Ninth *Hispana* was the weaker element in such an amalgamation, its men would have assumed the numeral and title of the larger legionary element, thus removing the Ninth from the army list . . . Yet again we wander into the realm of speculation and guess-work. The mysterious disappearance of the Ninth Legion remains unsolved. That is perhaps a good thing.

* * *

The increasingly professional armies of the late Republic, coupled with the ambitions of men like Caesar and Octavian, made it inevitable that civil wars would erupt, that the republican constitution of Rome would be overthrown and an imperial monarchy established in its place.

Caesar's legions bridge the gap between the militia army of the early Republic and the professional army of the Empire; the history of *legio IX*, as outlined above, demonstrates this. Legions remained the backbone of the Imperial army until the early fourth century AD. The status and seniority of legions in the army was undermined by the military reforms of the Emperor Constantine, but even in their reduced form the legions endured, and the history of some can be traced into the seventh century AD. The Ninth Legion may have disappeared in the mid-second century AD, but elements of the Fourth Scythian and Fifth Macedonian Legions, formed by Antony and Octavian respectively, soldiered on for centuries. The 'Macedonians' are last found strengthening the defences of Heliopolis (Baalbek) in AD 635/636 in advance of a Muslim assault. The fate of the Macedonians thereafter is unknown. The 'Scythians' (who probably won their title in the campaign in which Marcus Crassus claimed the *spolia opima*) defended Gaza against the Muslims in AD 637/639 (the precise date is disputed). When the city was taken the surviving Scythians were executed. They came to be revered as Christian martyrs.[62]

The courage exemplified by Caesar's centurions was demanded of the legionary, praetorian and auxiliary centurions of the Empire. Evidence of *fortia facta* (brave deeds) was a requirement for promotion to, and retention of, the rank. It comes as no surprise that Didius Saturninus, the last Roman known to have been awarded the civic crown (between AD 198 and 211), was a centurion. The decline of the centurionate in the fourth century AD went hand-in-hand with the decline of the legion, but the centurion maintained a traditional prestige, especially on the frontiers where units descended from the old legions survived. The essential officer class of the Roman army was still soldiering on in the early seventh century AD.[63]

The abolition of the praetorian cohorts in AD 312 appears to sever another link between the armies of the Republic and Empire, but Constantine replaced the cohorts with other guards units. Some of his guardsmen were actually praetorians under a different name: when he succeeded his father Constantius I, Emperor of the West, in AD 306, Constantine inherited a powerful field army with praetorian cohorts at its core. Even with evolution and periodic changes, there was always continuity at the heart of the Roman army.[64]

Chapter V

WARRIORS AND POETS

'Of all the nations of the world, the Romans have, without doubt, surpassed every other in the display of *virtus*.' (Pliny, *Natural History*, 7.130)

It is hoped that the foregoing chapters have dispelled the myth of the Roman fighting man, that erroneous image of him bringing civilisation to wild barbarian lands, populated by unruly warriors who are easily overcome by the purely professional soldier with his superior equipment, rational organisation and cunning tactics. The success of the Roman army boiled down to its origins in the war bands of the earliest kings and armed retinues of the great clans. As the army developed into a more sophisticated organisation, the warrior ethos was retained. Polybius stated that the legion would always overcome the phalanx because of the flexibility of its organisation. The legionary could fight equally well in a massed battle line, in an unsupported maniple, or on his own. Even when fighting in line he was given generous room in which to ply

235

his trade with *pilum* and *gladius*. The phalanx could only succeed if it kept its cohesion, the phalangites shoulder to shoulder and forming a greater entity. The phalangites were simply a group of soldiers, often tremendously brave, but useless when their formation was broken because they could not fight individually with the cumbersome *sarissa* or protect themselves adequately with their small shields. The legionary was always adaptable and ready to change from a group soldier to an individual warrior. Sometimes, however, the switch from soldier to warrior was sudden and drastic, resulting in bouts of serious indiscipline, berserk behaviour and acts of bloody atrocity.[1]

This final chapter provides further examples of that potent duality within the Roman fighting man. We shall also consider how poetry inspired him on his route to personal and national glory.

SORE LOSERS

The thing that really irritated the Romans was losing battles. Cannae (216 BC) was the biggest defeat of all. In a single day perhaps as many as 70,000 legionaries and Italian Allies were completely surrounded by Hannibal's army and butchered. When Hannibal's victorious troops plundered the Roman dead the next day, they discovered one of their own men, a Numidian, barely alive, trapped under an expired legionary whose arms had been shattered in the fighting. Despite this, the legionary had evidently used his teeth to tear the face off his enemy before he died. Brave deeds like this heartened the Romans but it took them another fourteen years to defeat Hannibal. We have seen how, during these years, men like Marcus Sergius Silus, fighting on with his left hand after he lost his right in combat, personified the indomitable spirit of Rome.

Gaius Acilius continued this tradition of fighting single-handed. Acilius was one of those Caesarian legionaries serving as marines during the sea fights against the Pompeians off Massilia (Marseilles) in 49 BC. Acilius grasped the stern of a Massiliote warship and was about to board it when a sword blow severed his right hand. Clearly a man of Sergius' ilk, he ignored this mere nick and clambered on to the enemy vessel and battered its crew into submission with his shield boss. We saw in Chapter III how partial the Roman soldier was to using his *umbo* (shield boss) as a weapon, despite shields which weighed up to twenty-two pounds and were held with a single horizontal handgrip. One of the sculptures from the monumental trophy at Adamklissi (early second century AD) appears to be a representation of this tactic. It shows a legionary about to thud the boss of his heavy *scutum* into the face of a Dacian warrior while he follows up with an underarm sword thrust.[2]

On the other hand, this kind of furious determination could also lead to serious bouts of group indiscipline. Even Caesar's experienced veterans were prone to it. At the battle of Thapsus (46 BC), where Caesar faced the forces still loyal to the Pompeian cause in Africa, his veteran legionaries were so eager to advance that they intimidated a trumpeter at the opposite end of the battle line into sounding the charge long before Caesar intended to give the order. The centurions appear to have been complicit in this; their half-hearted attempts to hold back the legionaries were surely just for show. Caesar himself was hardly surprised at their disobedience; he merely had his trumpeter sound 'Good fortune', and boldly charged forward with his cavalry at the opposing Pompeian line. The Pompeians were routed, but the maddened legionaries ignored Caesar's command to desist from the pursuit and slaughtered anyone attempting to surrender; then they turned on the senators who held high rank in Caesar's army. At least one senator was spitted on a *pilum* and the remaining senators fled the battlefield. It was not until the following day that Caesar was back in control of his army.[3]

The impatience and indiscipline displayed at Thapsus was still evident in the fourth century AD. The soldier-historian Ammianus Marcellinus paints a picture of legionaries and other Roman troops working themselves up into a state of near frenzy before battle, as at Argentoratum (Strasbourg) in AD 357: 'The soldiers gnashed and ground their teeth and showed their eagerness for battle by clashing their spears and shields together.' Sometimes it was impossible to get them to heed the recall, for example at Maiozamalcha in Mesopotamia (AD 363). In AD 359 legionaries transferred from Gaul to defend the city of Amida in Mesopotamia preferred not to guard the walls, but to sally out from the gates and fight the besieging Persians on open ground. When the gates of the city were barred to prevent their risky sorties, the legionaries threatened to kill their officers. Unsurprisingly the legionaries were permitted to make a final sortie at night. Armed with swords and axes they killed the Persian guards, entered the enemy camp and advanced on the tent of the king, Shapur II. They never reached it. Ammianus witnessed the fighting from the walls of Amida. He saw the legionaries cut down countless Persians, including noble commanders, but they were eventually forced to retreat by the volume of arrows being loosed by the Persian archers. Ammianus, who was fond of musical metaphors, describes with admiration how the legionaries retreated 'as if to music'. Four hundred legionaries were killed in the night-long engagement, perhaps a third or even a half of their total number (by this time legions were a fraction of the size of those fielded during the Republic and early Empire), but it persuaded the Persians to call a truce of three days.[4]

Centurions could also get a little impatient when it came to grappling with the enemy, and might take matters into their own hands. During the Cimbric War the *primus pilus* Gnaeus Petreius, tired of his tribune's reluctance to attack the German force which had surrounded the legion, gutted the cowardly officer with his *gladius* and led the legion out to victory. He was subsequently praised for this glorious action and rewarded with the highest military honours by Marius and Lutatius Catulus. Murder of senior officers was hardly encouraged (though it was the second such incident in the war – a young legionary had killed a tribune who attempted to rape him), but Petreius may have presented his act as a variation of *devotio*, deliberately sacrificing the tribune to secure the help of the gods. The incident may have happened at Vercellae in

101 BC. That battle was infamous for the huge volume of dust raised by the opposing armies and the confusion it caused (it was said that Marius advanced into the dust cloud expecting to meet the enemy but only succeeded in marching past them), perhaps allowing the Cimbri to surround Petreius' legion, but the encirclement of a legion would also fit with Catulus' chaotic retreat from the Cimbri down the Adige valley in winter 102–101 BC.[5]

SCALPING AND DRINKING BLOOD

We saw in Chapter III how the Romans had a passion for taking the heads of their opponents as trophies. Scalps were also taken as trophies – recall the helmet of Flaminius, decorated with human skin, perhaps a scalp, and crested with human hair – and to terrorise the enemy. Having slaughtered the Cimbric warriors on the battlefield of Vercellae the legionaries turned their attention to the Germans' wagon laager, defended by the women. The fighting here proved decidedly tough and in order to hasten the battle to its conclusion, the legionaries scalped those women they killed to terrify the rest into surrendering. It did not work. The Cimbric women killed their children and then themselves. The Romans respected suicide of this type (*see below*).[6]

Severed heads also presented a fine opportunity for amusement. Early in 43 BC Gaius Trebonius awoke to find a disgruntled centurion in his bedchamber. Trebonius had served Caesar loyally in Gaul but in 44 BC was persuaded to help Brutus and Cassius to assassinate the dictator. He fled to the province of Asia (now western Turkey) to avoid the recriminations of Caesar's veterans. Assuming the centurion intended to drag him before his enemy Dolabella (who had invaded the province), Trebonius declared that he would go willingly. The centurion famously retorted that Trebonius could go where he liked but would leave his head behind, and summarily decapitated him. In the morning Dolabella displayed the head as a warning to the other assassins, then threw it to his soldiers who used it for a game of catch until it was completely smashed.[7]

As if the taking of heads and scalping were not enough, we possess a few reports of soldiers drinking the blood of their opponents. Most graphically, following the disastrous battle of Adrianople (AD 378), where the Goths destroyed the field army of the Emperor Valens, they advanced on Constantinople, but were checked by a scratch force including Saracen auxiliaries. One completely naked Saracen was seen to slash the throat of a Goth, then clamp his lips to the open wound and drink the blood. Even the battle-hardened Goths thought this a tad much and fled the battlefield. This act might have been the result of battle rage but perhaps had some religious significance to the Saracen. Ammianus thought it bestial, but no more so than the Catilinarians who drank the blood of a sacrificed man, or the praetorian tribunes and centurions who were said to have 'tasted' Caligula's flesh when they killed him in a frenzy (*see below*).[8]

THE ROMAN WAY

Marcus Petreius, the son of centurion Petreius, became a general. His finest hour came in 62 BC when he defeated Catiline at Pistoria and was hailed as the saviour of the Roman Republic (*see* Chapter IV), but by 46 BC he found himself on the losing side in the civil war against Julius Caesar. After the disastrous defeat at Thapsus he entered into a kind of suicide pact with an allied king, Juba of Numidia. They fought an honourable duel 'so they could die like men', thinking it better than capture and execution at the hands of Caesar's men. This was, according to Martial, 'the Roman way', an honourable death by the sword that cheated the enemy of total victory, but other methods of suicide, such as hanging, poison and starvation, were considered cowardly and disgraceful in the extreme.

We saw in Chapter IV that, following the destruction of Caesar's Fourteenth Legion, the survivors who had managed to fight their way back to camp chose to commit suicide rather than suffer the final disgrace of having their camp overrun. This was not exceptional. In AD 28, 400 auxiliary soldiers were similarly cornered in a villa complex by rebellious Frisian Germans, who intended to set fire to the buildings. The soldiers fell on each other's swords. When the packed transport ships of the *legio Martia* were attacked and set on fire by Brutus' war fleet (42 BC), some soldiers committed suicide:

> The Martians, who excelled in courage, were exasperated that they should lose their lives uselessly, and so killed themselves rather than be burned to death. Others leaped on board the vessels of the enemy and sold their lives dearly. (Appian, *Civil Wars*, 4.116)[9]

INSULTS AND SONGS

The Gallic legionaries at Amida demonstrate the tenacity of Roman warriors under siege and their desire to take the fight to the enemy and to be seen performing *fortia facta*. When one of Caesar's legions was besieged by the Nervii (winter 54–53 BC), its centurions became fond of striding the ramparts to challenge prominent Gallic warriors to single combat. Infuriatingly, though, the enemy did not accept the challenges. Once nipping out to give the enemy a thrashing became tiresome, Roman soldiers would spend time making novel objects to lob at their besiegers. When Octavian besieged Mark Antony's wife Fulvia and his brother Lucius in Perusia (41–40 BC), the Antonian legionaries cast lead sling bullets (*glandes*) with legends that called doubt on Octavian's sexuality and masculinity, or boldly directed the missiles to strike him in the fundament. Octavian's legionaries took this badly and replied with their own suitably inscribed bullets in the hope they would hit Fulvia's nether regions or impact on Lucius' bald head. Other bullets identified the units and soldiers producing them. Most interesting is the bullet naming one Scaeva as *primus pilus* of Octavian's Twelfth Legion. This Scaeva is almost certainly the same man promoted by Caesar at Dyrrhachium (48 BC).[10]

The exchange of obscenely inscribed bullets clearly riled the troops. Most soldiers hated sling bullets because of the terrifying whizzing noise they made as they flew and the terrible injuries caused on impact. So, when Lucius Antonius attempted to break through the siege lines surrounding Perusia, Octavian's legionaries met him with a furious counter-attack and wave after wave of reinforcements forced the Antonians back towards the city walls. Many were trapped on the ramparts of the siege works or in the ditches between them and were slaughtered by a hail of javelins and other missiles. Octavian's triumphant men stripped the corpses of the Antonians, flung them in the ditches, and danced around clashing their weapons in wild celebration.

Lucius eventually surrendered unconditionally to Octavian but Caesar's heir gained little. Lucius and Fulvia were pardoned and set free (the redoubtable Fulvia died soon after, paving the way for the marriage of Octavia to Antony); Octavian did not want to fight Mark Antony. The city was about to be given over to Octavian's victorious army to plunder but an old soldier named Cestius Macedonicus (the *cognomen* he had taken for fighting in Macedonia), who had retired to the city, set fire to his house and threw himself into the flames. Whether he was just mad or had decided to combine the soldier's route of suicide with denying his property to the enemy is unclear, but the fire rapidly spread from his property and soon engulfed the whole city. Needless to say, Octavian's men were more than a little peeved at this outcome and it required the executions of a few local politicians to lift their spirits.[11]

Singing or chanting in battle was a favoured Roman practice. At Pharsalus Caesar's more psychotic legionaries sang gleefully as they killed. Regimental anthems were presumably popular, but at Pharsalus lyrical pronouncements on the parentage of the opponents, virtues of their mothers and reputation of their city were most prominent. This glorious tradition continued into the Imperial period. At the siege of Placentia (AD 69) German auxiliaries supporting the Emperor Vitellius thought it would be particularly heroic to advance on the walls bare-chested and clashing their weapons as they sang their battle hymn. The praetorians loyal to Emperor Otho found the musical pink blobs fifty feet below them to be perfect targets for their javelins. At the battle of Lugdunum

(Lyon) in AD 197 British legionaries fighting for Clodius Albinus feigned a retreat and drew the legionaries and praetorians of Septimius Severus on to concealed booby-trapped pits (*lilia* – 'lilies') and trenches. The Severan attack collapsed and Severus' attempts to send in reinforcements only added to the chaos. The legionaries of Britannia then turned from their apparently cowardly flight and bore down on the Severans screaming their paean of victory. Albinus' victory looked certain but unfortunately his now disordered legionaries were attacked from the rear by the Severan cavalry, which had been detached at the start of the battle to outflank the Britons. Severus later claimed to have rallied his panicked men by charging in among them, forcing them back into line with the flat of his sword, and declaring that he would rather die than retreat. The contemporary historian Herodian reports that Severus was actually attempting to flee when he was knocked from his horse and he tore off his purple imperial cloak to avoid recognition. Another (face-saving?) version has Severus forced to leave the battlefield because he was hit by a lead sling bullet.[12]

Singing was a vital element in immediate post-battle celebrations and during the triumphal processions through Rome, but the formal triumph was not exempt from the ribald ditties of the troops. Rather than sing about their countless victories, the veterans of Caesar's Gallic War regaled the citizens of Rome with tales of Caesar's gambling and sexual conquests (46 BC). Caesar was enjoying the songs until the legionaries, who became jealous and angry at the sight of centurions Caesar had promoted to exalted senatorial rank, bellowed that Caesar had been the passive participant in a sexual liaison with Nicomedes, king of Bithynia (northern Turkey). Caesar was mortified at the suggestion he was a *pathicus*, that is someone who willingly effeminised himself by submitting to penetrative sex – one of the insults directed at Octavian during the Perusine War. Caesar lived down this accusation of *effeminatio*, but it was a devastating charge and led to the death of more than one emperor at the hands of the soldiery.[13]

The Emperor Gaius (reigned AD 37–41) had been brought up in legionary camps on the Rhine and was affectionately nicknamed *Caligula* ('Little Boots') by the soldiers. He accordingly knew just how to wind up the proud officers of his bodyguard. One praetorian tribune came in for particular derision. Cassius Chaerea had made his name in Germany in AD 14 when, as a legionary centurion, he cut his way through a mob of mutinous soldiers who were intent on lynching him. By AD 41 he was a tribune of the Guard; to reach this important position he must have served as *primus pilus*, a rank that only the bravest and most talented centurions could aspire to. Josephus remarks that Chaerea could kill with his bare hands and was often employed to carry out the torture and execution of traitors. He was not a man you would intentionally irritate, unless you were a mad emperor. Gaius thought it amusing to imply that Chaerea was a *pathicus* and, among other public humiliations, would often present Chaerea with his hand to kiss and then suddenly withdraw it to make an obscene gesture with his middle finger, perhaps identical to the one used today. It did not take long for Chaerea and other incensed praetorian officers to plot Gaius' death. When the emperor was leaving a theatrical performance the praetorians pounced. Chaerea struck the first blow and the others soon followed, hacking and stabbing with their long daggers. It is not clear if Gaius was still alive when they castrated him.[14]

The first emperor to participate willingly in combat was Maximinus (reigned AD 235–238). This exertion stimulated the imperial appetite greatly. According to legend the giant Maximinus consumed forty pounds of meat and some six gallons of wine a day, but he did not like his greens and shunned all vegetables. When Maximinus was training recruits in Germany for a campaign against the Alamanni (AD 235), he played on the effeminate and cowardly reputation of the Emperor Severus Alexander; he was certainly dominated by his mother Julia Mamaea and her policies included cutting military pay, a sure way to alienate the soldiery. The recruits were thus encouraged to despise the emperor and worship the *bellator*

Maximinus. When it became known that the emperor planned to negotiate with the Alamanni and pay them a subsidy, centurions and recruits loyal to Maximinus pronounced him emperor, marched on Mainz and murdered Alexander and his entourage. As Alexander died he was taunted with cries of '*pathicus*' and 'lady-boy'.[15]

THE CENTURION POETS

In their spare time, when not extorting cash from recruits, beating civilians or performing acts of suicidal bravery in battle,[16] Roman centurions liked to compose poetry. This may come as a surprise to readers now familiar with centurions like Cornidius, striding into combat with a brazier of coals affixed to his helmet, or Scaeva, proud of the considerable number of arrow holes in his shield.

The satirist Perseus detested muscle-bound centurions who made a sport of baiting poets and philosophers, but the famous poet Martial knew this was merely cover for what went on behind the closed doors of the surprisingly plush apartments inhabited by off-duty centurions (think mosaic flooring and wall paintings). Martial complained that rough centurions on the frontiers were reading and distributing volumes of his poetry, yet he received not a penny in royalties. Virgil's epics, Catullus' heart-felt verses and, in the Greek-speaking East, Appian's military histories were also popular with the soldiers, and all this reading inspired more than a few centurions to reach for stylus and papyrus.[17]

The surviving results of the centurions' literary labours have met with a mixed response from modern scholars of Latin. This is due mainly to the variable quality of the Latin itself, but that is not surprising. In an empire stretching from the Scottish lowlands to the Saharan desert and with men recruited from every province and beyond the frontiers, few soldiers of the Imperial army could claim Latin as their mother tongue. Still, whatever their defects in style, the verses we possess attest the ambition, arrogance and general enthusiasm of these Roman successors of Archilochos, the famed Greek mercenary and poet.

Perhaps most famous is the verse inscription set up by an anonymous *primus pilus* in the province of Africa, probably in the early years of the second century AD and recalling his part in the conquest of Dacia (modern Romania). In a succession of boastful lines the centurion's gusto for combat and lechery is clear:

> I wanted to hold slaughtered Dacians: I held them.
>
> I wanted to sit on a chair of peace: I sat on it.
>
> I wanted to take part in illustrious triumphs: it was done.
>
> I wanted the full rewards of the chief centurionate: I had them.
>
> I wanted to see naked nymphs: I saw them. (*AE*, 1928, 37)

At the desert outpost of Bu Njem in Libya survive two lengthy examples of the acrostic – a poem in which the first letters of each line spell out the name of the author. One inscribed poem, dating to AD 202–203, names Q(uintus) Avidius Quintianus, centurion of the Third Augustan Legion, and reveals his devotion to the goddess Salus, a deity concerned with good health and safety, clearly of great importance to men who might garrison the exposed Bu Njem for up to three years before returning to the security and comforts of their mighty legionary fortress at Lambaesis.

The other acrostic names M(arcus) Porcius Iasucthan, also a centurion of the Third Legion. Iasucthan was of Punic origin (how Hannibal would have shuddered at the thought of his countrymen in Roman service!) and Latin was not his first language, but his acrostic is a splendid account of how the legionary detachment rebuilt a collapsed gatehouse in AD 222. The centurion revelled in the labour and savoured how the 'torrential valour' of his men made the construction easy. Iasucthan relates how the courses of masonry rose in time to the chanting of the legionaries (and one can imagine the centurion himself in full voice with them), until finally the new gatehouse was like 'a jewel set in gold'. Although we possess thousands of military inscriptions, many soldiers' private letters, and a mass of official military records, no other document relating to the Roman Imperial army exudes such pride and affection for regiment and comrades. Iasucthan should be of particular interest to the British reader because later in his career he was transferred to the Twentieth Legion, Valiant and Victorious, based at Chester.[18]

The great Ennius, father of Roman epic poets, served as a centurion in the Messapian Allied cohorts in the war against Hannibal before turning his hand to patriotic verse. Ennius encouraged the Roman *miles* to perform great deeds in battle for that secured the fame and glory that outlived a man and served as an inspiration to all. Marcus Porcius Iasucthan was evidently a brave man, otherwise he would not have been promoted to the rank of centurion, but he secured his posthumous glory (or 'eternal valour' as his poem suggests he would have put it) by means of enthusiastic and heartfelt poetry. Ennius would have approved.[19]

Lucius Pullius Peregrinus, a rich young Roman knight (*eques*) who served as a centurion, commissioned a sumptuous sarcophagus depicting him as a philosopher. Draped in a toga, he sits studying a scroll and is surrounded by a crowd of sages. The sarcophagus dates to the middle of the third century AD, a chaotic period of civil wars and foreign invasions often called 'The Crisis' by modern scholars. However, even in this period of perpetual warfare, the centurions maintained their interest in the arts and were concerned that their sons received a proper education.

The Emperor Maximinus, almost certainly a former *primus pilus* and to whom the title *bellator* is most appropriate, is depicted as a boor in hostile sources, but he took advantage of his supreme rank to ensure that his son Maximus was tutored by the finest minds of the age. Coming from a military family, Maximinus would have received the kind of good education that was essential for a man to advance through the ranks of the Imperial army.

It was the same in the legions of Caesar and Pompey. Courage played its part but without literacy or numeracy a man could not be a centurion; even Baculus and Scaeva were not exempt from the administrative burdens of command. In the final years of the Republic centurions who hoped their sons might attain even higher rank (Marcus Petreius is a key example of a son building on his father's advancement to the equestrian order via the primipilate) made sure their sons were properly educated; the father of the poet Horace was a former slave (perhaps a Sabellian captive taken during the Social War) and could not afford to send him to the same school in Venusia as attended by the 'sons of the great centurions'.[20]

Exposure to literature did not lessen the warlike nature of the Roman soldier. In many ways it reinforced it. The soldier was most likely to read (or hear being recited) passages from the classics of Ennius and Virgil. Their epic poems took the reader into the very heart of battle, with its dust and heat, blood and gore; Ennius wrote of decapitated heads with eyelids still twitching. As well as imitating Homeric models, Ennius may have drawn on his personal experience as a centurion and described the torture of enduring bombardments of javelins and sling bullets, of shields being punctured and helmets dented, of clothing soaked with sweat, and of aching limbs and burning lungs. Yet he also emphasised the personal and national glory to be won in war, that the battlefield was where a man proved his true worth and overcame fear. Virgil reminded the soldier not only of the need to defend the fatherland but his duty to extend it. Reading assured the *bellator* that he was involved in the just fight.[21]

* * *

Roman warriors fought for family and *patria* (fatherland). They also fought for personal glory and enrichment but remained loyal and honourable, steadfast and defiant. They were superstitious and devout, sometimes cruel, but more often heroic. The image of the crazed Caesarian legionaries at Thapsus should be tempered by the heroism displayed in the same battle by a veteran of *legio V Alaudae* who fought one of Scipio's war elephants:

> On the left wing an elephant, maddened by the pain of a wound, had attacked an unarmed camp follower, pinned him underfoot and then knelt upon him. With its trunk aloft and

trumpeting loudly, it was crushing the man to death. This was more than the veteran of the Fifth Legion could endure and, fully armed as he was, he attacked the beast. When the elephant became aware of him, advancing with his weapon ready to strike, the elephant abandoned the corpse of the camp follower, encircled the veteran with its trunk and lifted him off the ground. The veteran, realising that this dangerous crisis required determination on his part, hacked with his *gladius* at the encircling trunk with all his strength. The resulting pain caused the elephant to drop the veteran, turn about and, trumpeting shrilly, swiftly rejoin its fellow beasts. (Anonymous, *African War*, 84)

This episode, and other successful encounters of the *Alaudae* with the war elephants at Thapsus, resulted in the legion adopting the elephant as its emblem.[22]

Above all, Roman warriors were human. They laughed among themselves, sometimes at themselves and the places they ended up. *Clibanarius* – 'oven-' or 'furnace-man' – the descriptive term for a fully armoured cavalryman, surely resulted from soldiers' humour for the discomforts of such a panoply, while *noverca* ('step-mother' or 'mother-in-law') was their sardonic accolade for unfavourable terrain for a camp or battle. We have seen how they laughed at, and derided, the antics of their enemies. This helped carry them through to the day when they could sing with pride in the triumph and return home to their families with a deserved share of the spoils and perhaps even military decorations.

For all his fury in battle, the Roman warrior did have a mellower side, even a *carpe diem* philosophy. In death the Augustan legionary veteran Titus Cissonius still encourages the living to seize the day. The inscription on his still extant gravestone declares, 'While I was alive I drank freely; you who are alive, drink!'[23]

EPILOGUE

'To the gods of the Underworld. Vitalis, soldier of the Seventh Praetorian Cohort ... specially picked from the First Minervian Legion. He was a Suebian.' (*AE* 1990, 752)

When the original Ninth Legion was raised, some time before 59 BC, all of its recruits would have been Italians. When the legion disappeared in the second century AD, Italians were no longer the predominant element in the Roman army. When a new legion was raised during the first two centuries of Empire, its original complement of recruits was gathered in Italy by means of the *dilectus* (levy), but the legion would be sent to a far-off frontier, and when the legionaries retired from service they tended to settle in the vicinity of their old fortress, remaining close to friends and comrades. They married local women and their sons joined the legion. Other recruits were sought from the general population of the province in which the legion was based. Some regions, such as Illyricum and Thrace, had such reserves of willing manpower that shortfalls in local recruitment elsewhere could be easily made up.

Julius Caesar showed the way by recruiting *legio V Alaudae* from non-Italians. For much of the first century AD Italians still provided the majority of legionary recruits, but they came mostly from northern Italy. For reasons that cannot be readily explained, the descendants of the bellicose Samnites and Lucani and other Sabellian peoples supplied hardly any recruits to the Imperial legions. A respectable number of Imperial praetorians did come from southern Italy, but many were from the old Roman colonies originally established to control Sabellian territory. By the end of the second century AD, when the legions could be sustained by local and other provincial recruits (and sometimes by recruitment beyond the frontiers), the praetorian cohorts were the only units in the Roman army to be dominated by Italians. An inscription set up by a praetorian centurion in the AD 160s or 170s records his displeasure at serving in a field army alongside a 'barbarian legion'. But in AD 193 Septimius Severus disbanded the Italian praetorian cohorts for their role in the assassination of the Emperor Pertinax, and for 'auctioning' the Empire to Didius Julianus. Severus immediately reconstituted the cohorts from his legions, in which Pannonians, other Illyrians, and Thracians predominated.

The emperor, who, incidentally, was of Punic descent, also established a new legion, *II Parthica*, the first to be based on Italian soil for two centuries, but the major element in its manpower was Thracian. However, Italians made up a considerable portion of the legion's complement. It might be argued that the Italians of *legio II Parthica* were the last true Roman legionaries, but the non-Italian recruits who sustained the legions and other army units through the centuries of Empire were just as proud as any Italian that they served in the Roman army. The epitaph of an unnamed Frank who died, probably in battle, in the fourth century AD reads, 'I, a Frank, a Roman citizen, a soldier in arms', indicating equal pride in his German and Roman identities. The non-Italians of the Imperial army served loyally. They pursued *virtus* like the *bellatores* of old; the epitaph of the same Frank also reminded the world of his *'virtus* in war'. Courage hastened promotion to the highest ranks and it was officers and generals of provincial, German and other foreign origin, who led the late Roman army into battle. The Gallic legionaries who fought valiantly at Amida were the worthy successors of the legionaries who faced Pyrrhus and Hannibal. They were *bellatores* who fought and died for the glory of Rome.[1]

ABBREVIATIONS

AE	*L'Anneé Épigraphique*
BGU	*Aegyptische Urkunden aus den koeniglichen Museen zu Berlin. Griechische Urkunden.* Berlin: 1895–
CAH VII. 2	*The Cambridge Ancient History*, Volume VII, Part 2: *The Rise of Rome to 220 BC*, second edition. Cambridge: 1989.
CIL	*Corpus Inscriptionum Latinarum*
FGrH	Jacoby. F. (ed.), *Die Fragmente der griechischen Historiker.* Berlin & Leiden: 1923–
IGLS	*Inscriptiones grecques et latines de la Syrie*
ILLRP	Degrassi, A., *Inscriptiones Latinae Liberae Rei Publicae.* Florence: 1963
ILS	Dessau, H., *Inscriptiones Latinae Selectae.* Berlin: 1892–1916.
JRMES	*Journal of Roman Military Equipment Studies*
JRS	*Journal of Roman Studies*
P. Ross. Georg.	Zereteli, G. and O. Krueger, *Papyri Russischer u. Georgischer Sammlungen.* Tiflis: 1925.
RE	Pauly, A. Fr. von, G. Wissowa and W. Kroll (eds.), *Real-Encyclopädie der klassischen Altertumswissenschaft.* Stuttgart: 1893.
RIB	Collingwood, R. G. & R. P. Wright (eds.), *The Roman Inscriptions of Britain*, I. *Inscriptions on Stone.* Oxford: 1965.
SIG	Dittenberger, W., *Sylloge Inscriptionum Graecarum*, third edition. Leipzig: 1915–1924.

NOTES

Introduction *(pages 15-18)*

1. Phalanxes of Helvetii and Germans: Caesar, *Gallic War*, 1.24-25, 52.
2. Militaristic nature of Roman society, the Allies and the necessity of war: Cornell 1995, 364-8.

Chapter 1: The Pyrrhic War *(pages 19-77)*

1. Fame of Achilles: Plutarch, *Pyrrhus*, 7.4. Pyrrhus descended from Achilles: *ibid.*, 1; Pausanias, *Guide to Greece*, 1.11.1; Justin, *Epitome*, 17.3. Heracles: Florus, *Epitome*, 1.13.19; *De Viris Illustribus*, 25.1, *cf.* Plutarch, *Pyrrhus*, 22.5-6; Diodorus, 22.10.3: 'He vied to rank with Heracles.'
2. Pyrrhus' early life, role in wars of the *Diadochi*, Egyptian captivity, restoration and campaigns as king up to *c.* 282 BC (Aetolia, Macedonia, Thessaly, Illyria, Corcyra, etc.): Plutarch, *Pyrrhus*, 4-12. *Cf.* Pausanias, *Guide to Greece*, 1.6.7, 1.11.5-6; Justin, *Epitome*, 16.2-3, 17.3, 25.5.5.
3. Pyrrhus' military treatise: Cicero, *Letters to his Friends*, 9.25.1; Aelian, *Tactica*, 1.2; Plutarch, *Pyrrhus*, 8.2. Pyrrhus' tactics advocated by the Roman general Frontinus in his *Stratagems*, 2.6.9-10 (how to deal with an enemy made dangerous by desperation), 3.6.3 (how to lure an enemy from his defences). Hannibal on Pyrrhus: Livy, 35.14.8-9. *Cf.* Appian, *Syrian Wars*, 10: Pyrrhus was a great general 'because he [Hannibal] considered boldness the first qualification of a general'. Antigonus: Plutarch, *Pyrrhus*, 8.2 (note, however, that the comment may actually have been made by Antigonus Gonatas).
4. Recruiting officers: Frontinus, *Stratagems*, 4.1.3. Horned helmet and rich panoply: Plutarch, *Pyrrhus*, 11.5, 16.7. Pyrrhus' persuasiveness: *ibid.*, 4.4.
5. Franke's statement (1989, 467 f.) that Pyrrhus was 'not at all a man who thrived on the adventure of war', can hardly be reconciled with the king's career, which was dominated by warfare that he often instigated. *Cf.* Justin, *Epitome*, 25.4.2.
6. Although his conquests were short-lived, Pyrrhus was reckoned a better general than Alexander by the ancient historian Procles the Carthaginian: 'he was the better man in infantry and cavalry tactics and in the invention of stratagems of war' (quoted by Pausanias, *Guide to Greece*, 4.35.4).

7. Pantauchus versus Pyrrhus and Macedonians compare Pyrrhus to Alexander: *see also* Plutarch, *Demetrius*, 41.

8. The Eagle: Plutarch, *Pyrrhus*, 10.1. The king took an eagle as a pet: Plutarch, *Moralia*, 970c. Vision of Alexander: *Pyrrhus*, 11.2.

9. Lysimachus: Pausanias, *Guide to Greece*, 1.9.5–10.2; Plutarch, *Pyrrhus*, 11–12.

10. Pyrrhus chafes at inaction: Plutarch, *Pyrrhus*, 13. *See* chapter 1, note 2 for source references for Pyrrhus' Illyrian and Corcyra operations.

11. Tarentum's, power, wealth and beneficial position for trade and agriculture: Florus, *Epitome*, 1.13.2–3; Strabo, *Geography*, 6.3.1, 6.3.4, etc.; De Juliis 2000.

12. Tarentum's manpower: Brunt, 51.

13. Archidamus: Pausanias, *Guide to Greece*, 3.10.5; Diodorus Siculus, 16.63, 88.

14. Alexander the Molossian: Livy, 8.18.9; 8.24.

15. Cleonymus: Livy, 10.2 (10.2.3 for the Roman operation). Patavian gravestone: in the Museo Civico, Padua. The stele is reproduced in Salmon 1972, plate 44, and *Populi e civiltà dell'Italia antica* 4 (Roma, 1975), tav. 77.1.

16. Battle of Thurii: Valerius Maximus, 1.8.6; Ammianus Marcellinus, 24.4.24. If we remove the fantastic element from this battle, it seems that the Romans and Lucani did fight a rather desultory engagement before Thurii, but one legionary managed to break through the enemy battle line and climb the rampart of the siege camp. From there he called on his fellow soldiers to follow, the Lucani and Bruttii abandoned their battle line to defend the camp, and a second general engagement developed. Fabricius ascribed the victory to Mars probably because he had called on the god's aid immediately before or during the battle. The plumed helmet might have belonged to Sthenius Statilius or another enemy commander and was proudly displayed as a trophy – the spoils taken from an enemy general were always the most prized. All that the twin feathers signified were the courage of the wearer and his devotion to Mars/Mamers; Roman warriors also sported helmet plumes. But once Fabricius dedicated the victory to Mars, it would not have taken long for the story of the god's intervention to develop. The Romans who fought in the battle probably came to believe that the god had fought alongside them. (Pliny, *Natural History*, 34.32, gives Statilius the first name Sthen(n)ius; Valerius Maximus, etc., refer to him as Statius.) Twin feathers as crest of Mars: Virgil, *Aeneid*, 6.779. Romans wear plumes in helmet: Polybius, 6.22.12–13. Feathers identify Italic warriors with Mars: Salmon 1967, 108–9.

17. The Bacchanalia later spread to Rome. In 189 BC the Senate found it necessary to outlaw celebration of the festival.

18. Tarentum attacks Roman fleet and insults envoys: Dio, 9.39.5–8; Zonaras, 8.2, pp. 295–301; Dionysius of Halicarnassus, 19.5; Appian, *Samnite History*, 7.1–2. Orosius claims that the Tarentines also beat the envoys (*History Against the Pagans*, 4.1.2).

19. Tarentines supply fleet for Pyrrhus' Corcyra operation: Pausanias, *Guide to Greece*, 1.12.1.

20. Size of force promised to Pyrrhus: Plutarch, *Pyrrhus*, 13.6. Brunt, 59–60, doubts that 150,000 men of military age were available for active service in the south of Italy. Salmon 1967, 286 n.1, suggests that Pyrrhus' strained relations with the Samnites were influenced not only by their not sending any troops to fight at Heraclea, but by their number being much smaller than the Tarentines had led him to expect. Locri: Franke, 471–2. The payments were made from the treasury of the temple of Zeus Olympios. A considerable portion of the temple's wealth

derived from sacral prostitution. Locri's Roman garrison: Justin, *Epitome,* 18.1.9. Tarentine payments to Pyrrhus: Zonaras, 8.2, p. 309.

21. Pyrrhus dreams of empire: Plutarch, *Pyrrhus,* 14; Zonaras, 8.2, p. 307. New Trojan War: Pausanias, 1.12.2. Roman foundation myths: Momigliano, 56–62.

22. Oracular responses. Dodona: Dio, 9.40.6. Delphi: Cicero, *On Divination,* 2.56.116 = Ennius, *Annals,* frag. 174. Cicero believed Ennius used poetic licence to invent this response. The oracle at Dodona was said to have prophesised the death of Alexander the Molossian at Pandosia (Livy, 8.24.1). Paulus Orosius, a late Roman Christian, revels in Pyrrhus' 'deception' by the pagan oracle at Delphi (*History Against the Pagans,* 4.1.7, cf. *De Viris Illustribus,* 35.1–2).

23. Kings supply troops and materiel to Pyrrhus: Justin, *Epitome,* 17.2.13–15. Justin claims that Ptolemy Ceraunus offered 5,000 infantry and 4,000 cavalry, as well as 50 war elephants, but Plutarch, *Pyrrhus,* 15.1, reports only 20 elephants. The elephants were from Alexander the Great's original corps (Pausanias, *Guide to Greece,* 1.12.4). Macedonian troops, perhaps reinforcements, are reported at the battle of Ausculum. Much of Pyrrhus' cavalry was Thessalian. Following his success in Macedonia in 288 BC, Pyrrhus made substantial gains in Thessaly, though these also were mostly lost to Lysimachus.

24. Aemilius Barbula: Zonaras, 8.2, pp. 301–5; Frontinus, *Stratagems,* 1.4.1.

25. Pyrrhus' army, the advance force, crossing of the Adriatic, conscription of Tarentines, etc.: Plutarch, *Pyrrhus,* 15–16.2; Zonaras, 8.2, pp. 309–13. To the eminent classicist Tenney Frank Pyrrhus seemed like 'some Viking chieftain running amuck in a renaissance city' (Frank, 643). The Tarentines would probably have agreed.

26. Battle of Heraclea. The principal written sources are Plutarch, *Pyrrhus,* 16.3–17.5, and Zonaras, 8.3, pp. 317–27. Other sources are referred to in subsequent notes.

27. Laevinus' strategic force in Lucania: Zonaras, 8.3, p. 317.

28. Size of opposing armies. Justin, *Epitome,* 18.5.1, states that Pyrrhus was outnumbered, but the other ancient sources simply emphasise the large size of the Roman army and Pyrrhus' desire for reinforcements. Pyrrhus would have left a strong garrison at Tarentum, not only to counter a hostile move by Aemilius Barbula, but also to prevent an uprising by the discontented Tarentines. Franke, 466, estimates the Roman army at 30,000 and says it outnumbered Pyrrhus' force. Frank, 645, estimates the Romans at c. 24,000 (two legions of 4,000 and twice the number of Allies), and roughly the same number of Epirotes and Tarentines. Laevinus had also left troops in Lucania. Even before this, Zonaras (8.3, p. 317) suggests that his legions may not have been at full strength because a proportion of the army was left to garrison Rome. Cary & Scullard, 95, put the Roman army at 20,000. This may have been considered enough. The Romans had little, if any, experience of transporting large numbers of troops by sea and perhaps doubted that Pyrrhus had been able to ship many soldiers from Epirus. For more estimates of Epirote and Roman strength *see* Lévèque, 321–2.

29. Pyrrhus' letter and Laevinus' response: Dionysius of Halicarnassus, 19.9–10; Zonaras, 8.3, p. 319; Plutarch, *Pyrrhus,* 16.3–4.

30. Pyrrhus and Roman discipline: Plutarch, *Pyrrhus,* 16.4–5. Hannibal said Pyrrhus perfected the fortified camp, and the later Roman general Frontinus asserted that the Romans improved their camps by copying those of Pyrrhus (Livy, 35.14.8; Frontinus, *Stratagems,* 4.1.14).

31. Bandits: Livy, 10.1.1–6. Nequinum: Livy, 10.9.7–10.6

32. Fabricius enriches troops: Dionysius of Halicarnassus, 19.16.3.

33. Length of service, recruitment and organisation of Roman armies: Polybius, 6.19–26. Military age: Aulus Gellius, *Attic Nights*, 10.28.1.

34. Roman and Allied manpower. For the period before 225 BC *see* Brunt, 26–32. Livy, *Periochae*, 13 records the census return for 280 BC but Brunt sounds caution over their authenticity. For the varying size of the legion and proportion of Italian Allies in Roman armies, *see* Brunt, 671–86.

35. Laevinus and scout: Dionysius of Halicarnassus, 19.11; Zonaras, 8.3, p. 319.

36. Lucanian cows: Pliny, *Natural History*, 8.6.16.

37. Laevinus' speech: Zonaras, 8.3, p. 319.

38. Elephants held in reserve: Zonaras, 8.3, p. 323.

39. The Ferentani were probably of the Volsci (*cf.* Dionysius of Halicarnassus, 19.12.1, who gives Obsidius/Oblacus the *cognomen* 'Volsinius'), a powerful people from the central Apennines who fought Rome and her Latin Allies for control of Latium throughout the fifth century BC. The Ferentani were conquered in 316 BC. *See* Salmon 1967, 230, n.2.

40. Obsidius and Ferentani. The cavalry officer is called Obsidius by Florus, *Epitome*, 1.13.7. Plutarch, *Pyrrhus*, 16.8–10, calls him Oplax, probably a Greek version of Oblacus, as he is called by Dionysius of Halicarnassus, 19.12. Zonaras notes that Pyrrhus' men thought he had been killed (8.3, p. 323).

41. Macedonian phalanx: Polybius, 18.28–32 for a description of the phalanx and its strengths and weaknesses compared to the manipular legion. Connolly 2006, 78, for an illustration of a *speira*. File leaders form 'sword edge': Asclepiodotus, *Tactics*, 3.5.

42. Tactics and workings of the manipular legion and Allied cohorts: *see* Livy, 8.8.9–10.9.

43. Laevinus' bloody sword: Frontinus, *Stratagems*, 2.4.9.

44. Roman casualties: Plutarch, *Pyrrhus*, 17.4, following Hieronymus and so perhaps deriving from Pyrrhus' own 'memoirs', gives the total of Roman dead as 7,000. Dionysius of Halicarnassus (quoted by Plutarch) and Orosius, *History Against the Pagans*, 4.1.11, put the casualties at 14,880. The higher figures may derive from the historian Timaeus, a Sicilian Greek who was exiled by Agathocles in 315 BC and spent the next fifty years in Athens. He wrote a pro-Roman account of the Pyrrhic War but he was criticised in antiquity for inaccuracies and falsifications (Polybius, book 12). Roman captives: Eutropius, *Breviarium*, 2.11, says 1,800; Orosius, *ibid.*, gives the rather precise figures of 1,310 infantry and 802 cavalrymen (probably too good to be true), as well as 22 military standards (perhaps a reasonable estimate). Orosius, *ibid.*, recounts the deed of the centurion 'Minucius' against the elephant, but Florus, *Epitome*, 1.13.9, has the episode performed by the *hastatus* Gaius 'Numucius' at Ausculum in 279 BC. *Cf.* Jordanes, *Romana*, 7, placing the event at Ausculum and naming the *hastatus* as Gaius 'Minutius'. Note also Justin, *Epitome*, 18.1.7, who says Pyrrhus sustained a serious wound at Heraclea, perhaps confusing the wound caused by a *pilum* at Ausculum (*cf.* Plutarch, *Pyrrhus*, 21.9).

45. Pyrrhus' losses, his 'memoirs' and Hieronymus: Plutarch, *Pyrrhus*, 17.4, 21.8. Pyrrhus' inscription at Tarentum: Orosius, *History Against the Pagans*, 4.1.14 (following Ennius). Sulla: Plutarch, *Sulla*, 19; Livy, *Periochae*, 82. Memnon (frag. 32) states that the Pontic army was only *c.* 60,000 strong, thus underlining the absurdity of Sulla's claim. *See* Eutropius, *Breviarium*, 5.6–8 for more examples of Sulla's extraordinary casualty figures.

46. Pyrrhus inspects dead. *Cf.* Eutropius, *Breviarium*, 2.11. Livy, *Epitome*, 13: 'After this battle when Pyrrhus inspected the bodies of the Romans who had fallen, he found that they all faced their enemies.'

47. Cremation of Romans: Florus, *Epitome*, 1.13.15; Eutropius, *Breviarium*, 2.11, says they were buried. Pyrrhus asks Roman captives to join him: Dio, frag. 40.23. Dodona inscription: *SIG* 392. The inscription confirms that the battle was won without the aid of Italic or Italiote allies. The Messapians recruited after the crossing of the Adriatic were presumably enrolled into the Epirote or Tarentine phalanxes. Armour dedicated to Athena: *Chronicle of the Temple of Lindus*, FGrH 532, lines 114–21. Higbie, 138, suggests that the dedication of inscribed armour (the inscription itself is not recorded) be linked to Pyrrhus' victory over Antigonus and his Gallic mercenaries in 274 BC, *cf.* Plutarch, *Pyrrhus*, 26.10 and Pausanias, *Guide to Greece*, 1.13.2–3. Franke, 468, is happy to connect the dedication with Heraclea.

48. Late arrival of Pyrrhus' allies. Plutarch, *Pyrrhus*, 17.5, says that the king's anger died swiftly because he was so proud of having won the battle with only the Tarentines to support him, but there is no mention of sharing the spoils. Dio, frag. 40.21–22 and Zonaras, 8.3, pp. 327–9, report that Pyrrhus grudgingly gave the new allies a share of the spoils. Salmon, 1967, 286, believes Pyrrhus did not give any booty to the Samnites.

49. Sabellian reinforcements identified by Eutropius, *Breviarium*, 2.12. Epirote plundering: Dio, frag. 40.26–27. The Samnite contingent appears to have taken the opportunity to sack strategic Fregellae, where Rome had established a Latin colony in 328 BC to dominate the routes between Latium, Samnium and Campania. Fregellae was not in Samnium proper but fell under the sphere of Samnite influence and the establishment of the colony had triggered the Second Samnite War (Florus, *Epitome*, 1.13.24; Salmon 1967, 212, 286). Fabricius' and the Senate's criticism of Laevinus: Plutarch, *Pyrrhus*, 18.1, 19.5. Saepinum: Frontinus, *Stratagems*, 4.1.24.

50. Enrollment of *proletarii*: Orosius, *History Against the Pagans*, 4.1.3. Laevinus secures Capua and Naples: Zonaras, 8.4, p. 331. Pyrrhus at Praeneste: Florus, *Epitome*, 1.13.24; Eutropius, *Breviarium*, 2.12. Anagnia: Appian, *Samnite History*, 10.3. Plutarch, *Pyrrhus*, 17.5, says the king advanced to within forty miles of Rome.

51. Pyrrhus retreats before he is cut off by Coruncanius and protests of allies: Dio, frag. 40.27; Zonaras, 8.4, pp. 331–3. Laevinus confronts Pyrrhus in Campania and Roman army like the hydra: Zonaras, 8.4, pp. 333–5; Florus, *Epitome*, 1.13.19. Plutarch, *Pyrrhus*, 19.5, and Appian, *Samnite History*, 10.3, attribute the remark to Cineas after his embassy to Rome. The slaying of the Lernaean hydra was one of the twelve labours of Heracles, the supposed ancestor of Pyrrhus.

52. The sources for the negotiations are confused, for example whether Fabricius' embassy was sent to Pyrrhus before or after Cineas' trip to Rome; if Cineas made one or two trips to Rome; when exactly the prisoners were released. This section draws on the reconstruction of events in Franke, 470–1.

53. Pyrrhus' terms: Plutarch, *Pyrrhus*, 18.3–4; Zonaras, 8.4, p. 347. Cineas a student of Demosthenes: Plutarch, *Pyrrhus*, 14.1; Dio, 9.40.5; Appian, *Samnite History*, 10.1.

54. Caecus' speech and the Senate's rejection of Pyrrhus' terms: Plutarch, *Pyrrhus*, 18.5–19.5; Zonaras, 4.3, pp. 347–9. Later influence of the speech: Cicero, *On Old*

Age, 16; *Brutus*, 61. Rome a city of kings, or Senate a council of kings: Appian, *Samnite History*, 10.3; Justin, *Epitome*, 18.2.10.

55. Fabricius may also have led the initial delegation seeking the release of the prisoners.

56. Fabricius' embassy to Pyrrhus: Plutarch, *Pyrrhus*, 20, and Appian, *Samnite Wars*, 10.4–5, place this embassy after Cineas' trip to Rome. Dio, 9.40.29–38, Zonaras, 8.4, pp. 335–45, and Dionysius of Halicarnassus, 19.13–18, put it before Cineas' mission.

57. Pyrrhus' invasion of Apulia: Zonaras, 8.5, p. 351.

58. Plutarch's description of Ausculum: *Pyrrhus*, 21.5–10.

59. Pyrrhic and Cadmean victory: Dio, frag. 40.19; Zonaras, 8.3, p. 327; Diodorus, 22.6.1–2. 'Pyrrhic victory' as a modern expression: Keppie 1984, 235 n.8.

60. Size and battle order of armies: Dionysius of Halicarnassus, 21.1; Frontinus, *Stratagems*, 2.3.21 (the Homeric verse = *Iliad*, 4.299); Polybius, 18.28.10. Polybius certainly used Timaeus as a source, but was extremely critical of him. Pyrrhus unable to send to Epirus for more troops or money: Plutarch, *Pyrrhus*, 21.9–10. (Zonaras, 8.5, p. 355, says the opposite.)

61. First stage of battle and wagons versus elephants: Dionysius of Halicarnassus, 20.2.1–3.1; Zonaras, 8.5, pp. 353–5.

62. Alternative tactics against elephants: Florus, *Epitome*, 1.13.9–10; Orosius, *History Against the Pagans*, 4.1.21. *Cf.* Jordanes, *Romana*, 7.

63. Daunians and final stages of battle: Dionysius of Halicarnassus, 20.3.2–7; Zonaras, 8.5, p. 355.

64. Plutarch on Dionysius: *Pyrrhus*, 21.9. Ausculum as Roman victory: Frontinus, *Stratagems*, 2.3.21; Eutropius, *Breviarium*, 2.13; Orosius, *History Against the Pagans*, 4.1.19–23. Pyrrhus' retreat: Zonaras, 8.5, p. 355.

65. *Devotio*: Zonaras, 8.5, pp. 351–3, *cf.* Dio, frag. 40.43; Cicero, *Tusculan Disputations* 1.89 and *de Finibus* 2.61. Failed *devotio*: Skutsch, and Cornell 1987. Livy, 8.9.12, describes a ritual involving the burial of a statue of the failed, meaning a surviving, *devotus* and other sacrificial offerings to atone for the failure. The Capestrano Warrior has been identified as the statue of a Picente *devotus*, *see* Holland. Volsinii and consul of 265 BC: *De Viris Illustribus*, 36.1; Fulvius Flaccus' victory inscription of 264 BC: *AE* 1966, 13. Franke, 472, however, rejects the *devotio* tradition and accepts that Publius Decius Mus was again consul in 265 BC. *Cf.* Forsythe, 355: 'Its historicity is to be rejected as a later Roman patriotic fiction.'

66. Death of Ptolemy Ceraunus and appeal of Sicilians: Plutarch, *Pyrrhus*, 21.1–22.3; Diodorus, 22.7.2–6; Justin, *Epitome*, 24.4.8–5.7. Plot of Nicias and release of Roman prisoners: Zonaras, 8.5, pp. 355–7; Appian, *Samnite Wars*, 11; Plutarch, *Pyrrhus*, 21.1–3, though his chronology is out of step here; Eutropius, *Breviarum* 2.14, where the doctor actually comes in person to Fabricius and is sent back in chains to Pyrrhus. Roman pact with Carthage: Polybius, 3.25; Diodorus, 22.7.5. Tarentum left alone: note Zonaras, 8.5, p. 359.

67. Treatment of returned captives: Valerius Maximus, 2.7.15b; Frontinus, *Stratagems*, 4.1.18; Eutropius, *Breviarium*, 2.13.2. (Note also Cotta's treatment of noble officers in 252 BC: Frontinus, *Stratagems*, 4.1.30–31.) However, Zonaras, 8.4, p. 349, says that the former captives were split up, barred from service against Pyrrhus (*cf.* treatment of the later Cannae Legions) and put on garrison duty. Cannae Legions: Livy, 26.5.10–7.4; Valerius Maximus, 2.7.15c.

68. Anger of Tarentines and Pyrrhus' autocratic behaviour: Plutarch, *Pyrrhus*, 22.3. Milo (and Pyrrhus' son, Helenus?) left in command in Italy: Zonaras, 8.5, p. 357. Size of Pyrrhus' army: Appian, *Samnite Wars*, 11.2.

69. Pyrrhus in Sicily: Diodorus, 22.8, 22.10; Plutarch, *Pyrrhus*, 22.4–23.5; Dionysius of Halicarnassus, 22.8; Justin, *Epitome*, 23.3.1–10.

70. Alexander at Locri: Justin, *Epitome*, 1.18.12. Sea battle off Rhegium and battle with *legio Campana* and Mamertines: Appian, *Samnite Wars*, 12.1; Zonaras, 8.6, p. 363; Plutarch, *Pyrrhus*, 24. Pyrrhus' flagship later used by the Carthaginians in battle against the Romans at Mylae (260 BC): Polybius, 1.23.4. On the problematical size and status (whether Roman citizens, Allies, or a combined force), operations and intentions of the *legio Campana, see also* Polybius, 1.7; Dionysius of Halicarnassus, 20.4–5, 22.16; Diodorus, 22.1.3, 22.7.5; Livy, 31.31.6–7, *cf. Periochae*, 12, 14; Zonaras, 8.6, pp. 369–71; Valerius Maximus, 2.7.15f; Orosius, *History Against the Pagans*, 4.2.3–6, calling it the Eighth Legion. It was not until 270 BC that the Campanian legion was finally dealt with; Rhegium was stormed and the 300 surviving soldiers were taken to Rome where they were scourged and beheaded in the Forum. Robbing of temple of Persephone (called Proserpina by Romans and Italics) and her divine wrath: Dio, frag. 40.48; Dionysius of Halicarnassus, 20.9–10; Appian, *ibid.*, 12.1–2; Livy, 29.8, 29.18.3–7

71. Roman campaigns and appeals to Pyrrhus: Zonaras, 8.6, pp. 359–65; Plutarch, *Pyrrhus*, 25.1; Justin, *Epitome*, 23.3.5, 18.1.1 (Samnites). Fall of Croton: Zonaras, 8.6, p. 361, though not universally accepted. Heraclea: Cicero, *Pro Archia*, 6. Plague in Rome: Orosius, *History Against the Pagans*, 4.2.1. If the census figures recorded by Livy (*Periochae*, 13 and 14) are accepted, they demonstrate the decline in the number of citizens between 280 and 275 BC.

72. Size of Pyrrhus' army: Plutarch, *Pyrrhus*, 24.4. Plutarch does not mention the campaign against Rhegium (Zonaras, 8.6, p. 363), or the robbing of the temple of Persephone, presenting the Mamertines as ambushing Pyrrhus as he made his way back to Tarentum immediately after the sea battle in the Straits. Perhaps Plutarch was deliberately selective with events so that he could move quickly on to Pyrrhus' defeat at Malventum and embark on the next stage of the biography – the king's final campaigns in Greece.

73. Pyrrhus divides army and Curius waiting on reinforcements from Lentulus: Plutarch, *Pyrrhus*, 25.1–2. Malventum: *ibid.*, 25.2, says that the battle was fought near Beneventum – the name the Romans gave to the colony they founded at Samnite Malventum in 268 BC (*cf.* Livy, 9.27.14). Other sources place the battle at a place called the Arusine Plains in Lucania: Florus, *Epitome*, 1.13.11; Orosius, *History Against the Pagans*, 4.2.3; Jordanes, *Romana*, 7. However, Salmon 1967, 287, is content to site the Campi Arusini near Beneventum. Perhaps an action that occurred during Pyrrhus' initial advance through Lucania, or the operations of Pyrrhus' detached force, later became confused with the main battle at Malventum? Samnites: Plutarch, *Pyrrhus*, 25.1; Livy, 23.42.6 emphasises the ill-feeling the Samnites still bore against Pyrrhus sixty years after his departure from Italy.

74. Manius Curius Dentatus versus Samnites, Sabines and Gauls: Livy, *Periochae*, 11; Polybius, 2.19. Resistance to levy: Valerius Maximus, 6.3.4.

75. Strategic importance of Malventum/Beneventum: Salmon 1967, 20–3, 69. Curius' desire to engage Pyrrhus on rough terrain: Frontinus, *Stratagems*, 2.2.1.

76. Battle of Malventum. The principal sources are Plutarch, *Pyrrhus*, 25, Dionysius

of Halicarnassus, 20.10–12 (the detail about the young elephant and *principes/
triarii* are applied by the excerpts of Dionysius to the battle on the slopes but
Plutarch's account suggests that the details belong to the main battle; Dionysius'
statement that Pyrrhus' army was three times bigger than that of Curius is a gross
exaggeration), and Zonaras, 8.6, pp. 363–5. *See also* Florus, *Epitome*, 1.13.12.
Orosius, *History Against the Pagans*, 4.2.3–6, adds the detail about the flaming
missiles used against the elephants, but the size of Pyrrhus' army (86,000!) and
number of casualties (33,000) are to be rejected. *Cf.* Eutropius, *Breviarium*, 2.14,
where Pyrrhus sustains 23,000 casualties – perhaps more men than he was
actually able to put in the field. Pyrrhus' camp: Frontinus, *Stratagems*, 4.2.14.

77. Pyrrhus threatens Antigonus Gonatas: Justin, *Epitome*, 25.3.1–3; Pausanias,
    Guide to Greece, 1.13.1.

78. Size of army when Pyrrhus leaves Tarentum: Plutarch, *Pyrrhus*, 26.2. Milo and
    Helenus: Justin, *Epitome*, 25.3.3–6. Nicias chair: Zonaras, 8.6, p. 363.

79. Milo and final defeat of Sabellians: Zonaras, 8.6, pp. 367–71; Frontinus,
    Stratagems, 3.3.1. On the Roman settlement of Italy after Pyrrhic war, with
    particular reference to the measures taken against the recalcitrant Samnite tribes,
    see Salmon, 1967, 287–92. Ptolemy II: Zonaras, 8.6, p. 367; Dionysius of
    Halicarnassus, 20.14, etc.

80. Anio Vetus aqueduct: Frontinus, *Aqueducts of Rome*, 1.6.

81. Pyrrhus' last campaigns and death: Plutarch, *Pyrrhus*, 26–34; Justin, *Epitome*,
    25.3–5; Pausanias, *Guide to Greece*, 1.13.1–7, 2.21.4–5. Pyrrhus acknowledged
    the wrath of Persephone in his 'memoirs': Dionysius of Halicarnassus, 20.10.2.

82. Pyrrhus' *virtus*: Cicero, *On Offices*, 1.38 = Ennius, *Annals*, frag. 186–93.

Chapter II: Divine Intervention *(pages 78–101)*

1. Third Samnite War. On its origins and course *see* Salmon 1967, 255–79.

2. Battle at Camerinum: Livy, 10.26.7–13. Livy rightly dismissed alternative versions
   of the battle that made the Umbrians the principal enemy and Barbatus the
   victor, but he is confused about the location, placing the fight at Clusium, also
   known in antiquity as Camars. Polybius, 2.19.5–6, locates the battle at
   Camerinum and indicates that Samnites as well as Senones were present. Scipio
   Barbatus' handsomeness, *virtus* and accomplishments are laid out in his epitaph
   (*ILS*, 1 = *ILLRP*, 309), but the inscription was erased and re-carved, perhaps with
   embellishments, *c.* 200 BC, and is contrary to Livy's account of his campaigns as
   consul in 298 BC (10.12.3–8). It is not certain that Gellius Egnatius was the
   supreme commander of the confederate army; he may well have shared command
   with a Senonian chieftain or king, but he was certainly the leading personality of
   the campaign. Fulvius and Postumius in Etruria: Livy, 10.26.14–15, 26.5, 30.1–2;
   Orosius, *History Against the Pagans*, 3.21.3; Frontinus, *Stratagems*, 1.8.3. The
   tradition in the sources that the Etruscans (and some Umbrians) were actually
   with Egnatius at Sentinum but persuaded to return home a few days before the
   battle began because of the depredations of Fulvius and Postumius is perhaps to
   be rejected as the attempt of later Roman historians to make the confederate army
   at Sentinum appear overwhelming. It seems more likely that the Etruscans were
   deterred from crossing the Apennines in the first place. For a list of Italic members
   and sympathisers of Egnatius' anti-Roman coalition *see* Salmon 1967, 265.

   The legion that Fabius Rullianus put Barbatus in command of is identified
   by Livy as the Second (10.25.11). Rullianus' legions at the subsequent battle at

Sentinum had the numerals I and III (10.27.10). At 10.25.1–4 Rullianus selects 4,000' elite volunteer infantry and 600 cavalry from Rome, almost certainly a legion but with a larger than usual cavalry component. The two legions Rullianus took over from Appius Claudius Caecus in the camp at Aharna early in 295 BC were numbered I and IV and presumably given new numerals (10.18.4, 25.5). One suspects that Barbatus' *legio II* was one of the old legions and not the new formation recruited by Rullianus in Rome (*legio III* at Sentinum?), but this cannot be proven. A Second Legion was operating in Samnium in 295 BC under the proconsul Volumnius Flamma (10.27.11). This may have been another unit, given a numeral different to that it held in the previous year, but there remains the possibility that it was same unit as fought at Camerinum, though substantially reconstituted.

3. Rullianus' training methods: Livy, 10.25.10.

4. Battle of Sentinum. The principal source is Livy, 10.27–29 and is considered to be essentially authentic (Cornell 1989, 379). The seriousness and outcome of the battle is confirmed by Polybius, 2.19.6. *See also* Zonaras, 8.1, pp. 277–9, whose account was summarised from Dio, Book 8, and the brief mentions in *De Viris Illustribus*, 27.3–5, 28.4. Neither differs from Livy's account.

5. Size of Legions at Sentinum: Cornell 1989, 379, who also estimates the number of Roman and Allied soldiers as over 36,000. Polybius, 6.20.8–9, gives the standard complement of the manipular legion as 4,200 infantry (raised to 5,000 infantry in emergencies) and 300 cavalry. His figures may be more appropriate to the mid-second century BC than the time of Sentinum, but he does state that legions of approximately this size – the number of infantry is given as 4,000 – campaigned in Sicily in 263 BC (1.16.2). Allies in reserve lines at Sentinum: note Livy, 10.29.5, 10–11. Elite Campanian cavalry: *ibid.*, 10.26.14, 29.12.

6. Exaggerations of size of confederate army: Livy, 10.30.4–7. *Cf.* Diodorus Siculus, 26.6.1 for the notice that Duris, the Greek tyrant of Samos and also a historian who lived at the time of Sentinum, put the confederate casualties at 100,000. Salmon 1967, 265, suggests that the number of legionaries (perhaps nine legions – four consular, two with Volumnius, one each with Fulvius, Postumius, and Barbatus) and Allies the Romans mobilised in 295 BC totalled 100,000 and Duris assumed each Roman soldier 'accounted for one of the enemy'.

7. Rullianus asks for support of Decius: Livy, 10.25.11–26.7, noting the conflicting accounts in his sources.

8. Defence of intervals in battle lines. *See* Livy, 8.8–10 and 30.32; Herodian, 4.15.1.

9. *Devotio* practised by Picentes: Holland. *Devotio* understood and feared by Samnites and other Italians: Salmon 1967, 146. If the Capestrano Warrior statue represents a *devotus*, Picente *devoti* would appear to have gone to their deaths in full armour but perhaps of a recognisably ritual type. Picentes allied to the Romans and warn them of Egnatius' confederation: Livy, 10.11.7.

10. Samnite fugitives attacked by Paeligni: Livy, 10.30.3.

11. Sentinum veterans rewarded from spoils: Livy, 10.30.10.

12. Cremation of Decius: Zonaras, 8.1, p. 279. Altar of Victory grave: Forsythe, 330–3.

13. Gods intervene in battles. Lake Regillus: Livy, 2.20.12, 2.42.5; Valerius Maximus, 1.8.1a; Cicero, *On the Nature of the Gods*, 2.6, 3.11; Dionysius of Halicarnassus, 6.13; Frontinus, *Stratagems*, 1.11.8. Pydna: Plutarch, *Aemilius Paullus*, 25; Florus, *Epitome*, 1.28.14–15; Valerius Maximus, 1.8.1b–c. Vercellae: Florus,

Epitome, 1.38.19–21; Pliny, *Natural History*, 7.86. Silvanus: Livy, 2.7.1; Dionysius of Halicarnassus, 5.16; Valerius Maximus, 1.8.5.

14. Historicity of *devotiones*. Cornell 1989, 379, is emphatic about the *devotio* at Sentinum: '[an] undoubtedly historical incident'. The *devotio* at the Veseris (Livy, 8.6.9–13, 8.9) is sometimes considered fictitious, inspired by the deed at Sentinum, *e.g.* Forsythe, 289.

15. Appius Claudius and Bellona: Livy, 10.19.17–22. Regulus, Jupiter Stator and the yoke: Livy, 10.35.1–36.15; Zonaras, 8.1 (pp. 279–81). Although Livy settled on Regulus as the consul at Luceria, he noted that some earlier Roman historians disagreed about the identity of the Roman commander (10.37.13–16). Claudius Quadrigarius, writing around 80 BC, asserted that it was Postumius Megellus and he was defeated outright; the version of Fabius Pictor, the first Roman historian who composed his work at the end of the third century and was therefore much closer in time to the event, placed both consuls at Luceria, a temple vowed, and the fighting end, apparently in stalemate (cover for a Roman defeat?), with serious losses to both sides. If Postumius was at Luceria, it is interesting to note that he dedicated his temple to Victoria before setting out from Rome on campaign (perhaps the occasion of the burial of Decius Mus), presumably in the hope that this would prove propitious for the warfare ahead (10.33.9–10). Livy has Postumius successful in both Samnium and Etruria. He too is denied a triumph by the Senate and the majority of the plebeian tribunes, but disregards their will and holds one anyway (10.37.6–12). Was this simply caused by the machinations of his political enemies or does it lend credence to the tradition that he was present at Luceria? This highlights the difficulties of reconstructing early Roman history.

16. Linen Legion and the battle of Aquilonia: Livy, 10.38–42; Pliny, *Natural History*, 34.43; Dio, frag. 36.29; Zonaras, 8.1, pp. 279–81. For discussion *see* Salmon 1967, 182–6 & 270–2.

17. Cursor's vow to Jupiter: Livy, 10.42.7; Pliny, *Natural History*, 14.91. Bloodlust of legionaries and joy of Cursor in combat: Livy, 10.41.1, 42.6. Fighting at Cominium: Livy, 10.43.1–8. Statue of Jupiter: Pliny, *ibid.*, 34.43. Pliny suggests that the warriors Carvilius fought were also 'sworn'. The twenty Samnite cohorts, each of 400 men, were recalled before they reached Cominium (Livy, 10.40.6, 43.9). Their absence from Aquilonia was a considerable factor in the Roman success.

18. Eagle as the symbol and messenger of Jupiter: Pliny, *Natural History*, 10.15; Cicero, *Tusculan Disputations*, 2.10.24. Marius, *aquila* and other legionary standards: Pliny, *ibid.*, 10.16. The minotaur is connected to Jupiter Feretrius by Parker, 37–8. Parker also connects the boar to Quirinus (a deity similar to Mars, and from the third century BC associated with Romulus) and the horse to Jupiter Stator. However, von Domaszewski, 12 n.1, links the horse to Mars and states that he could find no link between the minotaur, as a creature of the Greek myths, and one of the Roman gods.

19. Silver eagles, Catiline: Cicero, *Catiline*, 1.9.24, *cf.* Sallust, *War with Catiline*, 59.3, for the origins of this standard. Brutus and Cassius: Appian, *Civil Wars*, 4.101. Gold eagles: Herodian, 4.7.7, though not necessarily indicative that the *aquila* was solid gold. Aurelian: Dexippus, *FGrH* 100, fr. 6. Live eagle standard of *II Parthica*: Balty & Van Rengen, pl. 18; *AE* 1991, 1572.

20. Eagles and siting of camps: Pliny, *Natural History*, 10.16. Idistaviso: Tacitus, *Annals*, 2.17–18. Eagles peck at standards: Appian, *Civil Wars*, 4.101.

21. Pompeian eagles: Dio, 43.35.4. Marcellus: Livy, 23.31; Plutarch, *ibid*12.1. Shield devices: Rossi 1971, 108–18. Lightning Miracle: Historia Augusta, *Marcus Antoninus*, 24.4; Aurelian column scenes 10–11.

22. Rain Miracle: Dio, 71.8, with additional comments at 71.9–10 about the Christian legion by his epitomator, the Byzantine monk Xiphilinus; Aurelian Column scene 16. *See* A.R. Birley 1987, 172–4, for a detailed discussion of both miracles. Titles of *legio XII Fulminata*: Keppie 1984, 209–10.

23. Scipio and Neptune: Livy, 26.45–46.

24. Sertorius' white doe: Plutarch, *Sertorius*, 11, 20; Appian, *Civil Wars*, 1.110, where the lost deer reappears in the midst of a battle.

25. Lunar eclipse, AD 14: Tacitus, *Annals*, 1.28. Constantine's Sun vision: *Panegyrici Latini*, 6(7).21; perhaps later reinterpreted by Constantine himself as a vision of the Cross superimposed on the sun: Eusebius, *Life of Constantine*, 1.28–32. Constantine's dream before the battle and the command to 'mark the heavenly sign of God on the shields of his soldiers and then engage in battle': Lactantius, *On the Deaths of the Persecutors*, 44.5. An excellent discussion of the evidence for the Sun/Cross vision, its date, and association with the dream before the battle of the Milvian Bridge, is to be found in Cameron & Hall, 204–13.

Chapter III: Single Combat *(pages 102–83)*

1. Acron versus Romulus and establishment of the *spolia opima*: Livy, 1.10.3–7. Dionysius of Halicarnassus, 2.33, places the fight between the kings within Caenina. *See also* Valerius Maximus, 3.2.3 and Propertius, 4.10.5–22. Plutarch, *Romulus*, 16.3–4, has the kings issue simultaneous challenges. The decapitation of Acron is deduced by Voisin, 280. Pyrrhus and Mamertines: Plutarch, *Pyrrhus*, 24.2–4. Mettius Curtius and Hostius Hostilius: Livy, 1.12.2–3.

2. *Spolia opima* and triumph: Plutarch, *Romulus*, 16.5–7; Oakley, 398. Thyrea: Herodotus, 1.82.

3. Fight of the Horatii and Curiatii and Publius Horatius' punishment: Livy, 1.24–26; Dionysius of Halicarnassus, 3.18–22. Treachery and death of Mettius Fufetius: Livy, 1.28. Roman armies forced under the yoke: Caudine Forks: Livy, 9.5–6. Jugurtha: Sallust, *War with Jugurtha*, 38. Tigurini: Caesar, *Gallic War*, 1.12; Livy, *Pericochae*, 65. Passing under the yoke symbolic of decapitation: Voisin, 281. Purification of blood guilt: Ogilvie, 117.

4. Umbrian judicial duels: Nicolaus of Damascus, *FGrH* 90, fr. 111.

5. Military and social importance of bronze belts to Sabellian Italians: Salmon 1967, 109; Schneider-Herrmann, 15–19. The military belt (*balteus*) remained key to the identity of the Roman soldier under the Empire. Juvenal, a former cavalry officer, called soldiers 'armed and belted men' (*Satires*, 16.48) and in AD 69 legionaries massacred civilian pranksters who had taken their military belts (Tacitus, *Histories*, 2.88). In AD 193 Praetorian Guardsman were dishonourably discharged by having their military belts taken from them (Herodian, 2.13.10). Depictions of Italic warriors with spoils (tunics, belts, shields, greaves hung from spears carried over the shoulder): Schneider-Herrmann, plates 4, 5, 10, 16, 21, 33, 46, 53, 62, 111, 118, 128. Trophy helmet from an Etruscan tomb: Turfa, 147–8. Legionaries singing in battle at Pharsalus: Dio, 41.6.5–6; Lugdunum: Herodian, 3.7.3; Forum Gallorum: Appian, *Civil Wars*, 3.70. Olive wreaths: Appian, *ibid.*, 3.74.

6. Siccius Dentatus. Summaries of the number of battles and duels he fought, etc.: Dionysius of Halicarnassus, 10.36–39, supplies the details of Dentatus' military

exploits in the form of a speech supposedly delivered by the man himself.
See also Pliny, *Natural History*, 7.101; Aulus Gellius, *Attic Nights*, 2.11, where
he is called the Roman Achilles; Valerius Maximus, 3.2.24. His heroic death:
Livy, 3.43.

7. Pompey and Gallic cavalry commander: Plutarch, *Pompey*, 7. Note also the one-on-one fight between Pompey and the Albanian prince Cosis: *ibid.*, 35.3.

8. Slave legionaries: Livy, 24.14–15. Probus: Historia Augusta, *Probus*, 14.2. Trajan's Column: scenes 24, 56–57, 71, 113, etc., *see* Cichorius. Aurelian Column: scene 65, *see* Petersen. Trajanic Frieze: Robinson, plate 238 (far left). Munda: Anonymous, *Spanish War*, 32. Orange: Voisin, 254 f.

9. Julius Mansuetus: Tacitus, *Histories*, 3.25.

10. Display of *spolia* in house: Polybius, 6.39.9–10. Falerii breastplate: Flower 1998 suggests that rather than stripped from a fallen opponent, this breastplate was taken as plunder from a tomb during the sack of Falerii. Fire of Rome: Suetonius, *Nero*, 38.2. Pompey's trophies: Historia Augusta, *Three Gordians*, 2.3, 3.6.

11. Capestrano Warrior: Holland.

12. Crowns: Polybius, 6.38. Scipio Aemilianus: Velleius Paterculus, 1.12.4. Grass crowns: Pliny, *Natural History*, 22.6–13.

13. Spurius Ligustinus: Livy, 42.34. Statius Marrax: *ILS*, 2638.

14. Vibillius: Velleius Paterculus, 2.78.3.

15. Antony and the centurion: Plutarch, *Antony*, 64.2. Scars of Aquilius: Cicero, *Against Verres*, 2.5.3; *In Defence of Flaccus*, 98; Livy, *Periochae*, 70.1. Bravery and corruption ran in the family. Aquilius' father, the consul of 129 BC, completed the suppression of the revolt of Aristonicus in Asia and was awarded a triumph for his efforts (126 BC). He was guilty of accepting bribes during his governorship of Asia but was also acquitted (Appian, *Civil Wars*, 1.22). Sertorius: Plutarch, *Sertorius*, 4.2.

16. Servilius' number of duels and scars: Livy, 45.39.16–17; Plutarch, *Aemilius Paullus*, 31.4. Galba had wide support among the veterans who fought in the Pydna campaign. Many experienced men and former centurions, including Spurius Ligustinus, had volunteered for service in 171 BC in the expectation of taking rich plunder (Livy, 42.32.6), but Paullus' strict discipline prevented them from doing much pillaging. Following Pydna the troops were permitted to sack the cities of Epirus, which had sided with Macedon, but Epirus was no longer a great kingdom and the plunder was meagre. The legionaries received no share of the riches taken from Macedon. Coins: Crawford, numbers 264 and 370 (mounted combats), and 327 (foot combat).

17. Displaying scars. Verres: Cicero, *Against Verres*, 2.15.32. Tactic of Cicero: *In Defence of Rabirius*, 36. Munda veteran: Seneca, *On Benefits*, 5.24.1–3.

18. Cornelius Cossus: Livy, 4.19–20, Dionysius of Halicarnassus, 12.5. *See also* Propertius, 4.10.23–38 and Valerius Maximus, 3.2.4.

19. Manlius Torquatus: Livy, 7.10.

20. *Gladius Hispaniensis*: Connolly 1997 and Quesada Sanz.

21. Sword fighting against Gauls, 225–223 BC: Polybius, 2.30.8, 33.1–6.

22. Rutilius and gladiatorial training methods: Valerius Maximus, 2.3.2. Polybius on Roman sword-fighting methods: 18.30.6–7. Vegetius on use of sword point rather than the edge: *Epitome*, 1.12. *Gladius* as cut-and-thrust weapon: Polybius, 2.33.6, 18.30.7. *Gladius Hispaniensis* used as cutting weapon in the First Macedonian War: Livy, 31.34.4.

23. Continuity of Roman fighting technique. Suetonius Paulinus: Tacitus, *Annals*, 14.36. Shields at Mons Graupius: Tacitus, *Agricola*, 36, *cf. Annals*, 2.21.1 for the Idistaviso campaign (AD 16). First Cremona: Tacitus, *Histories*, 2.42. Vetera: *Histories*, 4.29. Manlius Capitolinus: Plutarch, *Camillus*, 27.4–5. Acilius: Valerius Maximus, 3.2.22; Suetonius, *Divine Julius*, 68.4.

24. Valerius Corvus: Livy, 7.26; Dionysius of Halicarnassus, 15.1.1–4; Zonaras, 7.25, pp. 235–7. Eligibility to dedicate *spolia opima*: Valerius Maximus, 3.2.6.

25. Juno Sospita coins: Crawford, number 509.

26. Uniquely in Eutropius' *Breviarium*, (2.5), the raven lands on Valerius' arm as he advances to meet the Gaul. The raven then proceeds to attack the Gaul's eyes.

27. Winged helmet: Oakley, 394, *cf*. Diodorus Siculus, 5.30.2. For a metal eagle with moveable wings surmounting a Gallic helmet, *see* Rusu. The helmet was discovered in Romania, in a warrior's grave, perhaps that of a king, dating to the third century BC. Gunderstrup Cauldron: Cunliffe, 98–9. Winged Italian helmets: Bottini, 215–19; Pflug, 146. Torquatus coins: *e.g.* Crawford, number 295.

28. Drusus: Suetonius, *Tiberius*, 3.2. Identified with Livius Denter: F. Münzer, *RE* XIII, cols 853–4; Oakley, 395. Cestius Macedonicus: Appian, *Civil Wars*, 5.49. Gaius Valerius Arsaces: *CIL* IX 1460; Keppie 1983, 159–60 for discussion. Actiaci: *e.g.* 'Marcus Billienus Actiacus . . . served in legion XI, fought in the naval battle' (*ILS*, 2243); *see* Keppie 1971 and 1983, 111 for other examples. Helvius Rufus Civica inscription: *ILS*, 2637. *Expilator*: Salmon 1967, 398.

29. Corvus' duel invented to explain his name: Lendon, 133–4.

30. Raven at Aquilonia: Livy, 10.40.14.

31. Corvus' early consulship: Livy, 7.26.12; Eutropius, *Breviarium*, 2.6, giving Corvus' age as twenty-three.

32. Execution of the younger Torquatus: Livy, 8.6.13–8.1; Dio, frag. 35.2; Zonaras, 7.26, pp. 239–43; Polybius on Roman military punishments: 6.37–38 (*fustuarium* – being beaten to death with clubs and stones for falling asleep on guard duty or cowardice in battle); on death of younger Torquatus: 6.54.5. Contrary nature of Torquatus senior: Cicero, *On Offices*, 3.112. Mutiny of 342 BC: Livy, 7.38–42.

33. Order against single combat: Livy, 7.12.12. Unauthorised skirmishing at Veii: Livy, 5.19.9. Feats of Roman cavalrymen at Jerusalem: Josephus, *Jewish War*, 5.312–316, 6.161–163. Titus' order: *ibid.*, 5.316. Jonathon versus Priscus: *ibid.*, 6.169–176. Victory celebration of legionaries: Appian, *Civil Wars*, 5.37.

34. Roman junior centurion (actually an *optio*?) versus Latin senior centurion: Livy, 8.8.17–18.

35. Servilius' twenty-three duels: *see also* Plutarch, *Aemilius Paullus*, 31.4.

36. Metellus as *bellator*: Pliny, *Natural History*, 7.140. Marcellus' military decorations and reputation as a duellist: Plutarch, *Marcellus*, 2.1–2.

37. Marcellus in retreat at Clastidium: Frontinus, *Stratagems*, 4.5.4.

38. Marcellus decapitates Viridomaris: Propertius, 4.10.44–45. Valerius Maximus' use of *obtruncare* to describe Viridomarus' death (3.2.5) is also suggestive of decapitation, *cf*. Voisin, 245–7, 280.

39. Marcellus dedicated *spolia opima*: Plutarch, *Marcellus*, 8.1–5.

40. Flaminius at Trasimene: Silius Italicus, *Punica*, 5.131–139 (helmet); Livy, 22.6–7.

41. Replacement senators: Livy, 23.23.6.

42. Punishment of centurions at Canusium: Livy, 27.13.9.

43. Marcellus' campaigns during Second Punic War: Livy, books 20–27; Plutarch, *Marcellus*, 9–30. 'Sword of Rome': *ibid.*, 9.4. Virtually nothing of the *Clastidium*

survives. It is also possible that it was read when Marcellus' temple of Honour and Courage was finally dedicated in 205 BC. Naevius was not Roman, he was Campanian, and his satirical swipes at prominent Romans earned him a spell in prison and he ended his life in exile.

44. Fictitious duels of the Scipios at Ticinus: Silius Italicus, *Punica*, 4.264–310; at Zama: Appian, *Punic Wars*, 44–5.

45. Asellus versus Taurea: Livy, 23.46.12–47.18. Misidentified as 'not aristocrats, but men from lower down the social scale' by Goldsworthy, 266 and n. 58, who also cites Livy, 25.18, as a duel fought between ordinary cavalrymen but this single combat pitted a Campanian aristocrat against a future Roman consul!

46. Numerous single combats at Capua: Appian, *Hannibalic War*, 37. Badius versus Crispinus: Livy, 25.18. Importance of *hospitium*: Aulus Gellius, *Attic Nights*, 4.13.5.

47. Sergius Silus: Pliny, *Natural History*, 7.104–6. Coin: Crawford, number 286.

48. Aemilianus and mural crown: Livy, *Periochae*, 48; Valerius Maximus, 3.2.6b, Velleius Paterculus, 1.12.4; Pliny, *Natural History*, 37.9. The crown may actually have been a simple *corona aurea*.

49. Marius at Aquae Sextiae: Frontinus, *Stratagems*, 4.7.5. Aemilianus considered un-Roman: Polybius, 31.23–24. At Pydna: Livy, 44.44.1–3. Plutarch, *Aemilius Paullus*, 22.

50. Duellists held in respect: Polybius, 6.39.6, 54.3–4. Fragments of Polybius: 35.5.1–2. Effectiveness of Roman saddle: Connolly 1987. *Spolia opima*: Florus, *Epitome*, 1.33.11, *cf.* Valerius Maximus, 3.2.6.

51. Scipio Nasica: Plutarch, *Aemilius Paullus*, 16.3.

52. Metellus Macedonicus. This famous incident occurred at Contrebia in 143/142 BC: Velleius Paterculus, 2.5.2–3. Metellus also forced his young son to serve as a common legionary rather than have him in his staff: Frontinus, *Stratagems*, 4.1.11.

53. Duels and death of Q. Occius Achilles: Valerius Maximus, 3.2.21, Livy, *Periochae* (Oxyrhynchus) 53–4. Dentatus is called the Roman Achilles by Aulus Gellius, *Attic Nights*, 2.11.2. Possible influence of Occius' deeds on the Siccius Dentatus tales: Oakley, 396 n.33.

54. Marius at Numantia: Plutarch, *Marius*, 3.

55. Lucius Opimius: Ampelius, 22.4.

56. Aquilius versus Athenion probably not a formal single combat: Oakley, 397. Florus, *Epitome*, 2.7.11 says Aquilius forced Athenion into a set battle by cutting off his supplies.

57. Death of Aquilius: Appian, *Mithridatic Wars*, 19. Honourable fight to death of Sicilian captives: Diodorus Siculus, 36.10.3.

58. Sertorius' challenge to Metellus Pius: Plutarch, *Sertorius*, 13.3–4. Insults Metellus and Pompey: *Sertorius*, 19.5.

59. Author of *Spanish War* identified as a centurion and eyewitness: Macaulay quoted by Way, 303. Identified as an ordinary legionary or cavalryman: Carter, xxxv.

60. Centurions challenge Gauls: Caesar, *Gallic War*, 5.43. Valerius Flaccus: Caesar, *Civil War*, 3.53. Goldsworthy, 268, doubts that Turpio and Niger were of any great rank. Osgood, 44, identifies them as centurions.

61. Pompeius Niger. Compare how the Gallic grandfather of the Roman historian Pompeius Trogus was given citizenship by Pompey while serving, perhaps as a cavalry officer, in the war against Sertorius (Justin, *Epitome*, 43.5.11–12).

62. Cornidius' flaming helmet: Florus, *Epitome*, 2.26.16.

63. Elder Crassus killed by one of his own men: Dio, 40.27.2.

64. Crassus versus Deldo and subsequent campaigns: Dio, 51.23–24. Renovation of the temple of Jupiter Feretrius: Nepos, *Atticus*, 20.3.

65. Livy on Augustus' reading of the Cossus inscription: 4.20. Varro's assertion about the wide eligibility for the *spolia opima* is quoted by Festus, 204L. Some scholars have interpreted the passage to mean that any soldier could win the *spolia opima* but only a general could make the dedication. *See* Flower 2000, 37–8.

66. Drusus and *spolia opima*: Suetonius, *Claudius*, 1.4.

67. Torquatus and Corvus used to inspire legionaries before a battle with the Galatians (189 BC): Livy, 38.17.8–9. Antony's challenges to Octavian: Plutarch, *Antony*, 62.3, 75.1.

68. Caesar at the Sabis: Caesar, *Gallic War*, 2.25. Munda: Appian, *Civil Wars*, 2.104. Thapsus: Anonymous, *African War*, 83. Decius: Aurelius Victor, *De Caesaribus*, 29.3–5; Zosimus, 1.23; Historia Augusta, *Aurelian*, 42.6. The name Decius inevitably attracted comparison with the *devotiones* of the Decii at the Veseris and Sentinum.

69. Single combat in the sixth century AD. Althias: Procopius, *History of the Wars*, 4.13.11–17. Andreas: *ibid.*, 1.13.29–38. Note also 1.18.31 and 4.24.10–12, mounted single combats with bows; 7.4.21–30 and 8.31.11–16, duels of the classic type with tall Gothic warriors coming out to challenge Romans; 8.35.11 suggests challenges to single combat being made by Romans.

70. Valerius Maximianus: *AE* 1956, 124. This episode is perhaps commemorated on the Aurelian Column, scene 43. *See* A.R. Birley 1987, 175–6.

Chapter IV: Warlords and Their Warriors *(pages 184–234)*

1. We are now dealing with the legion of ten cohorts but its operation in battle was probably similar to that of the manipular legion. The centuries within the cohorts could function like maniples and the legion was still regularly deployed in three lines (*triplex acies*). *See* Cowan 2007.

   Effective strengths of legions. When Caesar relieved the camp of Quintus Cicero (54 BC), his two legions had a combined strength of 7,000 men (Caesar, *Gallic War*, 5.49). At Pharsalus the average strength of a Caesarian legion was 2,750; Pompey's legions were each about 4,000 strong (Caesar, *Civil War*, 3.88–89). When Caesar followed Pompey to Egypt, he took two legions, their combined strength only 3,200 (*ibid.*, 3.106). One of the legions was the Sixth. It suffered more casualties in Egypt and arrived at the battlefield of Zela (47 BC) with less than a thousand men (Anonymous, *Alexandrian War*, 69). The legions Mark Antony took to Parthia in 36 BC had an average strength of 3,750 (Plutarch, *Antony*, 37.3).

2. Battle with the Helvetii: Caesar, *Gallic War*, 1.21–29. Caesar was avenging the army of Cassius Longinus, which was defeated by the Tigurini, one of the subgroups of the Helvetii, in the Garonne valley in 107 BC. The grandfather of Caesar's third wife was killed in the battle. Popilius Laenas, the senior surviving Roman officer, managed to save the lives of the remaining Roman soldiers by surrendering half of their possessions and handing over hostages. This already disgraceful negotiation was compounded when the Romans were forced under the yoke (*Gallic War*, 1.12; Orosius, *History Against the Pagans*, 5.15.23; Livy, *Pericochae*, 65). Battle against Ariovistus: Caesar, *Gallic War*, 1.48–53.

3. Perhaps referring to paired prior ('front') and posterior ('rear') centuries, in this instance fighting side by side, or maybe used in a more general sense to mean 'ranks'.

4. Caesar's leadership: *e.g.* at Alesia, *Gallic War*, 7.86–88.

5. Battle of the Sabis and Atuatuci: Caesar, *Gallic War*, 2.18–33. Identification of the Sabis: Pelling, 747–9. For the tribute levied from Gaul *see* Suetonius, *Divine Julius*, 25.1

6. Germans: Caesar, *Gallic War*, 4.16–19. British expeditions: *ibid.*, 4.20–34, 5.8–23. Thanksgivings: *Gallic War*, 2.35, 4.38. Cato's proposal: Appian, *Gallic History*, 18.

7. Petrosidius as Sabellian name: Syme, 89 & 93; Salmon 1967, 391 n.1, doubts that he was a Samnite.

8. Eburones and Nervii attack wintering legions: Caesar, *Gallic War*, 5.24–52. Escape of Ambiorix: *ibid.*, 6.43

9. Vercingetorix's strategy and Avaricum: Caesar, *Gallic War*, 7.14–28.

10. Gergovia: Caesar, *Gallic War*, 7.34–53.

11. Cavalry battle: Caesar, *Gallic War*, 7.64–68.

12. Alesia: Caesar, *Gallic War*, 7.69–89. Mont Réa weapons: Verchère de Reffye. Execution of Vercingetorix: Dio, 43.19.4.

13. Uxellodunum: Hirtius, *Gallic War*, 8.40–44.

14. From the Rubicon to Pompey's escape from Brundisium: Caesar, *Civil War*, 1.1–29. *Legio V Alaudae*: Suetonius, *Divine Julius*, 24.2; Pliny, *Natural History*, 11.121. The lark in question was probably the shore lark, also called the horned lark after its horn-like tufts (Bishop). The 'horns' may have suggested to the Romans a connection with the crest of Mars.

15. Dyrrhachium and Thessaly: Caesar, *Civil War*, 3.23–83.

16. Battle of Pharsalus: Caesar, *Civil War*, 3.84–99. Death of Pompey and Caesar's reaction: *ibid.*, 3.104; Plutarch, *Pompey*, 79 and *Caesar*, 48.

17. Role of Fortune/luck in war: 'Fortune, a force universally powerful but especially so in war, brings about great changes by slight adjustments of her balance' (Caesar, *Civil War*, 3.68; in a similar vein, *Gallic War*, 6.42). Criticism and praise of Caesar by a modern soldier and historian: Fuller, 308–24. Avaricum: *Gallic War*, 7.17. Caesar's *dignitas*: *Civil War*, 1.7. Caesar's doubling of legionary pay may have coincided with his decision to embark on civil war, *see* Suetonius, *Divine Julius*, 26.3. Pull down heaven: Anonymous, *Spanish War*, 42.

18. Scaeva at Dyrrhachium: Valerius Maximus, 3.2.23; Lucan, *Civil War*, 6.144–262; Appian, *Civil Wars*, 2.60. Most of these details are missing from Caesar's own account (*Civil War*, 3.53) and may be dramatic inventions. Scaeva joined a legion prior to 58 BC and was promoted to centurion during Caesar's Gallic campaigns: 'serving in the ranks before the war with the Rhone's fierce races; there promoted from the lengthy ranks by shedding copious blood, he bears the Latian vine staff', (Lucan, *Civil War*, 6.144–147). The vine staff, or *vitis*, was the emblem of the centurion. Scaeva was later closely involved in the settlement of Caesar's legionary veterans on confiscated land in Italy (45–44 BC; Cicero, *Letters to Atticus*, 14.10.2). Cicero warned Atticus that he must be careful of Scaeva: 'When you speak to him you are speaking to Caesar' (*ibid.*, 13.23). Scaeva was also the commander of a cavalry unit (the *ala Scaevae, ILS*, 2490 = *ILLRP*, 498), and served Octavian as *primus pilus* of *legio XII* at the siege of Perusia (Perugia) in 41 BC (*ILLRP*, 1116a, *see* Chapter V).

19. Polybius noted that the centurions of the manipular legion were 'natural leaders ... those who will stand their ground even when worsted or hard-pressed, and will die in defence of their posts,' (6.24.9).

20. Baculus. Sabis: Caesar, *Gallic War*, 2.25. Octodurus: *ibid.*, 3.1-6. Aduatuca: *ibid.*, 6.35-41. *See also* Horn and Brown, 338.

21. Sabinus, Cotta and their centurions: Caesar, *Gallic War*, 5.28-37. Sabinus' previous valour and sound generalship against the Venelli: *ibid.*, 3.18-19.

22. Though note how just a few years later in the civil war of 44-43 BC, Cicero was happy to declare that the *legio Martia* and *legio IIII* (*Macedonica*) 'had no object but honour and glory', (*Philippics*, 12.12.29), despite their opponents being equally renowned Roman legions like *V Alaudae*.

23. Crastinus: Caesar, *Civil War*, 3.91, 99. Soldiers win their reputations under auspices of Caesar: *ibid.*, 1.7. Manner of Crastinus' death: Plutarch, *Pompey*, 71.3. His decorations and tomb: Appian, *Civil Wars*, 2.82. His mad rage: Lucan, *Civil War*, 7.471; Florus, *Epitome*, 2.13.46. *See also* Perrin.

24. Ariovistus: Caesar, *Gallic War*, 1.39-41, 52-53; Dio, 38.35.1-47.2. Mutiny of 47 BC and *Quirites*: Suetonius, *Divine Julius*, 70; Plutarch, *Caesar*, 51.2; Appian, *Civil Wars*, 2.92-93, etc. Doubt over effectiveness of the shame tactic: Chrissanthos.

25. Need to emulate old glories: Virgil, *Eclogues*, 4.26-27; *Aeneid*, 6.823. Vespasian: Josephus, *Jewish War*, 4.33. Imperative to establish courageous reputations: Polybius, 6.52.11. Centurions versus Sugambri: Caesar, *Gallic War*, 6.40.

26. Martyr centurion: Anonymous, *African War*, 44-46; Valerius Maximus, 3.8.7. In the quoted passage the figure of thirty-six years is probably a manuscript error and is sometimes emended to thirteen years.

27. Catiline's army: Sallust, *War with Catiline*, 56.1-3. The 2,000 original volunteers (56.2) are probably to be identified with the Sullani (16.4, 28.4).

28. Sullani at the Piraeus: Appian, *Mithridatic Wars*, 41. Chaeronea: Plutarch, *Sulla*, 18.2-3 (note also the joke at 18.5, made by a centurion about slaves in the enemy ranks). Catiline as executioner: Plutarch, *Sulla*, 32; Livy, *Periochae*, 88, for the details of the torture. Catiline's military expertise: Cicero, *Pro Caelio*, 12.

29. Aesernia: Sallust, *Histories*, frag. 1.46 (McGushin). *See* McGushin, 110-12, for Aesernia as the probable site of Catiline's siege. Ausculum: Catiline is among the members of Pompeius Strabo's staff listed on *ILS*, 8888 = *ILLRP*, 515, a document recording the award of military decorations and Roman citizenship to a Spanish cavalry unit in 89 BC.

30. Sulla's generosity to his legionaries: Plutarch, *Sulla*, 12.9, 25.2. Fufidius, a former *primus pilus*, is the only certain example of the promotion of a Sullan centurion to the Senate: Orosius, *History Against the Pagans*, 5.21.3; Syme, 70. Later impoverishment of the Sullani: Sallust, *War with Catiline*, 16.4. Manlius a former Sullan centurion: Cicero, *Against Catiline*, 2.14. Blood oath: Sallust, *ibid.*, 22. Sallust notes that some believed the blood and human sacrifice were subsequent inventions. *See also* Florus, *Epitome*, 2.12.4.

31. Battle of Pistoria: Sallust, *War with Catiline*, 57-61. Hybrida's gout: *ibid.*, 59.4; Dio, 37.39.2-3.

32. *Devotio* of Catiline. Note also Florus: 'He died a death which would have been glorious if he had fallen fighting for his fatherland' (*Epitome*, 2.12.12). Execution of Cicero: Plutarch, *Cicero*, 48.

33. Praetorian 'pimps': Cicero, *Against Catiline*, 2.24. *Cohors amicorum*: Keppie 1996,

103. Catiline, Pompey and Cicero together at Ausculum: *ILS*, 8888 (Catiline and Pompey); Cicero reveals his service there in *Philippics*, 12.27. Cicero's praetorian staff cohort: *Letters to Atticus*, 7.2.7. His fighting praetorian cohort: *Letters to his Friends*, 15.4.7. Tenth Legion: Caesar, *Gallic War*, 1.40, 42. Title *Equestris*: *e.g. AE* 1934, 152.

34. Bodyguards of the Scipios. Africanus: Festus, 223M. Aemilianus: Appian, *Spanish Wars*, 84. The type of men selected as Africanus' guards, and their greater pay, suggests similar procedures in the first century BC. Octavian's praetorians were almost certainly paid more than legionaries (Dio, 53.11.1, referring to 27 BC but probably continuing earlier bands of pay).

35. Petreius' Spanish 'praetorians': Caesar, *Civil War*, 1.75.

36. Bodyguards of Antony and Octavian: Appian, *Civil Wars*, 3.5, 40. Antony forms a praetorian cohort: *ibid.*, 3.45, 52. Battle of Forum Gallorum: Cicero, *Letters to his Friends*, 10.30 – the eyewitness account of Sulpicius Galba; the various praetorian cohorts are referred to at 10.30.1, 4 and 5. Appian's account of the battle (*Civil Wars*, 3.66–70) may derive from Asinius Pollio (note Pollio's keen interest in the fighting at Cicero, *ibid.*, 10.33.4).

37. New praetorians after Philippi: Appian, *Civil Wars*, 5.3. Destruction of Octavian's praetorian cohort and the *legio Martia*: *ibid.*, 4.115; Plutarch, *Brutus*, 47.3.

38. Praetorians at Perusia: Appian, *Civil Wars*, 5.24, 34. At Brundisium: *ibid.*, 5.59.

39. Praetorians in Parthian War: Plutarch, *Antony*, 39.2. Octavia secures praetorians in 37 BC: Appian, *Civil Wars*, 5.95. In 35 BC: Plutarch, *Antony*, 53.2; Dio, 49.33.4.

40. Battle of Actium: Plutarch, *Antony*, 61–68 (64.1–2 for the possible praetorian centurion); Dio, 50.13–35. Antony's coinage: Crawford, numbers 544.1, 544.8 (praetorian cohorts); 554.12 (cohort of *speculatores*); 544.9 (*legio XII Antiqua*). Octavian's praetorians: Orosius, *History Against the Pagans*, 6.19.8.

41. Policy of reconciliation after Actium and establishment of the Imperial legions: Keppie 1984, 134–44. Nine praetorian cohorts: Tacitus, *Annals*, 4.5. The number of cohorts was raised to twelve by Caligula or Claudius, *see* Keppie 1996, 107–11

42. Early Imperial praetorians on campaign: Keppie 1996, 119–21. Togas: Tacitus, *Annals*, 16.27; *Histories*, 1.38. Legionary demands in AD 14: *Annals*, 1.17.

43. Vitellius' new cohorts: Tacitus, *Histories*, 2.93; Suetonius, *Vitellius*, 10.1. Vespasian: *CIL* XVI 21. Domitian: *CIL* XVI 81. Severus: Dio, 74.1–2; Herodian, 2.13. Dio asserts that the youth of Italy were forced to become brigands or gladiators, but Italians could still enter the Urban Cohorts (Severus increased the size of each of the three cohorts to 1,500 men) and the newly established *legio II Parthica*, based outside Rome, also accepted Italian recruits. 'All the expeditions' inscription: *CIL* VI 2553. Diocletian, battle of the Milvian Bridge and final disbandment of the praetorians: Aurelius Victor, *De Caesaribus*, 39–40; Zosimus, 2.16–17. The defeat of the praetorians is depicted on the Arch of Constantine, illustrated in this volume.

44. Hadrian's thirty legions: Historia Augusta, *Hadrian*, 15.13. Inscribed columns: *ILS*, 2288. The surviving column can be seen in the Galleria Lapidaria of the Vatican Museums.

45. Lost eagles. *V Alaudae*: Velleius Paterculus, 2.97.1. *XII Fulminata*: suggested by Suetonius, *Vespasian*, 4.5. Possible disbandment (or loss of legionary status) of *III Gallica*: Ritterling, *RE* XII, cols 1525–7. Disbandment and restoration of *III Augusta*: Ritterling, *RE* XII, cols 1336, 1339, 1501; Cowan 2003, 12–13, 28–30.

46. *Legio XXII Deiotariana*. Last record of: *BGU* I, 140, a letter to the legion and its sister unit, *III Cyrenaica*, from Hadrian on the rights of soldier's sons to inherit their father's property; soldiers were of course not allowed to marry until the end of the second century AD, so the children were not legitimate. Lost in Bar Kochba revolt: Ritterling, *RE* XII, col. 1795; A.R. Birley 1997, 268; Eck 1999. Jewish revolt in Egypt: A.R. Birley 1997, 74. Keppie 1990 and Mor refute the suggestion that the legion was transferred to Judaea. Mor also suggests the possibility of destruction in Egypt in AD 121/122, but A.R. Birley 1997, 142, denies that there was any serious fighting.

47. Legions destroyed in battle. Teutoburg Forest: Dio, 56.18–22; Velleius Paterculus, 2.117–120. Kalkriese: Schlüter. *V Alaudae*: Keppie 1984, 214. *XXI Rapax*: Suetonius, *Domitian*, 6.1 with Ritterling, *RE* XII, col. 1789.

48. Ninth Legion at Ilerda: Caesar, *Civil War*, 1.45–46.

49. Ninth at Dyrrhachium: Caesar, *Civil War*, 3.45–46, 66–67. Antony's charge at Philippi: Appian, *Civil Wars*, 4.111. Ninth at Pharsalus: Caesar, *ibid.*, 3.89. The Ninth also fought on the left at the Sabis (Caesar, *Gallic War*, 2.23).

50. Uzitta and Thapsus: Anonymous, *African War*, 60, 81. The legion also had an adventurous crossing to Africa (*ibid.*, 53). Ninth re-formed by Ventidius for Antony: Cicero, *Letters to his Friends*, 10.33.4. The re-formed legion was presumably the basis for the Ninth that fought in the Actium campaign and is celebrated on Antony's legionary coinage, *see* Crawford, numbers 544.22–23. Octavian's Ninth: Ritterling *RE* XII, col. 1664. *Legio VIIII Gemella*: *AE* 1956, 160. *Cf.* Caesar, *Civil War*, 3.4, for the practice of calling amalgamated legions Twin. It is possible that the *Gemella* inscription dates to the period between Philippi and Actium, but Brunt, 596, suggests it may indicate an amalgamation after Actium.

51. Ninth brought up to strength: Tacitus, *Annals*, 14.38. Losses may have been greater, the draft from the German provinces being additional to local recruitment.

52. Vitellius' 8,000-strong British legionary guard: Tacitus, *Histories*, 2.57. Second Cremona: *ibid.*, 2.100, 3.1, 3.22 (3.25 for *III Gallica*).

53. Vexillation of Ninth in Chattan War: *ILS*, 1025; Ritterling *RE* XII, col. 1668. Legionaries of Ninth needed no help: Tacitus, *Agricola*, 26.

54. Ninth's titles. *Triumphalis*: *ILS*, 2240. There is much debate as to when this title was adopted. It may recall participation in Caesar's multiple triumphs of 46 BC, or the entry of the new triumvirs (Antony, Octavian and Lepidus) into Rome in 43 BC, or a role in the victory at Actium. *See* Ritterling *RE* XII, col. 1664 and Keppie 1983, 203. *Macedonica*: *CIL* III 551, about 25 BC. *Hispaniensis*: *ILS*, 2321. *Hispana*: *CIL* V 911. Ninth marches by Rome: Tacitus, *Annals*, 3.9. Involvement in AD 14 mutiny: *ibid.*, 1.23, 30. Selected for British invasion and Cerialis: Ritterling, *RE* XII, cols 1666–7. Inscription of AD 108 from York: *CIL* VII 241 = *RIB* 665.

55. British War: A.R. Birley 2002, 72–5. Losses: Fronto, *On the Parthian War*, 2.22 (Haines). Silchester eagle: Joyce, 363–4 and plate 17. Joyce proposed that the eagle was buried by a rebel *aquilifer* in the service of Allectus but the object is part of a statue, *cf.* Boon, 71, 119–20. Tribunes and legate of Ninth after AD 120: Ritterling, *RE* XII, col. 1668; E.B. Birley; Eck 1972; Mor, 267–9; Keppie 1989, and 2000, 92–4, but cautious about the later dates for service in the legion.

56. Ninth brick stamps, Carlisle and Nijmegen. The archaeological evidence is assessed by Keppie 2000, 93–4.

57. Aelius Asclepiades: *CIL* X 1769. Transfer from Misene fleet: Keppie 1989, 251. *I Adiutrix* recruited from marines: Tacitus, *Histories*, 1.6, 31, 36, 2.43, etc.; Miller; Morgan. Draft of marines to *X Fretensis*: *CIL* XVI, App. 13.

58. Later stages of Bar Kochba revolt, Aelia Capitolina, etc.: A.R. Birley 1997, 274-6. Jewish casualties: Dio, 69.14.1.

59. Alani: Dio, 69.15.1; Arrian, *Acies Contra Alanos*. Elegeia: Dio, 71.2.1; Lucian, *Alexander the False Prophet*, 27 ('silly Celt'); *How to Write History*, 21, 25-6 (length of battle and suicides). Doubt over involvement of a complete legion: Speidel 1983, 10-11.

60. Forgotten battles. Burnswark: Campbell 2003 demonstrates that Burnswark was the site of a major siege, hardly the training ground it is often described as. Dura-Europos: Campbell 2005, 47-9. Krefeld-Gellep: Reichmann 1995 and 1999. Third *Augusta* transfer:-*ILS*, 2487.

61. Second British Revolt: Ritterling, *RE* XII, col. 1668.

62. Macedonians: *IGLS* 2828. Scythians: Haldon, article V, page 14.

63. *Fortia facta*: Speidel 1992, 124-8; note also Tacitus, *Annals*, 1.44. Saturninus: *ILS*, 9194. Centurions in the fifth to seventh centuries AD: Keenan.

64. Constantine's praetorians: Zosimus, 2.9; Aurelius Victor, *de Caesaribus*, 39.42. Constantine's guardsmen carry praetorian-type standards on the Arch of Constantine: Speidel 1987, 378.

Chapter V: Warriors and Poets *(pages 235-49)*

1. Polybius on legion versus phalanx: 18.28-32.

2. Legionary mauls Numidian: Livy, 22.51.5-9. Seventy thousand killed at Cannae: Polybius, 3.117.3, but Livy's figure is a little under 50,000 (22.49.15; equally divided between Romans and Allies). Acilius: Valerius Maximus, 3.2.22; Suetonius, *Divine Julius*, 68.4. Adamklissi: Robinson, plate 477.

3. Battle of Thapsus: Anonymous, *African War*, 83-85.

4. Difficulty controlling Roman soldiers of the fourth century AD. Argentoratum: Ammianus Marcellinus, 16.12.13. Compare the behaviour of the Fimbrian legionaries in the first century BC: Plutarch, *Lucullus*, 19.3, 35.6. Maiozamalcha: Ammianus Marcellinus, 24.4.11. Amida: *ibid.*, 19.5-6.

5. Gnaeus Petreius: Pliny, *Natural History*, 22.11. Marius' nephew attempts to rape a young legionary but is killed and the recruit is praised by Marius: Cicero, *Pro Milone*, 9; Valerius Maximus, 6.1.12. Dust at Vercellae: Plutarch, *Marius*, 26.3. The detail about Marius failing to make contact with the enemy may derive from the malicious account of his enemy Sulla. Catulus' retreat: *ibid.*, 23.

6. Scalping at Vercellae: Orosius, *History Against the Pagans*, 5.16.17-19.

7. Trebonius: Appian, *Civil Wars*, 3.26.

8. Saracen and Goth: Ammianus Marcellinus, 31.16.6. Caligula: Dio, 59.29.7.

9. Petreius and Juba: Anonymous, *African War*, 94. Note also the 'suicide duel' of the younger Marius and Telesinus at Praeneste in 82 BC (Livy, *Periochae*, 88). 'Roman way': Martial, *Epigrams*, 1.78. Auxiliaries, AD 28: Tacitus, *Annals*, 4.73. *Legio Martia*: Octavian's praetorian cohort was also lost with the legion: Appian, *Civil Wars*, 4.115.

10. Perusia sling bullets: C. Zangemeister, *Ephemeris Epigraphica* VI (1885), 52-78; *ILLRP*, 1106-18; Hallett. Compare the earlier inscribed *glandes* from the siege of Ausculum with such legends as 'Hit Pompeius!'; Zangemeister, *ibid.*, 5-47.

11. Sling bullets, noise and wounds: Anonymous, *African War*, 83; Onasander,

The General, 19.3. Attempted breakout from Perusia: Appian, *Civil Wars,*
5.36–37. Cestius Macedonicus and execution of city council: *ibid.,* 5.48–49.

12. Battle songs and insults. Pharsalus: Dio, 41.59.3, 60.5–6. Placentia: Tacitus,
Histories, 2.22. Lugdunum: Dio, 75.6; Herodian, 3.7.2–4; Historia Augusta,
Severus, 11.2 (sling bullet).

13. Songs at Caesar's triumph: Suetonius, *Divine Julius,* 49, 51; Dio, 43.20.2–4.
Centurions in the Senate: Syme, 70.

14. Cassius Chaerea: Tacitus, *Annals,* 1.32 (AD 14); Josephus, *Jewish Antiquities,*
19.1.5–6, 19.1.11; Suetonius, *Caligula,* 56–58.

15. Maximinus in combat: Herodian, 7.2.6–8. His appetite: Historia Augusta,
Two Maximini, 4.1–3. Murder of Alexander Severus: Herodian, 6.8.3–5.

16. Centurions extort payments from soldiers for leave and exemption from duties:
Tacitus, *Histories,* 1.46. Centurion (perhaps in this case an *optio*) beats a
civilian: Apuleius, *The Golden Ass,* 9.39.

17. Poets complain about centurions: Perseus, *Satires,* 5.189–191; Martial, *Epigrams,*
11.3. Virgil and Catullus: Adams, 119–20, 127, Appian's *Mithridatic Wars* read
in the desert fortress of Dura-Europos: Welles *et al.,* 70–1.

18. Avidius Quintianus poem: *AE* 1929, 7b = 1999, 1760. Porcius Iasucthan poem:
AE 1995, 1641. *See* Adams for discussion. Iasucthan transferred to Britain:
ILS, 9293.

19. Ennius as centurion: Silius Italicus, *Punica,* 12.387–419, imagining the poet being
saved in battle by the intervention of the god Apollo. His exhortation of Roman
soldiers: *e.g. Annals,* frag. 434–5 (*see also 21 below*).

20. Pullius Peregrinus: *ILS,* 2669; for an illustration of the sarcophagus *see*
Huskinson, 115. Maximinus: Historia Augusta, *Two Maximini,* 27.3–5. Sons of
Late Republican centurions: Horace, *Satires,* 1.6.72–73.

21. Descriptions of battle in Ennius: *Annals,* fragments 342, 356–7, 406–15, 423,
434–5, 501–2. Virgil on duty to the state and the Roman destiny to conquer the
world: *Aeneid,* 4.267–276, 1.286–290, etc. The anonymous Caesarian author of
the *Spanish War* used quotes from Ennius to elevate his accounts of battle (23
and 31).

22. Elephant symbol of *legio V Alaudae*: Appian, *Civil Wars,* 2.96.

23. *Noverca*: Pseudo-Hyginus, *de Munitionibus Castrorum,* 57. Titus Cissonius: *ILS,*
2238.

Epilogue *(pages 250–3)*

1. New Imperial legions raised in Italy: Mann. Origins of legionaries: Forni, 116–41;
of praetorians: Passerini, 148–59, 174–80. Barbarian legion inscription: *ILS,* 2671.
Frank and Roman inscription: *ILS,* 2814; the translation follows Rigsby.

BIBLIOGRAPHY

Translations of the major ancient literary sources – Appian, Caesar, Dio, Livy, Plutarch, Polybius and so on – are not specifically listed in this bibliography but are readily available in various editions and series including the Penguin Classics and Oxford World's Classics. The facing page translations included in editions in the Loeb Classical Library are particularly useful for those with the necessary language skills because the English translation can be checked against the original Greek or Latin.

Adams, J.N., 'The Poets of Bu Njem: Language, Culture and the Centurionate', *JRS* 89 (1999), 109–34

Balty, J.C. and W. Van Rengen, *Apamea in Syria: The Winter Quarters of Legio II Parthica*. Brussels: 1993

Birley, A.R., *Marcus Aurelius: A Biography*, revised edition. London: 1987

——, *Hadrian: The Restless Emperor*. London & New York: 1997

——, *Garrison Life at Vindolanda: A Band of Brothers*. Stroud: 2002

Birley, E.B., The Fate of the Ninth Legion', in R.M. Butler (ed.), *Soldier and Civilian in Roman Yorkshire*. Leicester: 1971, 71–80

Bishop, M.C., 'Legio V Alaudae and the Crested Lark', *JRMES* 1 (1990), 161–4

Boon, G., *Silchester: The Roman Town of Calleva*. Newton Abbot: 1974

Bottini, A. (ed.), *Armi. Gli Instrumenti della Guerra in Lucania*. Bari: 1994

Brown, R.D., 'Two Caesarian Battle Descriptions: A Study in Contrast', *Classical Journal* 94 (1999), 329–57

Brunt, P., *Italian Manpower, 225 BC–AD 14*. Oxford: 1971

Campbell, D.B., 'The Roman Siege of Burnswark', *Britannia* 34 (2003), 19–33

——, *Siege Warfare in the Roman World, 146 BC–AD 378*. Oxford: 2005

Cameron, A. and S.G. Hall, (eds.), *Eusebius' Life of Constantine*. Oxford: 1999

Carter, J. (ed.), *Caesar: The Civil War*. Oxford: 1997

Cary, M. and H. H. Scullard, *A History of Rome: Down to the Age of Constantine*. London: 1975

Chrissanthos, S. G., 'Caesar and the Mutiny of 47 BC', *JRS* 91 (2001), 63–75

Cichorius, C., *Die Reliefs der Traianssäule*. Berlin: 1900

Connolly, P., *Greece and Rome at War*, new edition. London: 2006

——, 'The Roman Saddle', in M. Dawson (ed.), 'Roman Military Equipment: The Accoutrements of War', *Proceedings of the Third Roman Military Equipment Research Seminar*. Oxford: 1987, 7–27

——, 'Pilum, Gladius and Pugio in the Late Republic', *JRMES* 8 (1997), 41–57

Cornell, T. J., 'Book VI of Ennius' Annals: A Reply', *Classical Quarterly* 37 (1987), 514–16

——, 'The Conquest of Italy', in *CAH VII. 2*, 351–419

——, *The Beginnings of Rome: Italy and Rome from the Bronze Age to the Punic Wars (c. 1000-264 BC)*. London and New York: 1995

Cowan, R. H., *Imperial Roman Legionary, AD 161-284*. Oxford: 2003

——, *Roman Battle Tactics, 109 BC-AD 313*. Oxford 2007

Crawford, M. H., *Roman Republican Coinage*. Cambridge: 1974

Cunliffe, B., *The Ancient Celts*. Oxford: 1997

Davies, R. W., 'The *Medici* of the Roman Armed Forces', *Epigraphische Studien* 8 (1969), 83–99

De Juliis, E. M., *Taranto*. Bari: 2000

Domaszewski, A. von, 'Die Fahnen im römischen Heere', *Abhandlungen des Ärchäologische-Epigraphischen Seminars der Universität Wien*, Hefte V. Wien: 1885

Eck, W., 'Zum Ende der *legio IX Hispana*', *Chiron* 2 (1972), 459–62

——, 'The Bar-Kokhba Revolt: The Roman Point of View', *JRS* 89 (1999), 76–89

Flower, H., 'The Significance of an Inscribed Breastplate Captured at Falerii in 241 BC', *Journal of Roman Archaeology* 11 (1998), 224–32

——, 'The Tradition of the *Spolia Opima*: M. Claudius Marcellus and Augustus', *Classical Antiquity* 19 (2000), 34–64

Forni, G., 'Supplemento II', in *Esercito e marina di Roma antica: raccolta di contibuti*. Mavors volume 6. Stuttgart: 1992

Forsythe, G., *A Critical History of Early Rome: From Prehistory to the First Punic War*. Berkeley and Los Angeles: 2005

Frank, T., 'Pyrrhus', in *The Cambridge Ancient History*, Volume VII: *The Hellenistic Monarchies and the Rise of Rome*. Cambridge: 1928, 638–64

Franke, P. R., 'Pyrrhus', in *CAH VII.2*, 456–85

Fuller, J. F. C., *Julius Caesar: Man, Soldier and Tyrant*. London: 1965

Goldsworthy, A. K., *The Roman Army at War, 100 BC-AD 200*. Oxford: 1996

Haldon, J., *State, Army, and Society in Byzantium: Approaches to Military, Social, and Administrative History, 6th-12th Centuries*. Aldershot: 1995

Hallett, J. P., '*Perusinae Glandes* and the Changing Image of Augustus', *American Journal of Ancient History* 2 (1977), 151–71

Higbie, C., *The Lindian Chronicle and the Greek Creation of Their Past*. Oxford: 2003

Holland, L. A., 'The Purpose of the Capestrano Warrior', *American Journal of Archaeology* 60 (1956), 243–7

Horn, T., 'P. Sextius Baculus', *Greece and Rome* 8 (1961), 180–3

Huskinson, J., *Experiencing Rome: Culture, Identity and Power in the Roman Empire*. London: 1999

Joyce, J. G., 'Account of Further Excavations at Silchester', *Archaeologia* 46 (1881), 329–65

Keenan, J. G., 'Evidence for the Byzantine Army in the Syene Papyri', *Bulletin of the Society of Papyrologists* 27 (1990), 139–50

Keppie, L., 'A Note on the title *Actiacus*', *Classical Review* 85 (1971), 369–70. Reprinted in Keppie 2000a, 97–8

——, *Colonisation and Veteran Settlement in Italy 47–14 BC*. Rome: 1983

——, *The Making of the Roman Army: From Republic to Empire*. London: 1984

——, 'The History and the Disappearance of the Legion XXII *Deiotariana*', in A. Kasher *et al.* (eds.), *Greece and Rome in Eretz Israel: Collected Essays*. Jerusalem: 1990, 54–61. Reprinted in Keppie 2000a, 225–32

——, 'The Fate of the Ninth Legion: A Problem for the Eastern Provinces?', in D. H. French and C. S. Lightfoot (eds.), *The Eastern Frontier of the Roman Empire*. Oxford: 1989, 247–55. Reprinted in Keppie 2000a, 173–81

——, 'The Praetorian Guard Before Sejanus', *Athenaeum* 84 (1996), 101–24. Reprinted in Keppie 2000a, 99–122

——, 'Legio VIIII in Britain: The Beginning and the End', in R. Brewer (ed.), *Roman Legions and their Fortresses*. Cardiff & London: 2000, 83–100. Reprinted in Keppie 2000a, 201–18

——, *Legions and Veterans: Roman Army Papers 1971–2000*. Mavors volume 12. Stuttgart: 2000a

Lendon, J. E., *Soldiers and Ghosts: A History of Battle in Classical Antiquity*. New Haven and London: 2005

Lévèque, P., *Pyrrhos*. Paris: 1957

McGushin, P., *Sallust: The Histories, Volume 1*. Oxford: 1992

Mann, J. C., 'The Raising of New Legions During the Principate', *Hermes* 91 (1963), 483–9

Maxfield, V. A., *The Military Decorations of the Roman Army*. London: 1981

Miller, H. F., 'Legio I Adiutrix', *Greece and Rome* 28 (1981), 73–80

Momigliano, A., 'The Origins of Rome', in *CAH VII.2*, 52–112

Mor, M., 'Two Legions – The Same Fate?', *Zeitschrift für Papyrologie und Epigraphik* 62 (1986), 267–78

Morgan, G., 'Galba, the Massacre of the Marines, and the Formation of Legion I Adiutrix', *Athenaeum* 91 (2003), 489–515

Oakley, S. P., 'Single Combat in the Roman Republic', *Classical Quarterly* 35 (1985), 392–410

Ogilvie, R. M., *A. Commentary on Livy: Books 1–5*. Oxford: 1965

Osgood, J., *Caesar's Legacy: Civil War and the Emergence of the Roman Empire*. Cambridge: 2006

Parker, H. M. D., *The Roman Legions*. Oxford: 1928

Passerini, E., *Le Coorti Pretorie*. Rome: 1939

Pelling, C. B. R., 'Caesar's Battle Descriptions and the Defeat of Ariovistus', *Latomus* 40 (1981), 741–66

Perrin, B., 'The Crastinus Episode at Palaepharsalus', *Transactions and Proceedings of the American Philological Association* 15 (1884), 46–57

Petersen, E., A. von Domaszewski and G. Calderini, *Die Marcus-Säule auf Piazza Colonna in Rom*. Munich: 1896

Pflug, H., 'Chalkidische Helme', in A. Bottini *et al.*, *Antike Helme. Sammlung Lipperheide und andere Bestände des Antikenmuseums Berlin*. Mainz: 1988, 137–50

Quesada Sanz, F., '*Gladius Hispaniensis*: An Archaeological View from Iberia', *JRMES* 8 (1997), 251–70

Reichmann, C., 'Stadtarchäologie in Krefeld 1990–1994', in *Ein Land macht Geschichte Archäologie in Nordrhein-Westfalen*. Mainz: 1995

——, 'Archäologische Spuren der sogenennanten Bataverschlacht vom Novemeber 69 n. Chr. Und von Kämpfen des 3. Jahrhunderts n. Chr. im Umfeld Kastells *Gelduba* (Krefeld-Gellep)', in W. Schlüter and R. Wiegels (eds.), *Rom, Germanien und die Ausgrabungen von Kalkriese*. Osnabrück: 1999, 97–115

Rigsby, K. J., 'Two Danubian Epitaphs', *Zeitschrift für Papyrologie und Epigraphik* 126 (1999), 175–6

Ritterling, E., 'Legio', *RE* XII (1925), 1211–1829

Robinson, H. R., *The Armour of Imperial Rome*. London: 1975

Rossi, L., *Trajan's Column and the Dacian Wars*. London: 1971

Rusu, M., 'Das keltische Fürstengrab von Ciumesti in Rumänien', *50. Bericht der Römische-Germanischen Kommission 1969* (1971), 267–300

Salmon, E. T., *Samnium and the Samnites*. Cambridge: 1967

——, *The Making of Roman Italy*. London: 1972

Schlüter, W., 'The Battle of the Teutoburg Forest', in J. D. Creighton and R. J. A. Wilson (eds.), *Roman Germany: Studies in Cultural Interaction*. Portsmouth, Rhode Island: 1999, 125–59

Schneider-Herrmann, G., *The Samnites of the Fourth Century B.C. as Depicted on Campanian Vases and Other Sources*. London: 1996.

Skutsch, O., 'Book VI of Ennius' Annals', *Classical Quarterly* 37 (1987), 512–14

Speidel, M. P., 'The Roman Army in Asia Minor: Recent Epigraphical Discoveries and Researches', in S. Mitchell (ed.), *Armies and Frontiers in Roman and Byzantine Anatolia*. Oxford: 1983, 7–34

——, *Roman Army Studies II*. Mavors volume 8. Stuttgart: 1992

——, 'The Later Roman Field Army and the Guard of the High Empire', *Latomus* 46 (1987), 375–9. Reprinted in Speidel 1992, 379–84

Syme, R., *The Roman Revolution*. Oxford: 1939

Turfa, J. M., *Catalogue of the Etruscan Gallery of the University of Pennsylvania Museum of Archaeology and Anthropology.* Philadelphia: 2005

Verchère de Reffye, M., 'Les armes d'Alise', *Révue Archéologique* 10 (1864) 337–49

Voisin, J.-L., 'Les Romains, chasseurs de têtes', in *Du châtiment dans la cité: Supplices corporals et peine de mort dans le monde antique.* Rome: 1984

Way A. G. (ed.), *Caesar: Alexandrian, African and Spanish Wars.* London & Cambridge, Massachusetts. 1955

Welles, C. B., R. O. Fink and J. F. Graham, *The Excavations at Dura-Europos. Final Report V, Part 1: The Parchments and Papyri.* New Haven: 1959

INDEX

Index

Other books available from Greenhill include:

SPIES OF THE BIBLE
Espionage in Israel from the Exodus to the Bar Kokhba Revolt
Rose Mary Sheldon
ISBN 978-1-85367-636-9

GREEK AND ROMAN WARFARE
Battles, Tactics and Trickery
John Drogo Montagu
ISBN 978-1-85367-685-7

GREECE AND ROME AT WAR
Peter Connolly
Preface by Adrian Goldsworthy
ISBN 978-1-85367-303-0

BATTLES OF THE BIBLE
A Military History of Ancient Israel
Chaim Herzog and Mordechai Gichon
ISBN 978-1-85367-681-9

Greenhill offer a 10 per cent discount on any books ordered directly from us. In the UK please call 0208 458 6314 or email sales@greenhillbooks.com.

For more information on our other books, please visit www.greenhillbooks.com. You can write to us at Park House, 1 Russell Gardens, London NW11 9NN.